Shipbreaking in Developing Countries

This book explores the process of shipbreaking in developing countries, with a particular focus on Bangladesh.

In the past, shipbreaking (the disposal of obsolete ships) was a very common industrial activity in many developed countries. However, due to stringent domestic environmental and labour laws it is almost impossible for the increasing number of vessels to be disposed of domestically, and now developing nations including Bangladesh, China, India, Turkey and Pakistan regularly participate in this activity. The shipbreaking yards in these countries are not only detrimental to the marine and coastal environment but also represent significant health hazards to local people and workers. Given the global importance of the issue, an effective legal and institutional framework for a sustainable operation of the shipbreaking industry is desperately needed.

Sitting at the intersection of three distinct fields – environmental justice, international environmental law and international maritime law – this book offers an innovative take on the issues surrounding the shipbreaking process. Drawing on the case study of Bangladesh due to its prominence in the shipbreaking industry, the author implements an environmental justice framework to examine the issues of sustainability surrounding shipbreaking, and analyses the relationship between social development, economic development and environmental protection. Maritime perspectives of environmental justice will also be highlighted through a discussion of the International Maritime Organization's role in the implementation of the Hong Kong Convention in developing countries.

This book will be of great interest to scholars of environmental justice, international maritime law and international environmental law.

Dr Md Saiful Karim is a Senior Lecturer at the Faculty of Law, Queensland University of Technology (QUT), Brisbane, Australia.

IMLI Studies in International Maritime Law

Series Editor: Professor David Joseph Attard, Director of the IMO International Maritime Law Institute

For a full list of titles in this series, please visit www.routledge.com

The IMO International Maritime Law Institute (IMLI) was established under the auspices of the International Maritime Organization, a specialised agency of the United Nations.

The Institute is an international centre for the training of specialists in international maritime law. It contributes to the development and dissemination of knowledge and expertise in the international regime of merchant shipping and related areas of maritime law and the general law of the sea, with special reference to the international regulations and procedures for safety and efficiency of shipping and the prevention of marine pollution. For further information on the Institute please visit its website at: www.imli.org.

The series is dedicated to publishing original, scholarly contributions which analyse key issues in international maritime law. The works published in the series will be of interest to an audience of students and scholars in maritime law, maritime lawyers and barristers, and professionals in the shipping industry.

Available titles:

Serving the Rule of International Maritime Law
Essays in Honour of Professor David Joseph Attard
Edited by A. Martínez Gutiérrez

Extension of Coastal State Jurisdiction in Enclosed or Semi-enclosed Seas
A Mediterranean and Adriatic Perspective
Mitja Grbec

European Sustainable Carriage of Goods
The Role of Contract Law
Ellen Eftestøl-Wilhelmsson

Shipbreaking in Developing Countries
A Requiem for Environmental Justice from the Perspective of Bangladesh
Md Saiful Karim

Shipbreaking in Developing Countries

A Requiem for Environmental Justice from the Perspective of Bangladesh

Md Saiful Karim

Routledge
Taylor & Francis Group
LONDON AND NEW YORK

First published 2018
by Routledge

2 Park Square, Milton Park, Abingdon, Oxfordshire OX14 4RN
52 Vanderbilt Avenue, New York, NY 10017

Routledge is an imprint of the Taylor & Francis Group, an informa business

First issued in paperback 2019

British Library Cataloguing-in-Publication Data
A catalogue record for this book is available from the British Library

Library of Congress Cataloging-in-Publication Data
Names: Karim, Saiful, author.
Title: Shipbreaking in developing countries : a requiem for environmental justice from the perspective of Bangladesh / Dr. Md Saiful Karim.
Description: Abingdon, Oxon ; New York, NY : Routledge, 2018. | Series: IMLI studies in international law | Includes bibliographical references and index.
Identifiers: LCCN 2017033075 | ISBN 9781138818200 (hardback)
Subjects: LCSH: Ships—Scrapping—Law and legislation—Bangladesh. | Recycling industry—Law and legislation—Bangladesh. | Environmental law, International. | Labor laws and legislation, International. | International and municipal law—Bangladesh.
Classification: LCC KNG1018.R43 K37 2018 | DDC 344.549204/62—dc23
LC record available at https://lccn.loc.gov/2017033075

ISBN: 978-1-138-81820-0 (hbk)
ISBN: 978-0-367-87120-8 (pbk)

Typeset in Galliard
by Apex CoVantage, LLC

Dedicated to
Jamal Nazrul Islam (24 February 1939–16 March 2013)

Day-labourers

Those who with hard labour broke the rugged hills
With hammer, shovel and pick-axe,
Their bones today are strewn on either side
Of those very roads. Those who, in order to render
You service, became day-labourers.
Those who covered their cherished bodies with dust
Only to carry you and your belongings,
They are indeed the real human beings,
they are the saints.

–Kazi Nazrul Islam

Kazi Nazrul Islam, 'Day-Labourers; (translated by Amir Hossain Chaudhury), in Mohammad Nurul Huda (ed), *Poetry of Kazi Nazrul Islam in English Translation* (Vol. 1, Nazrul Institute, 4th ed., 2014) 314.

Contents

Tables

Treaties

1919 *Constitution of the International Labour Organization*, opened for signature 28 June 1919, Part XIII of Treaty of Versailles (1919)

1930 *Convention Concerning Forced or Compulsory Labour*, opened for signature 28 June 1930, 39 UNTS 55 (entered into force 1 May 1932)

1948 *Convention Concerning Freedom of Association and Protection of the Right to Organise*, opened for signature 17 July 1948, 68 UNTS 17 (entered into force generally 4 July 1950)

Convention on the International Maritime Organization, opened for signature 6 March 1948, 289 UNTS 48 (entered into force 17 March 1958)

1949 *Convention Concerning the Application of the Principles of the Right to Organise and to Bargain Collectively*, opened for signature 1 July 1949, 96 UNTS 257 (entered into force generally 18 July 1951)

1951 *Convention Concerning Equal Remuneration for Men and Women Workers for Work of Equal Value*, opened for signature 29 June 1951, 165 UNTS 303 (entered into force 23 May 1953)

1954 *International Convention for the Prevention of Pollution of the Sea by Oil*, opened for signature 12 May 1954, 327 UNTS 3 (entered into force 26 July 1958)

1957 *Convention Concerning the Abolition of Forced Labour*, opened for signature 25 June 1957, 320 UNTS 291 (entered into force 17 January 1959)

1958 *Convention Concerning Discrimination in Respect of Employment and Occupation*, opened for signature 25 June 1958, 362 UNTS 31 (entered into force 15 June 1960)

1960 *Convention Concerning the Protection of Workers against Ionising Radiations*, adopted on 22 June 1960, ILO Convention 115 (entered into force 17 June 1962)

1966 *International Covenant on Civil and Political Rights*, opened for signature 16 December 1966, 999 UNTS 171 (entered into force 23 March 1976)

International Covenant on Economic, Social and Cultural Rights, opened for signature 16 December 1966, 999 UNTS 3 (entered into force 3 January 1976)

1969 *International Convention Relating to Intervention on the High Seas in Cases of Oil Pollution Casualties*, opened for signature 29 November 1969, 9 ILM 25 (entered into force 6 May 1975) as amended by the 1973

Vienna Convention on the Law of Treaties, opened for signature 23 May 1969, 1155 UNTS 331, (entered into force 27 January 1980)

1971 *Convention Concerning Protection and Facilities to be Afforded to Workers' Representatives in the Undertaking*, opened for signature 23 June 1971, 883 UNTS. 111 (entered into force 30 June 1973)

1972 *Convention Concerning the Protection of World Cultural and Natural Heritage*, opened for signature 23 November 1972, 1037 UNTS 151 (entered into force 15 December 1975)

Convention for the Protection of the Marine Environment of the North-East Atlantic, opened for signature 22 September 1972, 2354 UNTS 67 (entered into force 25 March 1998)

Convention on the Prevention of Marine Pollution by Dumping of Wastes and Other Matter, opened for signature 29 December 1972, 11 ILM 1294 (entered into force 30 August 1975)

Convention on Wetlands of International Importance Especially as Waterfowl Habitat, opened for signature 2 February 1972, 996 UNTS 245 (entered into force 21 December 1975)

1973 *Convention Concerning Minimum Age for Admission to Employment*, opened for signature 26 June 1973, 1015 UNTS 297 (entered into force 19 June 1976)

Protocol Relating to Intervention on the High Seas in Cases of Marine Pollution by Substances other than Oil, opened for signature 2 November 1973, 13 ILM 650 (entered into force 30 March 1983)

International Convention for the Prevention of Pollution from Ships, opened for signature 2 November 1973, 1340 UNTS 184 as modified by the Protocol of 1978 to the 1973 Convention, opened for signature 17 February 1978, 1341 UNTS 3 (entered into force 2 October 1983)

1974 *Convention Concerning Prevention and Control of Occupational Hazards caused by Carcinogenic Substances and Agents*, adopted on 24 June 1974, ILO Convention 139 (entered into force 10 June 1976)

1977 *Convention Concerning the Protection of Workers against Occupational Hazards in the Working Environment Due to Air Pollution, Noise and Vibration*, adopted on 20 June 1977, ILO Convention 148 (entered into force 11 July 1979)

1981 *African Charter on Human and Peoples' Rights*, opened for signature 27 June 1981, 1520 UNTS 217 (entered into force 21 October 1986)

1982 *United Nations Convention on the Law of the Sea*, opened for signature 10 December 1982, 1833 UNTS 3 (entered into force 16 November 1994)

1985 *Convention Concerning Occupational Health Services*, adopted on 25 June 1985, ILO Convention 161 (entered into force 17 February 1988)

Vienna Convention for the Protection of the Ozone Layer, opened for signature 22 March 1985, 1513 UNTS 324 (entered into force 22 September 1988)

1986 *Convention Concerning Safety in the Use of Asbestos*, adopted on 24 June 1986, ILO Convention 162 (entered into force 16 June 1989)

1987 *Montreal Protocol on Substances that Deplete the Ozone Layer*, opened for signature 16 September 1987, 1522 UNTS 3 (entered into force 1 January 1989)

1988 *Additional Protocol to the American Convention on Human Rights in the Area of Economic, Social, and Cultural Rights (San Salvador Protocol)*, opened for signature 17 November 1988, OASTS 69 (entered into force 16 November 1999)

1989 *Basel Convention on the Control of Transboundary Movements of Hazardous Wastes and Their Disposal*, opened for signature 22 March 1989, 1673 UNTS 126 (entered into force 24 May 1992)

1990 *Convention Concerning Safety in the use of Chemicals at Work*, adopted on 25 June 1990, ILO Convention 170 (entered into force 4 November 1993)

International Convention on Oil Pollution Preparedness, Response and Cooperation, opened for signature 30 November 1990, 30 ILM 733 (entered into force 13 May 1995)

1992 *Convention on Biological Diversity*, opened for signature 5 June 1992, 1760 UNTS 143 (entered into force 29 December 1993)

United Nations Framework Convention on Climate Change, opened for signature 9 May 1992, 1771 UNTS 107 (entered into force 21 March 1994)

1994 *Arab Charter on Human Rights*, opened for signature 15 September 1994, 12 International Human Rights Report 893 (2005) (entered into force 15 March 2008)

1995 *United Nations Agreement for the Implementation of the Provisions of the United Nations Convention on the Law of the Sea of 10 December 1982 Relating to the Conservation and Management of Straddling Fish Stocks and Highly Migratory Fish Stocks*, opened for signature 4 December 1995, 34 ILM 1542 (entered into force 11 December 2001)

1996 *Protocol to the Convention on the Prevention of Marine Pollution by Dumping of Wastes and Other Matter*, opened for signature 7 November 1996, 36 ILM 1 (entered into force 24 March 2006)

1998 *Rotterdam Convention on the Prior Informed Consent Procedure for Certain Hazardous Chemicals and Pesticides in International Trade*, opened for signature 10 September 1998, 2244 UNTS 337 (entered into force 24 February 2004)

Convention on Access to Information, Public Participation in Decision-making and Access to Justice in Environmental Matters, opened for signature 25 June 1998, 2161 UNTS 447 (entered into force 10 October 2001)

1999 *Convention Concerning the Prohibition and Immediate Action for the Elimination of the Worst Forms of Child Labour*, opened for signature 17 June 1999, 2133 UNTS 161 (entered into force 19 November 2000)

Convention Concerning the Promotional Framework for Occupational Safety and Health, adopted on 15 June 1999, ILO Convention 187 (entered into force 20 February 2009)

2000 *Protocol on Preparedness, Response and Co-operation to Pollution Incidents by Hazardous and Noxious Substances*, opened for signature 15 March 2000, 2007 ATS 41 (entered into force 14 January 2007)

2001 *Stockholm Convention on Persistent Organic Pollutants*, opened for signature 22 May 2001, 2256 UNTS 119 (entered into force 17 May 2004)

International Convention on the Control of Harmful Anti-fouling Systems on Ships 2001, IMO Doc. AFS/CONF/26 (5 October 2001) (entered into force 17 September 2008)

2004 *International Convention for the Control and Management of Ship's Ballast Water and Sediments*, IMO Doc. BWM/CONF/36 (16 February 2004) (entered into force 8 September 2017)

2007 *Nairobi International Convention on the Removal of Wrecks*, opened for signature 18 May 2007, IMO Doc LEG/CONF.16/19 (entered into force 14 April 2015)

2009 *Hong Kong International Convention for the Safe and Environmentally Sound Recycling of Ships*, opened for signature 1 September 2009, IMO Doc. SR/CONF/45 (19 May 2009) (not yet in force)

National laws

Bangladesh Coast Guard Act, 2016 (Act no. XI of 2016)
Bangladesh Labour Act, 2006 (Act No. XLII of 2006)
Constitution of the People's Republic of Bangladesh, 1972
Draft Bangladesh Ship Recycling Act, 2017 (Bangladesh National Parliament, Bill No 16/2017)
Environment Conservation Act 1995 (Act No. I of 1995)
Hazardous Wastes and Shipbreaking Wastes Management Rules, 2011 (SRO No 369-Law/2011)
Import Policy Order 2006–2009 (No. S.R.O. 73-LAW/2007)
Import Policy Order 2009–2012 (No. S.R.O. 22-LAW/2010)
Import Policy Order 2012–2015 (No. S.R.O. 411-Ain/2012)
Import Policy Order 2015–2019 (No. S.R.O. 28-Law/2016)
Imports and Exports (Control) Act, 1950 (Act No. XXXIX of 1950)
Merchant Shipping Ordinance, 1983 (Ordinance No. XXVI of 1983)
Penal Code, 1860 (Act No. XLV of 1860)
Ship Breaking and Recycling Rules, 2011 (Ministry of Industries Gazette Notification dated 12 December 2011, an amended gazette notification published on 11 January 2012)
Territorial Waters and Maritime Zones Act, 1974 (Act No. XXVI of 1974)

International and regional cases

Bladet Tromsø A/S and Stensaas v. Norway (2000) 29 EHRR 125 (Judgment of 20 May 1999)

Claude-Reyes et al. v. Chile (Judgment of 19 September 2006), Inter-American Court of Human Rights

Fadeyeva v. Russian Federation (2007) 45 EHRR 10, (Judgment of 9 June 2005)

Gabčíkovo-Nagymaros Project (Hungary v. Slovakia), Judgment, ICJ Rep 1997, p. 7

Guerra and ors v. Italy (1998) 26 EHRR 357 (Judgment of 19 February 1998)

Hamer v. Belgium, European Court of Human Rights, Application no. 21861/03) (Judgment of 27 November 2007)

Hatton and ors and Friends of the Earth (intervening) v. United Kingdom and British Airways (intervening) (2003) 37 EHRR 28, (Judgment of 8 July 2003)

Iron Rhine Arbitration (Belgium v. Netherlands) (2008) 27 RIAA 35

Kawas-Fernández v. Honduras (Judgment of 3 April 2009), Inter-American Court of Human Rights

Legality of the Threat or Use of Nuclear Weapons, Advisory Opinion, ICJ Rep 1996 (I), p. 226

López Ostra v. Spain (1995) 20 EHRR 277 (Judgment of 9 December 1994)

Mangouras v. Spain (2010) ECHR 1364 (Judgment of 28 September 2010)

Netherlands v. France (Rhine Chlorides Arbitration), Award, ICGJ 374 (PCA 2004)

Öneryıldız v. Turkey (2005) 41 EHRR 20 (Judgment of 30 November 2004)

Powell and Rayner v. United Kingdom (1990) 12 EHRR 335 (Judgment of 21 February 1990)

Pulp Mills on the River Uruguay (Argentina v. Uruguay), Judgment, ICJ Rep 2010, p. 14
Saramaka People v. Suriname (Judgment of 28 November 2007) Inter-American Court of Human Rights
Yakye Axa Indigenous Community v. Paraguay (Judgment of 17 June 2005) Inter-American Court of Human Rights

National cases

Aftab Uddin v. Bangladesh (1996) 48 DLR (HCD) 1

Bangladesh Environment Lawyers Association v. Shafique Alam Mehedi and Others, Contempt Petition(H) 304 of 2014 (Bangladesh Supreme Court High Court Division)

Bangladesh Environmental Lawyers Association v. Bangladesh (Writ Petition No. 2911 of 2003) (Bangladesh Supreme Court High Court Division)

Bangladesh Environmental Lawyers Association v. Bangladesh, Writ Petition No. 3916 of 2006 (Unreported judgment delivered 6 July 2006, Bangladesh Supreme Court High Court Division, (*MT Alfaship* case)

Bangladesh Environmental Lawyers Association v. Ministry of Shipping, Writ Petition no 7260 of 2008, Bangladesh Supreme Court High Court Division, (Unreported judgment dated 17 March 2009) (*MT Enterprise* case [Judgment])

Bangladesh Environmental Lawyers Association v. Ministry of Shipping (*MT Enterprise*), Writ Petition no 7260 of 2008, Bangladesh Supreme Court High Court Division, (Unreported order dated 30 November 2008)

Bangladesh Environmental Lawyers Association v. Ministry of Shipping, Writ Petition no 7260 of 2008, Bangladesh Supreme Court High Court Division) (*MT Enterprise*) (Unreported order dated 11 May 2010)

Bangladesh Sangbadpatra Parishad v. Bangladesh (1991) 43 DLR (AD) 126

Bangladesh Ship Breakers Association v. Commissioner of Customs (Writ Petition No 2048 of 1997), Bangladesh Supreme Court High Court Division, (10 April 1997)

Charan Lal Sahu v. Union of India (1990) AIR SC 1480

Dada Match Workers Union v. Government of Bangladesh (1977) 29 DLR (HCD) 188

Dr Mohiuddin Farooque v. Bangladesh and Others (1996) 48 DLR (HCD) *438* (Radiated Milk Case)

Dr Mohiuddin Farooque v. Bangladesh and Others (1997) 49 DLR (AD) 1 (FAP 20 Case [Standing])
Dr Mohiuddin Farooque v. Bangladesh and Others (1998) 50 DLR (HCD) 84 (FAP 20 Case Merits)
Dr Mohiuddin Farooque v. Bangladesh and Others (2003) 55 DLR (HCD) 69 (Industrial Pollution Case)
Francis Coralie Mullin v. Union Territory of Delhi (1981) AIR SC 746
Human Rights for Peace for Bangladesh v. Bangladesh (2011) 19 BLT (HCD) 107
Kazi Mukhlesur Rahman v. Bangladesh (1974) 26 DLR (AD) 44 (Berubari Case)
Kudrat-E-Elahi Panir v. Bangladesh (1992) 44 DLR (AD) 319
M Saleem Ullah v. Justice M A Quddus Chowdhury (1994) 46 DLR (HCD) 691
M. C. Mehta v. Union of India (1988) AIR SC 1037
M. C. Mehta v. Union of India (1996) 4 SCC 351
M. C. Mehta v. Union of India (1996) 4 SCC 750
M. C. Mehta v. Union of India (1987) AIR 1086
Major-General KM Safiullah v. Bangladesh (2010) 18 BLT (Special Issue – 01) 1
Minerva Mills v. Union of India (1980) AIR SC 1789
Neeraja Chaudhary v. State of MP (1984) AIR (SC) 1099
Olga Tellis v. Bombay Municipal Corporation (1986) AIR SC 180
Rabia Bhuiyan, MP v. Ministry of LGRD (2007) 59 DLR (AD) 176
Research Foundation for Science v. Union of India, Writ Petition No. 657 of 1995, (Unreported judgment delivered on 6 September 2007, India), <www.legalservicesindia.com/judgments/sep/case_6a_9_07.htm>
Rural Litigation and Entitlement Kendra v. State of U P (1991) AIR SC 2216
Rural Litigation and Entitlement Kendra v. State of U.P. (1985) AIR SC 652
Shehla Zia v. WAPDA (1994) PLD SC 693
Subhash Kumar v. State of Bihar (1991) AIR SC 420
V Mathur v. Union of India (1996) 1 SCC 119
Virender Gaur v. State of Haryana (1995) 2 SCC 577
Wahab v. Secretary Ministry of Land (1996) 1 MLR (HC) 338

Acknowledgements

This book is a result of my many years of research that started in Chittagong, Bangladesh, and then continued for more than 12 years in six cities in three countries. I would like to thank all the institutions at which I was either a student or a staff member, including the University of Chittagong, the National University of Singapore (NUS), Bangladesh Environmental Lawyers Association (BELA), Infinitus Law Corporation (Singapore), Macquarie University, Southern Cross University and the Queensland University of Technology (QUT). I would also like to thank the University of Sydney and the University of the South Pacific, where I had visiting appointments.

Research on this topic would not have been possible without the help and encouragement of some friends, colleagues and well-wishers from Bangladesh. I would like to express sincere thanks and gratitude to my friend Anwarul Karim for collecting many important documents from Bangladesh. I would also like to thank Abdullah Al Faruque, Jakerul Abedin, Ridwanul Hoque, Masum Saifur Rahman, Ismail Hossain, Ariful Kaiser, Abul Hasanat and Nazimuddin Pradhan.

I would like to thank Justice Md. Imman Ali for kindly giving me an appointment during my visit to Bangladesh.

I would like to thank all my colleagues at QUT. Particular thanks are due to Tracey Carver for reading the first draft of one of my book proposals. I would also like to thank Belinda Carpenter, Ben Mathews, Des Butler, Reece Walters, Richard Johnstone, Allan Chay, Felicity Deane, Andrew Garwood-Gowers, Amisha Mehta and Lucy Cradduck for their support and encouragement.

My sincere thanks also go to Natalie Klein, Alan Tan, Rafiqul Islam, M Shah Alam, Koh Kheng Lian, Lye Lin-Heng, Simon Tay, Nicholas A Robinson, Robert Beckman, Rocque Reynolds and Rosemary Lyster for their help as my teachers or colleagues.

This book incorporates some material from my previously published article: Md Saiful Karim, 'Environmental Pollution from Shipbreaking Industry: International Law and National Legal Response' (2010) 22 *Georgetown International Environmental Law Review* 185. I would like to thank the editors and publisher of this journal.

This book is dedicated to the late Professor Jamal Nazrul Islam, Professor Emeritus and Director, Research Centre for Mathematical and Physical Sciences,

Chittagong University, Bangladesh. He was one of the discussants on my first keynote paper highlighting the issues of labour rights violation in the shipbreaking industry, presented at a seminar held in Chittagong 12 years ago. This book honours his commitment and contributions to the people and the environment of Bangladesh.

Last but not least, my heartfelt gratitude and love go to my family.

Md Saiful Karim
Brisbane, QLD, Australia
September 2017

Abbreviations

AFS	Anti-fouling system
ASEAN	Association of Southeast Asian Nations
BAN	Basel Action Network
BELA	Bangladesh Environmental Lawyers Association
BIMCO	Baltic and International Maritime Council
BSBA	Bangladesh Ship Breakers Association
BWM	Ballast water management
CBDR	Common but differentiated responsibilities
CoP	Conference of Parties
DLR	Dhaka Law Report
ECSA	European Community Shipowners' Associations
EC WSR	European Council Waste Shipment Regulation
EU	European Union
FAP	Food Action Plan of Bangladesh
FIDH	International Federation for Human Rights
FOEI	Friends of the Earth International
HCB	Hexachlorobenzene
HCD	High Court Division
HNS	Hazardous and noxious substances
ICCPR	International Covenant on Civil and Political Rights
ICESCR	International Covenant on Economic, Social and Cultural Rights
ICS	International Chamber of Shipping
ILO	International Labour Organization
IMDG	International Maritime Dangerous Goods
IMO	International Maritime Organization
INTERCARGO	International Association of Dry Cargo Shipowners
INTERTANKO	International Association of Independent Tanker Owners
IPTA	International Parcel Tankers Association
MARPOL	International Convention for the Prevention of Marine Pollution from Ships
MDGs	Millennium Development Goals
MEPC	Marine Environment Protection Committee

NBR	National Board of Revenue
NGO	Nongovernmental organisation
NIEO	New International Economic Order
NOC	No Objection Certificate
OCIMF	Oil Companies' International Marine Forum
OECD	Organization for Economic Co-operation and Development
OHS	Occupational health and safety
OPRC	Oil Pollution Preparedness, Response and Cooperation
PAH	Polycyclic aromatic hydrocarbon
PCB	Polychlorinated biphenyl
PIC	Prior informed consent
PIL	Public interest litigation
POP	Persistent organic pollutant
SBSRB	Ship Building and Ship Recycling Board
SDGs	Sustainable Development Goals
SRFP	Ship recycling facility plan
SRP	Ship recycling plan
TBT	Tributyltin
UDHR	Universal Declaration of Human Rights
UK	United Kingdom
UN	United Nations
UNCLOS	United Nations Convention on the Law of the Sea
UNESCO	United Nations Educational, Scientific and Cultural Organization
UNDP	United Nations Development Programme
UNEP	United Nations Environment Programme
UNFCCC	United Nations Framework Convention on Climate Change

1 Introduction

1.1 Introduction

Shipbreaking is a phrase describing the disposal of obsolete ships. The process is also called ship recycling, ship dismantling or ship scrapping. International organisations refer to it differently depending on the nature and mandate of their work. In this book, I use these terms interchangeably. On average, the commercial life of ships may extend to 25–30 years, after which ships go to shipbreaking yards for breaking or recycling. In the past, shipbreaking was a highly mechanised industrial activity in some developed countries. Due to the increasing costs associated with environmental, health and safety requirements in developed countries, this industry was transferred to the beaches of developing countries including India, Bangladesh, China, Turkey and Pakistan.[1]

The major catalysts for this shifting of the shipbreaking industry are cheap labour, weak regulatory systems and ever-increasing demand for steel. On average, each year 1,000 ships are sent to shipbreaking yards for disposal.[2] Three South Asian countries, Bangladesh, India and Pakistan, are currently responsible for disposal of around 70% of global obsolete ships.[3] In the year 2015, 20.4 million gross tonnage of ships was disposed of, and the Bangladeshi shipbreaking industry contributed 33% of this, making it the largest shipbreaking operation in the world.[4]

Shipbreaking activities in Bangladesh began almost by accident. In the mid-1960s, a devastating cyclone drove ashore a large ship on the Chittagong coast, which perforce had to be broken up.[5] This event led to the beginnings of

1 Widha Kusumaningdyah, Agustina Eunike and Rahmi Yuniarti, 'Modelling Tradeoff in Ship Breaking Industry Considering Sustainability Aspects: A System Dynamics Approach' (2013) 17 *Procedia Environmental Sciences* 785.

2 NGO Shipbreaking Platform, *Substandard Shipbreaking: A Global Challenge* (February 2016) <www.shipbreakingplatform.org/shipbrea_wp2011/wp-content/uploads/2016/04/Worldwide-overview_FINAL.pdf>.

3 Ibid.

4 Ibid.

5 Ataur Rahman and A. Z. M. Tabarak Ullah, *Ship Breaking: A Background Paper*, International Labour Organization Report (1999) 1.

shipbreaking as an industry in the early 1970s.[6] Shipbreaking mainly established as an industry in Bangladesh in the 1980s. At present, around 40 shipbreaking yards are in operation, all located on an 18-km stretch of the Chittagong Coast.[7] The industry maintains no proper employment records, but it is estimated that the shipbreaking yards employ around 22,000 workers.[8] These shipbreaking yards are managed in a very disorganised and primitive way.

A report published in a Bangladeshi newspaper revealed a proposal for a new shipbreaking industry in an Ecologically Critical Area[9] near the Sundarbans.[10] The Sundarbans is the largest contiguous mangrove forest in the world. It is a UNESCO World Heritage Site under the World Heritage Convention and also a Wetland of International Importance under the Ramsar Convention.[11]

Shipbreaking is an ultra-hazardous industry and is also one of the most polluting industries. Death and serious injury are regular occurrences in South Asian shipbreaking, particularly in Bangladesh. The operations of the shipbreaking industry in Bangladesh raise serious doubts about international and national legal frameworks ensuring environmental justice.

The shipbreaking industry has found in Bangladesh a fertile place for its growth. This is because, on one hand, the environmental laws of Bangladesh are not strictly enforced and the rights of workers are not adequately safeguarded, for the promotion of employers' interests. On the other hand, the government of Bangladesh cares more about earning revenue from this industry than protecting the quality of the marine environment and the safety of the workers engaged in the industry. Widespread corruption is possibly the main reason why repeated violations of environmental laws and labour rights by the industry are not given

6 Ibid.

7 Maria Sarraf et al., *The Ship Breaking and Recycling Industry in Bangladesh and Pakistan*, World Bank Report No. 58275-SAS (2010) <http://documents.worldbank.org/curated/en/2010/12/13695952/ship-breaking-recycling-industry-bangladesh-pakistan>.

8 Ibid.

9 An Ecologically Critical Area is an area declared under section 5 of the Bangladesh *Environment Conservation Act 1995*, the conservation and protection of which from destructive activities is needed due to its unique biodiversity and environmental importance. *Environment Conservation Act 1995* (Act No. I of 1995) s 2 and s 5.

10 Iftekhar Mahmud, '150 Industrial Projects around Sundarbans' *Daily Prothom Alo* (online) 9 August 2016 <http://en.prothom-alo.com/bangladesh/news/115689/150-industrial-projects-around-Sundarbans>; Pinaki Roy, 'Critical Area at a Stake: Nearly 150 Industrial Units Springing up within 10 kms of Sundarbans' *The Daily Star* (online) 4 October 2016 <www.thedailystar.net/frontpage/critical-area-stake-1293748>.

11 *Convention Concerning the Protection of World Cultural and Natural Heritage*, opened for signature 23 November 1972, 1037 UNTS 151 (entered into force 15 December 1975); *Convention on Wetlands of International Importance Especially as Waterfowl Habitat*, opened for signature 2 February 1971, 996 UNTS 245 (entered into force 21 December 1975); UNESCO World Heritage Centre, *The Sundarbans* <http://whc.unesco.org/en/list/798>; Ramsar Sites Information Service, *Sundarbans Reserved Forest* (1 January 2003) <https://rsis.ramsar.org/ris/560>.

due attention by the government or any of its responsible departments. As a result, it is understandable that the shipbreaking industry has rapidly expanded in Bangladesh, causing a serious threat to the marine and coastal environment and violating labour rights.[12] The government may consider that shutting down the industry is not a reasonable solution to the problem and that it is not advisable to return the industry to the industrialised nations where it can be carried out in a more environmentally sound way. The best solution would be to maintain the industry in Bangladesh by effectively applying relevant international and national laws. However, that does not necessarily mean that the Bangladeshi shipbreaking industry should be allowed to continue in its presently unsafe and environmentally harmful condition.

The shipbreaking industry in Bangladesh is causing significant marine environmental and human catastrophes in Bangladesh. From the perspective of the Bangladesh government, the industry is playing an important role in the country by supplying iron. As people are directly or indirectly dependent on shipbreaking for their livelihoods, phasing out this industry in Bangladesh may not be the best option; therefore, safe and environmentally sound operation of this industry should be ensured as a matter of priority.[13] Further, from a global environmental and economic perspective, the recycling of ships is a good option for environmentally sound disposal of obsolete ships. However, current shipbreaking practice in Bangladesh should not be treated as recycling. Rather, it should be acknowledged as dumping of developed countries' wastes in a developing country under the guise of recycling. The industry should not be allowed to operate if worker casualties continue unabated. Continuation of current practices causing death and injury of workers is a clear violation of the right to life enshrined in the Constitution of Bangladesh, as well as a gross violation of international human rights legal instruments to which Bangladesh is a party.[14]

This introductory chapter presents an overview of the issues related to ensuring environmental justice in the Bangladeshi shipbreaking industry. Section 1.2 examines the environmental, occupational health and safety (OHS) and other associated issues with shipbreaking operations in Bangladesh. Section 1.3 presents the scope and overview of the book.

12 Md Saiful Karim, 'Violation of Labour Rights in the Ship-Breaking Yards of Bangladesh: Legal Norms and Reality' (2009) 25 *The International Journal of Comparative Labour Law and Industrial Relations* 379.

13 See generally, Md M. Maruf Hossain and Mohammad Mahmudul Islam, *Ship Breaking Activities and Its Impact on the Coastal Zone of Chittagong, Bangladesh: Towards Sustainable Management* (Young Power in Social Action [YPSA], 2006).

14 *Constitution of the People's Republic of Bangladesh*, arts 31 and 32; *Universal Declaration of Human Rights*, GA Res 217(III), UN Doc. A/RES/3/217A (10 December 1948); *International Covenant on Civil and Political Rights*, opened for signature 16 December 1966, 999 UNTS 171 (entered into force 23 March 1976); *International Covenant on Economic, Social and Cultural Rights*, opened for signature 16 December 1966, 999 UNTS 3 (entered into force 3 January 1976).

1.2 The environmental and human costs

Shipbreaking involves a sequential chain of activities in the intertidal zone, on the beach and on shore. Prior to beaching, oily wastes, chemicals and other hazardous substances are discharged into the sea to ready the vessel for scrapping. This process severely impairs water quality in the adjacent sea area, which has harmful effects on the marine ecosystem.[15] Scientific studies have demonstrated high levels of heavy metals, polychlorinated biphenyls (PCBs), tributyltin (TBT) and asbestos in shipbreaking yards.[16] Even asbestos collected from various parts of ships are omnipresent in the shipbreaking yards.[17] Shipbreaking operators make no effort to safely dispose of these hazardous substances.[18] Apart from soil and water pollution, this industry is also releasing serious organic contaminants into the air in the surrounding area.[19]

These shipbreaking yards are not only detrimental to the marine and coastal environment, but they also impose significant health hazards on the local people and workers. Bangladesh does not require pre-cleaning or a 'gas-free-for-hot-work' certificate prior to the import of ships and tankers to Bangladesh for breaking.

Environmental justice in the shipbreaking industry involves more issues than just transboundary movement of obsolete ships and their environmentally sound disposal. Violation of labour rights is rampant in the industry. Worker death and disability arising from accidents at work are common occurrences in shipbreaking yards in Bangladesh. Although specific information is not available, it has been estimated that 'some 1000–2000 workers have died in the last 30 years, and many more have suffered serious injuries'.[20] The major causes of these causalities are the almost non-existent safety systems, the use of archaic methods for cutting

15 Md M. Maruf Hossain and Mohammad Mahmudul Islam, 'Shipbreaking Activities and Its Impact on the Coastal Zone of Chittagong, Bangladesh: Towards Policy Implications' (2006) 6 *Social Action* 3, 3.

16 Asma Binta Hasana et al., 'Enrichment Factor and Geo-Accumulation Index of Trace Metals in Sediments of the Ship Breaking Area of Sitakund Upazilla (Bhatiary – Kumira), Chittagong, Bangladesh' (2013) 125 *Journal of Geochemical Exploration* 130; Asma Binta Hasana et al., 'Trace Metals Pollution in Seawater and Groundwater in The Ship Breaking Area of Sitakund Upazilla, Chittagong, Bangladesh' (2013) 71 *Marine Pollution Bulletin* 317; Hasan Muhammad Abdullah et al., 'Monitoring the Drastic Growth of Ship Breaking Yards in Sitakunda: A Threat to the Coastal Environment of Bangladesh' (2013) 185 *Environmental Monitoring and Assessment* 3839; M. Jamaluddin Ahmed et al., 'Physicochemical Assessment of Soil Pollutants Due to the Ship Breaking Activities and Its Impact on the Coastal Zone of Chittagong, Bangladesh' (2013) 2 *European Chemical Bulletin* 1053; Aage Bjørn Andersen, Erik Bjørnbom and Terje Sverud, *Technical Report: Decommissioning of Ships – Environmental Standards: Ship-Breaking Practices/On Site Assessment: Bangladesh – Chittagong*, Det Norske Veritas Report No. 2000–3158 (12 May 2000) <www.shipbreakingplatform.org/shipbrea_wp2011/wp-content/uploads/2011/11/dnvbangladesh.pdf>.

17 Andersen, Bjørnbom and Sverud, ibid.

18 Ibid.

19 Therese H. Nøst et al., 'High Concentrations of Organic Contaminants in Air from Ship Breaking Activities in Chittagong, Bangladesh' (2015) 49 *Environmental Science and Technology* 11372.

20 YPSA, *Overview of Ship Breaking in Bangladesh* (2012) <www.shipbreakingbd.info/overview.html>; another estimate is that around 700 workers were killed and 10,000 injured in explosions at shipbreaking yards over the last three decades. Many injured workers were left

gigantic ships and the total absence of precautionary measures. This scenario of fatal accidents and injury continues unabated to this day. Workers are subject to regular exposure to hazardous substances in the shipbreaking yards of Bangladesh. Many of the workers are not local (mainly from the northern parts of the country), and are illiterate and extremely poor.

In 2004, under the auspices of the International Labour Organization (ILO), a set of guidelines called Safety and Health in Shipbreaking: Guidelines for Asian Countries and Turkey (hereinafter ILO Guidelines) was adopted.[21] The ILO Guidelines identify a number of issues including 'lack of an inventory of hazardous material; decontamination and gas-freeing; planning for safe demolition; and recycling and safe waste management' in the shipbreaking industry.[22] They also identify a number of common hazards that are responsible for death, injury, ill health and disease among shipbreaking workers.[23] Some of the most frequent causes of accidents in the shipbreaking yards identified in the guidelines are 'fire, explosion, falling objects, poor illumination, falls from heights, oxygen deficiency, moving objects, lack of personal protective equipment, lack of hazard communication and inhalation in confined and enclosed spaces'.[24] The ILO Guidelines also identify a number of hazardous substances, wastes and physical hazards responsible for worker injury, death and ill health, including 'asbestos'; heavy and toxic metals such as 'lead, mercury, cadmium, copper and zinc'; organometallic substances such as TBT, PCBs, 'polyvinyl chloride'; 'volatile organic compounds' and 'compressed gas'.[25] The guidelines also identify other hazards responsible for death, injury, ill health and disease among shipbreaking workers, including 'mechanical', 'biological', 'ergonomic and psychosocial hazards'.[26] Finally, they identify a number of serious violations of occupational safety procedures and rights of workers including, inter alia, unsatisfactory 'work organisation' and absence of proper 'safety and health training', lack of proper systems for 'accident prevention', and inadequate 'first aid, rescue and medical facilities'.[27]

Despite the global and national attention given to this industry, death is a regular occurrence. International and national legal frameworks have failed to ensure workers' safety in this industry. More than a decade after the adoption of the ILO Guidelines and despite the introduction of many more regulations at international and national levels, in 2016 alone at least 22 workers were killed and 30 were seriously injured in the Bangladeshi shipbreaking yards.[28] Table 1.1 shows

---

disabled. M. Zahid Hossain, 'A Few Data on the Accident of Shipbreaking, Chittagong' (2006) 6 *Social Action* 13.

21 International Labour Organization (ILO), *Safety and Health in Shipbreaking: Guidelines for Asian Countries and Turkey* (ILO, 2004).

22 Ibid., 4.

23 Ibid.

24 Ibid., 8.

25 Ibid.

26 Ibid.

27 Ibid.

28 NGO Shipbreaking Platform, *Substandard Shipbreaking: A Global Challenge* (February 2017) <www.shipbreakingplatform.org/shipbrea_wp2011/wp-content/uploads/2017/01/Worldwide-overview_FINAL_2017.pdf>.

Table 1.1 Number and Causes of Deaths in the Shipbreaking Industry: 2006–2016[29]

Year	*Number of worker deaths*	*Some known or common causes*
2006	11	Fall from height Slipping on wet surfaces Explosion Suffocation by toxic gases Smashed by heavy iron plate
2007	8	Fall from height Smashed by heavy iron plate
2008	14	Suffocation by toxic gases Smashed by heavy iron plate Fall from height Smashed by a sharp iron plate Fire from gas
2009	25	Fall from height Slipping on wet surfaces Suffocation by toxic gases Smashed by heavy iron plate Gas explosion Explosion of oil tank
2010	12	Smashed by iron plate Fire from fuel tank Fall of heavy metal
2011	15	Explosion in the fuel tank Fall of heavy metal plate
2012	15	Fire Smashed by iron plate
2013	20	Fall of large iron plate Fall of object Fire
2014	16	Fire while cutting a pipe Fall from height Tank explosion Suffocation by toxic gases
2015	16	Fall from height Cylinder blast Smashed by Steel plate Explosion
2016	22	Fall from height Falling steel plates Cylinder blast Inhaling toxic gas

29 This table was developed using information from the following sources: YPSA, *Death Trap! A List of Dead Workers from the Year of 2005 to 2012 (September)* (2012) <www.shipbreakingbd.info/death_trap.html>; YPSA, *Death Trap! Accident Information for 2012* (2012) <www.shipbreakingbd.info/death_trap_2012.html>; International Federation for Human Rights (FIDH), *Bangladesh Shipbreaking Still Dirty and Dangerous with at Least 20 Deaths in 2013* (13 December 2013) <www.fidh.org/en/region/asia/bangladesh/14395-bangladesh-shipbreaking-still-dirty-and-dangerous-with-at-least-20-deaths>; Industri ALL, *Four Workers Die in a Series of Accidents in Bangladeshi Shipbreaking Yards* (7 June 2016)

the number and probable causes of death in this industry in the last decade, signifying the failure of national and international regulations.

The causes of worker casualties listed in Table 1.1 clearly show that these were preventable deaths. Proper gas-free-for-hot-work procedures, pre-cleaning of vessels in developed countries or in state-of-the-art facilities within Bangladesh and robust OHS procedures could prevent most of these casualties. The table shows an incomplete record of deaths in the shipbreaking industry, representing only incidents about which local media and nongovernmental organisations (NGOs) were able to collect information. Accurate figures for casualties are most likely higher. Moreover, these figures do not include deaths of workers after leaving shipbreaking yards due to exposure to dangerous and hazardous substances. A recent study of 101 workers in the Bangladeshi shipbreaking industry showed that 33 had asbestos deposits on 60% of their bodies' and eight had 'a build-up of the toxic mineral in 60% of their lungs'.[30] Because of the obscure process of

---

<www.industriall-union.org/four-workers-die-in-a-series-of-accidents-in-bangladeshi-shipbreaking-yards>; Star Online Report, 'Worker Killed in Ctg Ship Breaking Yard' *The Daily Star* (online) 3 June 2013 <www.thedailystar.net/news/worker-killed-in-ctg-ship-breaking-yard>; Star Online Report, '3 Burnt in Ctg Ship-Breaking Yard Fire' *The Daily Star* (online) 19 January 2014 <http://archive.thedailystar.net/news2014/3-burnt-in-ctg-ship-breaking-yard-fire-7455>; Staff Correspondent, 'Ship-Breaking Worker Killed' *The Daily Star* (online) 3 June 2014 <www.thedailystar.net/ship-breaking-worker-killed-26819>; Arun Bikash Dey, 'Two Ship Breaking Yard Burn Victims Groaning at CMCH' *The Daily Star* (online) 22 January 2014 <www.thedailystar.net/two-ship-breaking-yard-burn-victims-groaning-at-cmch-7908>; Staff Correspondent, 'Worker Dies in Ctg Ship Breaking Yard Accident' *The Daily Star* (online) 7 June 2015 <www.thedailystar.net/city/worker-dies-ctg-ship-breaking-yard-accident-93400>; Star Online Report, 'Cylinder Blast Hurts 8 at Ctg Ship Breaking Yard' *The Daily Star* (online) 5 September 2015 <www.thedailystar.net/country/cylinder-blast-hurts-4-ctg-ship-breaking-yard-138238>; Staff Correspondent, 'Ctg Ship Breaking Yard Worker Dies' *The Daily Star* (online) 7 July 2015 <www.thedailystar.net/city/ctg-ship-breaking-yard-worker-dies-108625>; Staff Correspondent, 'Burnt Worker of Ctg Ship-Breaking Yard Dies in CMCH' *The Daily Star* (online) 10 September 2015 <www.thedailystar.net/city/burnt-worker-ctg-ship-breaking-yard-dies-cmch-140662>; Staff Correspondent, 'Four Workers Die Due to Toxic Gas in Sitakunda Shipbreaking Yards' (title translated from Bengali), *The Daily Prothom Alo* (online) 4 April 2014 <www.prothom-alo.com/bangladesh/article/184267/সীতাকুণ্ডে-জাহাজভাঙা-ইয়ার্ডে-বিষক্রিয়ায়-চার>; Shashank Bengali, 'Adult and Underage Workers Risk Their Lives in Bangladesh's Rising Ship-Breaking Industry' *Los Angeles Times* (online) 9 March 2016 <www.latimes.com/world/asia/la-fg-bangladesh-ships-20160309-story.html>; Mike Schuler, *NGO Shipbreaking Platform: Use of 'Polluting' South Asia Scrap Yards Accelerating* (1 February 2017) <http://gcaptain.com/ngo-shipbreaking-platform-use-of-polluting-south-asia-scrap-yards-accelerating/>; NGO Shipbreaking Platform, *Platform News – Surge of Fatal Accidents in Chittagong: 10 Shipbreaking Workers Killed or Severely Injured in One Month Only* (27 June 2016) <www.shipbreakingplatform.org/platform-news-surge-of-fatal-accidents-in-chittagong/>; Staff Correspondent Ctg, 'Worker Dies at Chittagong Shipbreaking Yard' *The Daily Star* (online) 18 April 2016 <www.thedailystar.net/backpage/worker-dies-shipbreaking-yard-ctg-1210384>; NGO Shipbreaking Platform, ibid.

30 Staff Correspondent, 'One-Third of Bangladesh Ship-Breaking Workers at High Risk of Lung Diseases: Study' *Bdnews24.com* (online) 2 February 2017 <http://bdnews24.com/bangladesh/2017/02/02/one-third-of-bangladesh-ship-breaking-workers-at-high-risk-of-lung-diseases-study>.

appointment of workers, many of whom are not local to Chittagong, it is almost impossible to collect information about death and disease among workers due to exposure to hazardous substances in shipbreaking yards after they leave the yard.

In recent times, the increasing number of casualties has raised serious questions about so-called 'initiatives' of international and national authorities. In 2016, at least 10 workers were killed or severely injured in just one month.[31] This industry is a blight on humanity. It is surprising that the global and national community allows this rampant killing of poor workers. The regularity of these incidents proves that they are not just accidents; they are nothing but the killing of poor workers. When shipbreaking owners ask workers to cut a vessel using an oxy-acetylene torch, knowing that the ship is not pre-cleaned and is not in a proper gas-free-for-hot-work condition, they risk killing workers.

For doing this dangerous job, Bangladeshi shipbreaking workers are paid only 24 to 52 cents (U.S.) per hour.[32] A report by a human rights organisation shows that shipbreaking workers are deprived of almost all recognised labour rights, including inter alia, a legal wage structure, sick leave, medical facilities, safety gear and other OHS arrangements, a weekly paid day off, overtime, identification documents or proper records of appointment and freedom of association.[33] In fact, neither the industry nor the government care for these unfortunate workers. As observed by one worker:

> The lives of the shipbreaking workers have no value to the government and local shipbreaking owners. They do not consider us as a [sic] human beings. If a worker dies in an accident, the owners can get away with paying 100,000 taka [$1,284] to the family. To them the value of a worker is no more than 100,000 taka [$1,284].[34]

Most of the workers are not local to the Chittagong region and are mainly from relatively poor northern districts of Bangladesh.[35] Most are appointed using a separate contractor through an obscure system, and face a modern form of economic slavery.[36] Moreover, a 2005 estimate showed that around 11% of workers were children.[37]

31 NGO Shipbreaking Platform, above n 29.

32 Charles Kernaghan, *Murder in the Shipbreaking Yards, Chittagong, Bangladesh*, Report, Institute for Global Human and Labour Rights (November 2015) <www.globallabourrights.org/reports/document/Murder-in-the-Shipbreaking-Yards-1.pdf>.

33 Ibid.; see also, FIDH, *Where Do the 'Floating Dustbins' End Up? Labour Rights in Shipbreaking Yards in South Asia: The Cases of Chittagong (Bangladesh) and Alang (India)*, Report, FIDH (December 2002) <www.fidh.org/IMG/pdf/bd1112a.pdf>.

34 Ibid, Kernaghan.

35 YPSA, *Workers in Shipbreaking Industries: A Base Line Survey of Chittagong (Bangladesh)* (Young Power in Social Action, 2005) 29.

36 Karim, above n 12.

37 YPSA, above n 35. See also Ruben Dao, *Childbreaking Yards – Child Labour in the Ship Recycling Industry in Bangladesh*, Report, FIDH and YPSA (2008) <www.fidh.org/IMG/pdf/bgukreport.pdf>.

1.3 Scope and overview of the book

This book aims to critically examine the issue of global and national environmental injustice using the shipbreaking industry as an example. It examines possible ways of establishing a just, equitable and effective legal regime for ensuring environmentally sound disposal of obsolete ships by critically analysing the legal framework for disposal of obsolete ships using the lens of environmental justice. There are many critical issues relevant to ensuring environmental justice in the shipbreaking industry. Perhaps the concept is best understood by identifying what constitutes environmental injustice. It follows that the shipbreaking industry represents a clear example of environmental injustice. Despite the location of most shipbreaking in the least developed countries, the owners of shipbreaking companies are very wealthy local businessmen. The ultimate burden of environmental pollution and accidents in the industry is borne by poor workers and people resident in nearby areas. Nevertheless, owners of shipbreaking companies and middleclass people from these countries benefit from the industry as a source for building materials and furniture.[38] The burden has been shifted to the most marginalised segment of society.

Moreover, the shipbreaking industry involves a broader issue of global environmental injustice. It is not uncommon for developed countries to externalise their hazards or environmental harms to others. For example, it is common for hazardous wastes to be disposed of in least developed countries, whose ability to assess and manage the risks associated with such hazards is very limited. This practice imposes adverse environmental and socio-economic consequences in many of these countries. The shipbreaking industry is an example of this practice. Further, the burden of recycling of developed countries hazardous substances has been shifted to the least developed countries. This is a clear derogation of the 'polluter pays' principle. Recently developed international legal instruments also fail to change this unsatisfactory status and have proven to be counterproductive.

This introductory chapter concisely presents the environmental justice issues related to shipbreaking and the scope of the book. Chapter 2 presents a critical analysis of environmental justice from the perspective of the Bangladeshi shipbreaking industry. In defining the concept of environmental justice, the chapter uses the notion of *nyaya* or the 'comprehensive concept of realized justice' as explored in the Amartya Sen's *Idea of Justice*. The chapter paves a foundation for subsequent chapters by discussing the fundamentals of environmental justice in both the international and Bangladeshi contexts.

Chapter 3 examines the role of existing international environmental conventions in ensuring a safe and environmentally sound operation of shipbreaking. The chapter particularly highlights the role of the International Maritime Organization (IMO) marine environmental conventions and international conventions for transboundary movement and environmentally sound disposal of hazardous

38 Nicky Gregson et al., 'Following Things of Rubbish Value: End-of-Life Ships, "Chock-Chocky" Furniture and the Bangladeshi Middle Class Consumer' (2010) 41 *Geoforum* 846.

wastes and other hazardous substances including, inter alia, the International Convention for the Prevention of Pollution from Ships (hereinafter MARPOL Convention or MARPOL 73/78),[39] the Basel Convention on the Control of Transboundary Movements of Hazardous Wastes and Their Disposal (hereinafter Basel Convention),[40] the Stockholm Convention on Persistent Organic Pollutants (hereinafter Stockholm Convention)[41] and the Rotterdam Convention on Certain Hazardous Chemicals and Pesticides (hereinafter Rotterdam Convention).[42] This chapter shows that although these international legal instruments may be relevant for the shipbreaking industry, practical implementation is lacking due to multifarious causes, including lack of political will from the governments; the unwillingness of shipping and shipbreaking companies to adhere to the conventions; and the culture of 'flags of convenience' that allows ship owners and shipbreaking business owners to circumvent legal requirements.

Chapter 4 introduces regulatory developments at global and regional levels, including the Hong Kong International Convention for the Safe and Environmentally Sound Recycling of Ships (hereinafter Hong Kong Convention)[43] and the European Union Ship Recycling Regulation (hereinafter EU SRR), which implements the Hong Kong Convention in EU member states.[44] Although it is expected that the Hong Kong Convention will establish a more effective and comprehensive regulatory framework, it has a number of fundamental flaws that may make it largely ineffective. The convention treats shipbreaking as a mere technical issue and fails to adequately address the issue of environmental injustice and violation of labour rights.

Chapter 5 comprehensively examines the legal and institutional framework of Bangladesh for ensuring environmental justice in the shipbreaking industry. The chapter argues that because of global awareness, activism by local environmental groups and interventions from the Supreme Court, the government recently

39 *International Convention for the Prevention of Pollution from Ships*, opened for signature 2 November 1973, 1340 UNTS 184 as modified by the Protocol of 1978 to the 1973 Convention, opened for signature 17 February 1978, 1341 UNTS 3 (entered into force 2 October 1983).

40 *Basel Convention on the Control of Transboundary Movements of Hazardous Wastes and Their Disposal*, opened for signature 22 March 1989, 1673 UNTS 126 (entered into force 24 May 1992).

41 *Stockholm Convention on Persistent Organic Pollutants*, opened for signature 22 May 2001, 2256 UNTS 119 (entered into force 17 May 2004).

42 *Rotterdam Convention on the Prior Informed Consent Procedure for Certain Hazardous Chemicals and Pesticides in International Trade*, opened for signature 10 September 1998, 2244 UNTS 337 (entered into force 24 February 2004).

43 *Hong Kong International Convention for the Safe and Environmentally Sound Recycling of Ships*, opened for signature 1 September 2009, IMO Doc. SR/CONF/45 (19 May 2009) (not yet in force).

44 *Regulation (EU) No. 1257/2013 of the European Parliament and of the Council of 20 November 2013 on Ship Recycling and Amending Regulation (EC) No. 1013/2006 and Directive 2009/16/EC*, 2013, OJ (L 330) 1.

developed regulations for this industry. However, practical implementation and enforcement of these regulations is seriously lacking due to the unwillingness of the shipbreaking industry and their influence in regulatory institutions. The chapter argues that the regulatory system in Bangladesh has failed due to frequent changes to laws that protect the interests of shipbreaking company owners. The human rights of shipbreaking workers have been flouted in flagrant violation of the Constitution of Bangladesh and applicable laws of the country. The relevant departments of the government have been more interested in safeguarding the interests of shipbreaking company owners. Consequently, the rampant killing of poor shipbreaking workers continues unabated with full impunity. The decisions of the highest court of the country are routinely violated, not only because of the lack of proactive steps by the relevant government departments, but also due to the notoriously ingenious and deliberate misinterpretation of the court's decisions by government officials, presumably to safeguard the interests of the influential shipbreaking industry.

2 Environmental justice

2.1 Introduction

This chapter critically examines the issue of environmental justice at both international and national levels in the context of shipbreaking. Globally, the burden of obsolete ship disposal has been transferred to the least developed countries, taking advantage of their corruption and serious failures in environmental governance. Nationally, the main burden of environmental pollution and occupational hazards is borne by poor workers.

Ensuring environmental justice in the shipbreaking industry may involve consideration of many aspects of justice. It may involve broader aspects of socio-economic rights as well as issues of sharing the disproportionate burden of environmental harms by a marginalised segment of society.

Section 2.2 aims to conceptualise environmental justice in the context of the shipbreaking industry. The section defines environmental justice, mainly relying on Amartya Sen's *Idea of Justice*, particularly using the concept of *nyaya* or a 'comprehensive concept of realized justice.' Section 2.3 examines the concept of environmental justice under international law. It particularly highlights the issues of human rights and the environment; environmental justice and international environmental law principles; environmental justice and labour rights; and the United Nations Convention on the Law of the Sea (UNCLOS)[1] and protection of the marine environment in a just and equitable way. This list indicates the multidimensional aspects of environmental justice in the context of the shipbreaking industry.

Section 2.4 discusses the concept of environmental justice in the context of Bangladesh. It specifically examines the relationship between environmental justice and the realisation of aspirational socio-economic rights included in the Constitution of Bangladesh as fundamental principles of state policy. This section also examines the relationship between fundamental rights under the Constitution of Bangladesh – particularly the right to life – and environmental justice in the shipbreaking industry. This chapter argues that, in the context of the Bangladeshi

1 *United Nations Convention on the Law of the Sea*, opened for signature 10 December 1982, 1833 UNTS 3 (entered into force 16 November 1994), (hereinafter UNCLOS).

shipbreaking industry, implementation of socio-economic rights is inherently interlinked with ensuring environmental justice. The process should be guided by the concept of *nyaya* (realised justice). It is critical to have a society based on realised justice (in Bengali ন্যায়ভিত্তিক সমাজ [*nyayabhittik somaj*]) for ensuring environmental justice or for elimination of environmental injustice in the true sense.

2.2 Defining environmental justice

It is not easy to define environmental justice, which is a relatively new concept that can be considered a special area of social justice. In the last few decades, environmental justice has been elaborately examined by scholars of different areas of social sciences.[2] The environmental justice framework has been influenced by several theoretical developments of justice including, inter alia, distributive,[3] recognition,[4]

2 Karen Bell, *Achieving Environmental Justice: A Cross-National Analysis* (Policy Press, 2014); Rhuks Ako, *Environmental Justice in Developing Countries: Perspectives from Africa and Asia-Pacific* (Routledge, 2013); Gordon Walker, *Environmental Justice: Concepts, Evidence and Politics* (Routledge, 2012); Florence Margai, *Environmental Health Hazards and Social Justice: Geographical Perspectives on Race and Class Disparities* (Routledge, 2010); Filomina Chioma Steady, *Environmental Justice in the New Millennium: Global Perspectives on Race, Ethnicity, and Human Rights* (Springer, 2009); David Schlosberg, *Defining Environmental Justice: Theories, Movements, and Nature* (Oxford University Press, 2007); Kristin Shrader-Frechette, *Environmental Justice: Creating Equity, Reclaiming Democracy* (Oxford University Press, 2002); Marie-Claire Cordonier Segger and Christopher Gregory Weeramantry (eds), *Sustainable Justice: Reconciling Economic, Social and Environmental Law* (Martinus Nijhoff Publishers, 2005); Ruchi Anand, *International Environmental Justice: A North – South Dimension* (Ashgate, 2004); Joni Adamson, Mei Evans and Rachel Stein, *The Environmental Justice Reader: Politics, Poetics, & Pedagogy* (University of Arizona Press, 2002); Laura Westra, *Environmental Justice and the Rights of Indigenous Peoples: International and Domestic Legal Perspectives* (Earthscan, 2012); Francis O. Adeola, 'Cross-National Environmental Injustice and Human Rights Issues: A Review of Evidence in the Developing World' (2000) 43 *American Behavioral Scientist* 686; David Naguib Pellow and Robert J. Brulle (eds), *Power, Justice, and the Environment: A Critical Appraisal of the Environmental Justice Movement* (MIT Press, 2005); Andrew Dobson (ed), *Fairness and Futurity: Essays on Environmental Sustainability and Social Justice* (Oxford University Press, 1999); Bunyan I. Bryant, *Environmental Justice: Issues, Policies, and Solutions* (Island Press, 1995); Luke W. Cole and Sheila R. Foster, *From the Ground up: Environmental Racism and the Rise of the Environmental Justice Movement* (New York University Press, 2001).

3 Brian Barry, 'Sustainable and Intergenerational Justice' in Andrew Dobson (ed), *Fairness and Futurity: Essays on Environmental Sustainability and Social Justice* (Oxford University Press, 1999) 94–117; Tomilola Akanle Eni-Ibukun, *International Environmental Law and Distributive Justice* (Routledge, 2014); Andrew Dobson, *Justice and the Environment: Conceptions of Environmental Sustainability and Theories of Distributive Justice* (Oxford University Press, 1998). For distributive justice, see generally, John Rawls, *A Theory of Justice* (Oxford University Press, 1971).

4 Iris Marion Young, *Justice and the Politics of Difference* (Princeton University Press, 1990); Nancy Fraser, *Justice Interruptus: Critical Reflections on the 'Postsocialist' Condition* (Routledge, 1997); Robert Doyle Bullard, *Dumping in Dixie: Race, Class, and Environmental Quality* (Westview Press, 2000); Robert Doyle Bullard, *The Quest for Environmental Justice: Human Rights and the Politics of Pollution* (Sierra Club Books, 2005); Cole and Foster, above n 2.

capability[5] and procedural justice.[6] Environmental justice has gone far beyond the distribution of environmental risks and has expanded in many ways.[7]

Despite the theoretical development of environmental justice discourses, the issue of disproportionate burden of environmental risk is a central issue for environmental injustice at local, national and international levels. As observed by Shrader-Frechette, '[i]n every nation of the world poor people and minorities face greater environmental risks, have less access to environmental goods, and have less ability to control the environmental insults imposed on them'.[8] This aspect of environmental justice is highly relevant in the shipbreaking industry in Bangladesh.

The disproportionate burden of environmental pollution to poor shipbreaking workers reminds us of some fundamental theoretical issues. The most important of this is what should be the central focus of justice. Even if it is not possible to establish a perfectly just society, it is highly desirable that we eliminate at least remediable injustice.[9] According to Amartya Sen, identification of redressable injustice should be central to the theory of justice.[10] Contemporary justice scholarship mainly focusses on the identification and establishment of 'just institutions'.[11] Establishment of just institutions and rules are important but 'realized actuality' may involve more than just institutions and rules.[12] Actual realisation-based theoretical development of justice may be explained using the concepts of *niti* and *nyaya*. *Niti*, as understood in Sanskrit and Bengali, reflects a version of justice based on 'organizational propriety and behavioural correctness'.[13] In contrast, the term *nyaya* means a 'comprehensive concept of realized justice'.[14] Another concept of ancient Indian jurisprudence is *matsyanyaya* (justice of fish), where big fish can freely eat small fish.[15] It is essential to avoid *matsyanyaya* to ensure *nyaya*.[16] Eliminating *matsyanyaya* to ensure *nyaya* may be an important aspect of justice or environmental justice in the shipbreaking industry of

5 Martha Nussbaum and Amartya Sen (eds), *The Quality of Life* (Oxford University Press, 1992); Jérôme Ballet, Jean-Marcel Koffi and Jérôme Pelenc, 'Environment, Justice and the Capability Approach' (2013) 85 *Ecological Economics* 28; Ortrud Lessmann and Felix Rauschmayer (eds), *The Capability Approach and Sustainability* (Routledge, 2016).

6 Walker, above n 2, 47–50; Shrader-Frechette, above n 2, 27; Schlosberg, above n 2, 25–28; Brian J. Preston, 'The Effectiveness of the Law in Providing Access to Environmental Justice: An Introduction' in Paul Martin et al. (eds) *The Search for Environmental Justice* (Edward Elgar Publishing, 2015) 23, 34–38.

7 David Schlosberg 'Theorising Environmental Justice: The Expanding Sphere of a Discourse' (2013) 22 *Environmental Politics* 37.

8 Shrader-Frechette, above n 2, 3.

9 Amartya Sen, *The Idea of Justice* (Allen Lane, 2009) vii.

10 Ibid.

11 Ibid., xi.

12 Ibid., 18.

13 Ibid., 20.

14 Ibid.

15 Ibid.

16 Ibid.

Bangladesh where it is effectively accepted by the government and society that the right to life of poor workers is not as important as the right to life of rich or middleclass people. It is important for emerging economies like Bangladesh to recognise that it is important to fare well, not just fare forward.[17]

Poor and mostly non-local workers bear the main burden of environmental risk in the shipbreaking industry of Bangladesh. A critical question in this aspect is why the poor bear the disproportionate – in the case of shipbreaking – burden of environmental risk. The related question here is why they work in the shipbreaking industry despite this risk. As mentioned by Sen, '[d]evelopment consists of the removal of various types of unfreedoms that leave people with little choice and little opportunity of exercising their reasoned agency'.[18] He further said, 'development requires the removal of major sources of unfreedom: poverty as well as tyranny, poor economic opportunities as well as systematic social deprivation, neglect of public facilities as well as intolerance or overactivity of repressive states'.[19] Despite some success, substantive freedom is yet to be achieved for marginalised segments of society in Bangladesh.[20] The interrelationship of some crucial instrumental freedoms, including 'economic opportunities, political freedoms, social facilities, transparency guarantees and protective security' is worth examining to ensure substantive freedom for individuals.[21] The shipbreaking industry may be an example of how the cumulative consequence of these factors may lead to environmental injustice. The main reasons for people to work in a hazardous industry like shipbreaking is poverty and ignorance. Impoverished people have little choice but to work in this type of industry, thereby risking their lives. Sustainable development should be ensured to provide freedom to these people. Sustainable development will give them the power of decision making. As observed in the 1972 Stockholm Declaration on Human Environment (hereinafter Stockholm Declaration):

> In the developing countries most of the environmental problems are caused by under-development. Millions continue to live far below the minimum levels required for a decent human existence, deprived of adequate food and clothing, shelter and education, health and sanitation. Therefore, *the developing countries must direct their efforts to development, bearing in mind their priorities and the need to safeguard and improve the environment.* For the same purpose, the industrialised countries should make efforts to reduce the gap themselves and the developing countries.[22]

17 Ibid., 24.

18 Amartya Sen, *Development as Freedom* (Oxford University Press, 1999) xii.

19 Ibid., 1.

20 The Economist, 'Bangladesh and Development: The Path through the Fields' *The Economist* (online) 3 November 2012 <www.economist.com/news/briefing/21565617-bangladesh-has-dysfunctional-politics-and-stunted-private-sector-yet-it-has-been-surprisingly>.

21 Sen, above n 18, xii.

22 *Declaration of the United Nations Conference on the Human Environment*, UN Doc. A/Conf.48/14/Rev.1 (1972), (hereinafter Stockholm Declaration) (emphasis added).

However, economic development of a country may not fully ensure justice or environmental justice for marginalised segments of society. Because of serious limits to their freedom and capabilities, a group of people even in a developed country may face a lower standard of living than even average people in some developing countries.[23] In the context of shipbreaking, environmental justice involves a number of issues including equality, disproportionate burden, lack of knowledge, access to decision and law making processes and access to justice. In the case of the victims of environmental injustice in the shipbreaking industry, poverty makes all of these other aspects redundant. People are forced to work in conditions that are totally unacceptable under any circumstances.

2.3 Environmental justice and international law

Environmental justice is a critical discourse of international law involving distributive, procedural, corrective and social aspects.[24] Historically, developed countries have been more responsible than developing countries for global environmental degradation. Even today, despite remarkable development of some leading developing countries, per capita consumption of resources by the developed world is far higher than in the developing world. Despite the developed world's greater abilities, the developing world still bears a greater burden of environmental harms The shipbreaking industry is a clear example of this, where vessels that served the economy of the developed world go to developing countries for disposal. In fact, developed country ship owners sell their obsolete ships to developing country shipbreaking yards. Rather than internalising the cost of disposal of wastes, they profit from them.

An important question in this regard is why developed countries accept/import wastes. The answer to this question involves issues dealing with the broader aspect of economic development. Some of the countries that import hazardous wastes, particularly Bangladesh, were colonised by a European power for a long time. The colonial power used these countries to produce raw materials for the rapid industrialisation of Europe. In doing so, they completely destroyed the agriculture-based sustainable economics of these countries and created extreme poverty that even led to famine.[25] Many developing countries are yet to fully recover from many years of oppression that not only destroyed their economy but also divided societies and countries because of the 'divide and rule' policy of the colonisers. Colonial rulers not only destroyed the economy of the colonies,

23 Sen, above n 9, 226.

24 Carmen G. Gonzalez, 'Environmental Justice and International Environmental Law' in Shawkat Alam et al. (eds) *Routledge Handbook of International Environmental Law* (Routledge, 2013) 77.

25 Janam Mukherjee, *Hungry Bengal: War, Famine and the End of Empire* (Oxford University Press, 2015); see also Sen, above n 18; see generally, Shashi Tharoor, *An Era of Darkness: The British Empire in India* (Aleph Book Company, 2016).

but they also institutionalised corruption and bribery.[26] As observed by one commentator, during the colonial period in India, 'a government officer accepting money for favours rendered in his official capacity was as legal as the unwritten British Constitution, regardless of the stringent punishment provided against it in the written law'.[27] Environmental justice in the post-colonial global south cannot be understood fully without acknowledging this historic background. It is difficult for the developing world to emerge from its colonial past because most post-colonial developing countries began their journey as independent states with the leftovers of the former colonial administration, which was highly corrupt. In other words, former colonies inherited a corrupt bureaucracy and an anti-people governance system. Many former colonies still follow the legal system introduced by the colonisers. For example, Bangladesh has inherited, with some exceptions, environmental and resource-related laws and institutions that were established by the British to exploit natural resources to supply raw materials for their own industries.[28] Therefore, environmental and natural resources laws in Bangladesh are still use-oriented, ignoring the rights of local people who are historically dependent on those resources.[29] Economic and political colonisation is still alive in different forms throughout international institutions as well as the economic and military might of the former colonisers. Economic conditions and a colonial legacy of corruption and misgovernance are important factors in understanding why the least developed countries still accept hazardous wastes. As will be discussed later in this book, although this historical background is important to understand global environmental justice, developing countries like Bangladesh should not use this as an excuse for not eliminating 'redressable injustice', particularly in cases where it is possible to ensure environmental justice using their own capacity.

Following the decolonisation era, an initiative for establishing a New International Economic Order (NIEO)[30] was taken to transform the global economy for

26 This is not to say there was no corruption in pre-colonial rule. For example, corruption was common in bureaucracy in ancient and medieval South Asia. Akbar Ali Khan, *Gresham's Law Syndrome and Beyond: An Analysis of the Bangladesh Bureaucracy* (University Press Limited, Dhaka, 2015) 33–37.

27 M.B. Lal, 'How Our British Rulers "Legalised" Bribery' *The Hindu* (online) 10 September 2011 <www.thehindu.com/opinion/open-page/how-our-british-rulers-legalised-bribery/article2442485.ece#comments>.

28 Anjan Kumer Dev Roy, Khorshed Alam and Jeff Gow, 'A Review of the Role of Property Rights and Forest Policies in the Management of the Sundarbans Mangrove Forest in Bangladesh' (2012) 15 *Forest Policy and Economics* 46; Md Saiful Karim, 'Proposed REDD+ Project for the Sundarbans: Legal and Institutional Issues' (2013) 3 *International Journal of Rural Law and Policy* 1.

29 Mohiuddin Farooque, 'Regulatory Framework and Some Examples of Environmental Contamination in Bangladesh' in Bangladesh Environmental Lawyers Association (BELA) (ed) *Selected Writings of Mohiuddin Farooque: Environmental Order the Security of Survival* (BELA, 2004) 20.

30 Three important United Nations (UN) General Assembly Resolutions for a New International Economic Order (NIEO), *Declaration on the Right to Development*, UN Doc.

redirecting benefit to the global south, to make the decolonisation process meaningful.[31] NIEO was full of obstacles, partly due to the structure of international institutions – in particular monetary institutions, which favour the developed world.[32] Moreover, some developed countries tried their best to undermine this initiative and NIEO is now almost forgotten.[33] However, it is arguably true that economic conditions in the global south are better now than during the time of initiation of the NIEO, and some of the objectives of the NIEO have arguably been achieved.[34] However, this development is not evenly distributed, creating a further division between developing and least developed countries.

Despite the above foundational and inherent inadequacies, the international legal system has developed a framework for environmental justice. It is mainly established through international human rights instruments and some basic principles of international environmental law.

2.3.1 Human rights and environment

During the adoption of major global legal instruments for human rights after World War II, environmental human rights were not considered for inclusion. The Universal Declaration of Human Rights (UDHR) of 1948,[35] the International Covenant on Civil and Political Rights (ICCPR) of 1966[36] and the International Covenant on Economic, Social and Cultural Rights (ICESCR) of 1966[37] made no explicit mention of environmental human rights. National constitutions of states at that time also did not refer to such rights. However, many countries

A/41/53 (1986); *Declaration on the Establishment of a New International Economic Order*, UN Doc. A/RES/S-6/3201 (1974); *Permanent Sovereignty Over Natural Resources*, UN Doc. A/5217 (1962).

31 Nils Gilman, 'The New International Economic Order: A Reintroduction' (2015) 6 *Humanity* 1.

32 Ervin Laszlo et al., *Obstacles to the New International Economic Order* (Pergamon Press, 1980).

33 'The NIEO today is almost entirely forgotten, at least when referred to by its proper name . . . Already in the early 1980s, the conventional wisdom among main-stream analysts in the Anglophone academy was that NIEO had always been doomed to failure. The explanations for this inevitability were legion: the political solidarity of the Third World was bound to unravel; the logic of collective action meant that commodity cartels were destined to defection and failure; the attempt to use international law to rein in the sovereign prerogatives of powerful countries was fated to succumb to jurisdictional fragmentation and forum shopping; and the north was always going to have been willing and able to flex its vastly greater economic, political, and (if ultimately necessary) military might to restrain the rise of the south'. Gilman, above n 31, 9 (citations omitted).

34 Ibid.

35 *Universal Declaration of Human Rights*, GA Res 217(III), UN Doc. A/RES/3/217A (10 December 1948) (hereinafter UDHR).

36 *International Covenant on Civil and Political Rights*, opened for signature 16 December 1966, 999 UNTS 171 (entered into force 23 March 1976) (hereinafter ICCPR).

37 *International Covenant on Economic, Social and Cultural Rights*, opened for signature 16 December 1966, 999 UNTS 3 (entered into force 3 January 1976) (hereinafter ICESCR).

later recognised the right to a healthy environment as a constitutional right, or incorporated environmental protection-related provisions in their constitutions.[38]

Environmental protection became an increasingly central issue following the United Nations Conference on the Human Environment, held in Stockholm in 1972. The Stockholm Declaration recognised the 'fundamental right to freedom, equality and adequate conditions of life, in *an environment of a quality that permits a life of dignity and well-being*' for everyone.[39] This is, obviously, not a recognition of a separate environmental right. Rather, it incorporates environmental rights in the pre-existing human rights, including the rights to freedom, to equality and to life. Similarly, Principle 1 of the 1992 Rio Declaration on Environment and Development (hereinafter Rio Declaration) recognises that human beings 'are entitled to a healthy and productive life in harmony with nature'.[40]

Although global human rights and environmental conventions do not expressly incorporate a separate right to a healthy environment, a number of regional human rights legal instruments explicitly recognise the right to a healthy environment. Article 24 of the 1981 African Charter on Human and Peoples' Rights (the Banjul Charter) states that '[a]ll peoples shall have the right to a general satisfactory environment favourable to their development'.[41] This is a clear recognition of a collective right regarding the environment. Similarly, the right to a healthy environment was recognised by the Additional Protocol to the American Convention on Human Rights in the area of Economic, Social, and Cultural Rights (the San Salvador Protocol). Article 24 of the San Salvador Protocol states that '[e]veryone shall have the right to live in a healthy environment and to have access to basic public services'.[42] Article 38 of the Arab Charter on Human Rights incorporates the right to a healthy environment in the context of the right

38 On human rights and environment, see generally, Ben Boer, *Environmental Law Dimensions of Human Rights* (Oxford University Press, 2015); Anna Grear and Louis J. Kotzé, *Research Handbook on Human Rights and the Environment* (Edward Elgar Publishing, 2015); Lyuba Zarsky, *Human Rights and the Environment: Conflicts and Norms in a Globalizing World* (Earthscan, 2012); Romina Picolotti and Jorge Daniel Taillant, *Linking Human Rights and the Environment* (University of Arizona Press, 2010); Donald K. Anton and Dinah L. Shelton, *Environmental Protection and Human Rights* (Cambridge University Press, 2011).

39 Stockholm Declaration, Principle 1.

40 *Rio Declaration on Environment and Development*, UN Doc. A/CONF.151/26 (Vol. I) (1992) (hereinafter Rio Declaration). For human rights and environment in the context of Rio Erath summit, see generally, Dinah Shelton, 'What Happened in Rio to Human Rights?' (1992) 3 *Yearbook of International Environmental Law* 75.

41 *African Charter on Human and Peoples' Rights*, opened for signature 27 June 1981, 1520 UNTS 217 (entered into force 21 October 1986); Emeka Polycarp Amechi, 'Enhancing Environmental Protection and Socio-Economic Development in Africa: A Fresh Look at the Right to a General Satisfactory Environment under the African Charter on Human and Peoples' Rights' (2009) 5 *Law, Environment and Development Journal* 60.

42 *Additional Protocol to the American Convention on Human Rights in the Area of Economic, Social, and Cultural Rights (San Salvador Protocol)*, opened for signature 17 November 1988, OASTS 69 (entered into force 16 November 1999).

to an adequate standard of living.[43] The 'right to a safe, clean and sustainable environment' in the context of the 'right to an adequate standard of living' has been recognised by the 2012 ASEAN (Association of Southeast Asian Nations) Human Rights Declaration.[44] In Europe, the 1998 Aarhus Convention on Access to Information, Public Participation in Decision-Making and Access to Justice in Environmental Matters, adopted under the auspices of the UN Economic Commission for Europe, recognises that 'every person has the right to live in an environment adequate to his or her health and well-being'.[45]

Although (unlike regional human rights instruments) global human rights instruments do not explicitly recognise the right to a healthy environment, enjoyment of many aspects of human rights recognised by the international human rights instruments may be jeopardised by environmental degradation and destruction of the natural environment.[46] Resolution 16/11 of the UN Human Rights Council provides that 'sustainable development and the protection of the environment can contribute to human well-being and the enjoyment of human rights', and 'environmental damage can have negative implications, both direct and indirect, for the effective enjoyment of human rights'.[47] A healthy environment is related to a number of civil and political rights, as well as economic, social and cultural rights, including, inter alia, the inherent right to life,[48] right to equality before the law and equal protection of the law,[49] freedom of association,[50] right to economic, social and cultural development,[51] right to work,[52] right to

43 *Arab Charter on Human Rights*, opened for signature 15 September 1994, 12 International Human Rights Report 893 (2005) (entered into force 15 March 2008).

44 *ASEAN Human Rights Declaration* (2012) <http://aichr.org/?dl_name=ASEAN-Human-Rights-Declaration.pdf>; Catherine Shanahan Renshaw, 'The ASEAN Human Rights Declaration 2012' (2013) 13 *Human Rights Law Review* 557; Gerard Clarke, 'The Evolving ASEAN Human Rights System: The ASEAN Human Rights Declaration of 2012' (2012) 11 *Northwestern University Journal of International Human Rights* 1.

45 *Convention on Access to Information, Public Participation in Decision-Making and Access to Justice in Environmental Matters*, opened for signature 25 June 1998, 2161 UNTS 447 (entered into force 10 October 2001). Also see generally for Europe: Richard Desgagne, 'Integrating Environmental Values into the European Convention on Human Rights' (1995) 89 *American Journal of International Law* 26.

46 Human Rights and Environment, Final Report Prepared by Mrs Fatma Zohra Ksentini, Special Rapporteur, UN. E/CN.4/Sub.2/1994/9 (6 July 1994); Report of the Independent Expert on the issue of human rights obligations Relating to the Enjoyment of a Safe, Clean, Healthy and Sustainable Environment, John H Knox, UN Doc. A/HRC/22/43 (24 December 2012).

47 Resolution of Human Rights Council 16/11 Human Rights and the Environment, UN Doc. A/HRC/RES/16/11 (12 April 2011).

48 ICCPR, art 6, UDHR art 3.

49 ICCPR, art 3, UDHR art 7.

50 ICCPR, art 22, UDHR art 20.

51 ICESCR, art 1. See also, *Declaration on the Right to Development*, UN Doc. A/41/53 (1986).

52 ICESCR, art 6, UDHR art 23.

health,[53] right to safe and healthy working conditions[54] and the right to an adequate standard of living.[55]

Environmental activists and other aggrieved parties have linked various human rights for environmental matters to judicial proceedings in different contexts. The right to life has been widely interpreted by some national courts to include the right to a healthy environment, health and strength of workers, livelihood, provision of bare necessaries of life, improvement to public health by government and ensuring a quality of life consistent with human dignity.[56] In these cases, national courts have also expanded the scope of access to justice by allowing *locus standi* to environmental activist organisations.[57] In some such cases, the court intervened in government projects or instructed the government to take proper action for environmental protection, mainly by liberally interpreting the scope of the fundamental right to life.[58] Similarly, some regional human rights courts have considered human rights, such as the right to a private life, right to life, right to health, right to food and right to property, to ensure government action for combating environmental threats, enforcement of environmental law, access to environmental information and adoption of precautionary measures – with mixed results.[59]

53 ICESCR, art 12, UDHR art 25.

54 ICESCR, art 7.

55 ICCPR, art 11, UDHR art 25.

56 For example, *Rural Litigation and Entitlement Kendra v. State of U P* (1985) AIR SC 652. *Francis Coralie Mullin v. Union Territory of Delhi* (1981) AIR SC 746; *Charan Lal Sahu v. Union of India* (1990) AIR SC 1480; *V Mathur v. Union of India* (1996) 1 SCC 119; *M C Mehta v. Union of India* (1996) 4 SCC 351; *Rural Litigation and Entitlement Kendra v. State of U P* (1991) AIR SC 2216; *M C Mehta v. Union of India* (1996) 4 SCC 750; *M C Mehta v. Union of India* (1988) AIR SC 1037; *Olga Tellis v. Bombay Municipal Corporation* (1986) AIR SC 180; *Subhash Kumar v. State of Bihar* (1991) AIR SC 420; *Dr Mohiuddin Farooque v. Bangladesh and Others* (1996) 48 DLR (HCD) 438 (Radiated Milk Case); *Dr Mohiuddin Farooque v. Bangladesh and Others* (1997) 49 DLR (AD) 1 (hereinafter FAP 20 Case [Standing]); *Dr Mohiuddin Farooque v. Bangladesh and Others* (2003) 55 DLR (HCD) 69 (Industrial Pollution Case); *Virender Gaur v. State of Haryana* (1995) 2 SCC 577; *Rabia Bhuiyan, MP v. Ministry of LGRD* (2007) 59 DLR (AD) 176; *Shehla Zia v. WAPDA* (1994) PLD SC 693.

57 Ibid.

58 Ibid.

59 For example: *Saramaka People v. Suriname* (Judgment of 28 November 2007) Inter-American Court of Human Rights; *Yakye Axa Indigenous Community v. Paraguay* (Judgment of 17 June 2005) Inter-American Court of Human Rights; *Claude-Reyes et al. v. Chile* (Judgment of 19 September 2006) Inter-American Court of Human Rights; *Kawas-Fernández v. Honduras* (Judgment of 3 April 2009) Inter-American Court of Human Rights; *Powell and Rayner v. United Kingdom* (1990) 12 EHRR 335 (Judgment of 21 February 1990); *López Ostra v. Spain* (1995) 20 EHRR 277 (Judgment of 9 December 1994); *Guerra and ors v. Italy* (1998) 26 EHRR 357 (Judgment of 19 February 1998); *Fadeyeva v. Russian Federation* (2007) 45 EHRR 10, (Judgment of 9 June 2005); *Hatton and ors and Friends of the Earth (Intervening) v. United Kingdom and British Airways (Intervening)* (2003) 37 EHRR 28, (Judgment of 8 July 2003); *Hamer v. Belgium*, European Court of Human Rights, Application no. 21861/03 (Judgment of 27 November 2007); *Bladet Tromsø A/S and Stensaas v. Norway* (2000) 29 EHRR 125 (Judgment of 20 May 1999); *Öneryıldız v.*

The Inter-American Court of Human Rights held, in *Kawas-Fernández v. Honduras*, that 'there is an undeniable link between the protection of the environment and the enjoyment of other human rights'.[60]

Resolution 16/11 of the UN Human Rights Council stated that 'environmental damage is felt most acutely by those segments of the population already in vulnerable situations'.[61] Similarly, a report by a UN independent expert on the question of human rights and extreme poverty acknowledges that '[e]nvironmental degradation disproportionately affects those living in extreme poverty'.[62] This is particularly relevant to the shipbreaking industry, where the burden of environmental degradation is disproportionately borne by workers, and to some extent the local community. It is imperative to explore how existing human rights – both substantive and procedural rights – may be used for prevention of disproportionate environmental harm to vulnerable communities. As will be demonstrated in this book, despite jurisprudential development by the liberal interpretation of national and regional courts, the practical impact of this development in the life of the most marginalised segment in the least developed countries is minimal. In many respects, the decisions of the court are routinely ignored by the government. Moreover, the international community as a whole has failed to consider its human rights obligations to marginalised people by allowing ship owners to send obsolete ships with hazardous materials to developing countries. The developed world has also failed to provide any meaningful technical and financial assistance for environmentally sound operation of the shipbreaking industry, thereby directly or indirectly violating many recognised human rights. As observed by Okechukwu Ibeanu, the UN Special Rapporteur, on the adverse effects of the movement and dumping of toxic and dangerous products and wastes on the enjoyment of human rights:

> By any standards, the demolition of ships is a dirty and dangerous occupation. The conditions prevailing at many shipbreaking yards in the world, and in particular in South Asian countries where ships are dismantled directly on tidal beaches, risk adversely affecting the enjoyment of several human rights, including the right to life, the right to the highest attainable standard of physical and mental health, and the right to safe and healthy working conditions.[63]

Turkey (2005) 41 EHRR 20 (Judgment of 30 November 2004); *Mangouras v. Spain* (2010) ECHR 1364 (Judgment of 28 September 2010).

60 *Kawas-Fernández v. Honduras* (Judgment of 3 April 2009) Inter-American Court of Human Rights.

61 *Resolution of Human Rights Council 16/11 Human Rights and the Environment*, UN Doc. A/HRC/RES/16/11 (12 April 2011).

62 *Report of the Independent Expert on the Question of Human Rights and Extreme Poverty*, UN Doc. A/65/259 (9 August 2010).

63 *Report of the Special Rapporteur on the Adverse Effects of the Movement and Dumping of Toxic and Dangerous Products and Wastes on the Enjoyment of Human Rights*, UN Doc. A/HRC/12/26 (15 July 2009).

As discussed later in this book, the most depressing aspect of the entire discourse is the remarkable absence of human rights within the shipbreaking industry in international negotiations regarding the development of international regulation of this industry. The shipbreaking industry in Bangladesh clearly illustrates the hollow foundation of the international and national legal and human rights system. The systemic violation of human rights in this industry is totally ignored at the global and national levels to maximise the economic interests of international and national elites.

2.3.2 Environmental justice and international environmental law principles

This section critically examines the relationship between environmental justice and the implementation of principles of international environmental law in the context of international legal frameworks for environmentally sound disposal of end-of-life vessels. The discussion specifically highlights four major principles of international environmental law: the polluter pays principle; the principle of prevention, the principle of common but differentiated responsibilities (CBDR) and the principle of sustainable development. The polluter pays principle is vitally important for the shipbreaking industry because the existing system has failed to establish a legal obligation for people or entities responsible for the resulting pollution; rather, it shifts the burden to the poor workers of least developed countries. The principle of CBDR is also relevant in the development of an international legal framework for the environmentally sound disposal of obsolete ships. The principle of sustainable development is an important principle of international environmental law relevant to the shipbreaking industry. As mentioned earlier, shipbreaking is not a simple issue of waste trafficking. When we talk about shipbreaking, we must consider the realities on the ground. Phasing out this industry may be difficult for Bangladesh because a degree of dependency on this industry has been created. Thus, the most reasonable solution is to develop a sustainable shipbreaking industry in which labour rights are enforced and environmental protection is respected.

2.3.2.1 The principle of sustainable development

Sustainable development is the most important international environmental principle in the contemporary world. It is a culmination of apparently conflicting or complementary principles and concepts of collective rights to development and rights to the environment. The widely accepted definition of sustainable development as coined in the *Our Common Future* report is development that ‘meets the needs of the present without compromising the ability of future generations to meet their own needs’.[64] According to Principle 4 of the Rio Declaration,

64 *Report of the World Commission on Environment and Development: Our Common Future*, UN Doc. A/42/427 (4 August 1987), annex.

'In order to achieve sustainable development, environmental protection shall constitute an integral part of the development process and cannot be considered in isolation from it'.[65] Similarly, Principle 25 provides that 'Peace, development and environmental protection are interdependent and indivisible'.[66] In fact, sustainable development was more central in two world summits on the environment and development subsequent to the Rio summit; these two summits were entitled 'World Summit on Sustainable Development' and 'United Nations Conference on Sustainable Development, Rio+20'.[67]

In a sense, sustainable development is a culmination of emerging norms, principles and concepts of international environmental law including, inter alia, intergenerational equity, access to information, transparency, access to justice, public participation, the precautionary principle, the polluter pays principle, common heritage of humankind, cooperation and good governance. As observed by the International Court of Justice in the *Gabčíkovo – Nagymaros Project* case:

> Throughout the ages, mankind has, for economic and other reasons, constantly interfered with nature. In the past, this was often done without consideration of the effects upon the environment. Owing to new scientific insights and to a growing awareness of the risks for mankind – for present and future generations – of pursuit of such interventions at an unconsidered and unabated pace, new norms and standards have been developed, set forth in a great number of instruments during the last two decades. Such new norms have to be taken into consideration, and such new standards given proper weight, not only when States contemplate new activities but also when continuing with activities begun in the past. This need to reconcile economic development with protection of the environment is aptly expressed in the concept of sustainable development.[68]

In his Separate Opinion, Vice-President of the Court, Christopher Gregory Weeramantry went further and said:

> The Court has referred to it [sustainable development] as a concept in paragraph 140 of its Judgment. However, I consider it to be more than a mere concept, but as a principle with normative value. Since sustainable development is a principle fundamental to the determination of the competing considerations in this case, and since, although it has attracted attention only

65 Rio Declaration, Principle 4.

66 Rio Declaration, Principle 25.

67 *Johannesburg Declaration on Sustainable Development*, UN Doc. A/CONF.199/20 (4 September 2002); *The Future We Want, General Assembly Resolution 66/288*, UN Doc A/RES/66/288 (11 September 2012).

68 *Gabčíkovo-Nagymaros Project (Hungary v. Slovakia)*, Judgment, ICJ Rep 1997, 7, 78 (hereinafter *Gabčíkovo-Nagymaros Project* case).

> recently in the literature of international law, it is likely to play a major role in determining important environmental disputes of the future.[69]

It is pertinent to question what role the sustainable development principle plays in the contemporary development agenda. Eight Millennium Development Goals (MDGs) were adopted at the Millennium Summit in September 2000, at which the global community pledged to achieve these goals by 2015.[70] A number of MDGs represent the core elements of the principle of sustainable development including, inter alia, Goal 1: Eradicate Extreme Hunger and Poverty, Goal 7: Ensure Environmental Sustainability and Goal 8: Develop a Global Partnership for Development. The MDGs era officially ended in 2015. Although there were significant achievements with respect to these goals in the reference period, the 'progress has been far from uniform across the world-or across the Goals. There are huge disparities across and within countries. Within countries, poverty is greatest for rural areas, though urban poverty is also extensive, growing, and underreported by traditional indicators'.[71] Hundreds of millions of people are still facing extreme poverty, and environmental pollution and destruction of habitat is widespread in many parts of the world.

The principle of sustainable development played an even more central role in the 2030 Agenda for Sustainable Development, which include 17 Sustainable Development Goals (SDGs).[72] As the name indicates, all the goals are related to sustainable development. However, Goal 14 deserves special mention in the context of marine and coastal pollution from the shipbreaking industry, as this goal relates to the conservation and sustainable use of oceans, seas and marine resources for sustainable development.[73]

Finally, it is pertinent to highlight the role of sustainable development principles in the shipbreaking industry. An Additional Secretary to the Ministry of Industries of Bangladesh said in 2011 that 'the ship-breaking industry is a big recycler and important for keeping the macro- and micro-economic balance'.[74] However, he did not say whose trash the country is recycling or whether this operation can be called recycling at all given that hazardous substances are simply dumped into the coastal and marine area. The then Minister for Industries went further and said '[t]he industrial development of Bangladesh depends much on the ship-breaking industry'.[75] However, no hard evidence was supplied to

69 Ibid., 85.

70 UNDP, *Millennium Development Goals* (2006) <www.undp.org/content/undp/en/home/sdgoverview/mdg_goals.html>; see also, *United Nations Millennium Declaration*, GA Res 55/2, UN Doc A/RES/55/2 (18 September 2000).

71 Ibid.; see also, UN, *The Millennium Development Goals Report 2015* (UN, 2015).

72 *Transforming Our World: The 2030 Agenda for Sustainable Development*, GA Res 70/1, UN Doc. A/RES/70/1 (21 October 2015).

73 Ibid.

74 Star Business Report, 'Barua Praises Role of Ship-Breakers' *The Daily Star* (online) 11 February 2011 <www.thedailystar.net/news-detail-173747>.

75 Ibid.

support this claim. Nevertheless, a World Bank report shows that shipbreaking meets around 20% to 25% of the steel consumption needs in Bangladesh.[76] It seems that the government is sacrificing the environment and life of workers for a cheap, low-quality steel supply. The shipbreaking industry in Bangladesh is a clear example of unsustainable development and the way it is currently operating is a gross violation of all of the elements of the principle of sustainable development. However, this is not a failure of the Bangladesh government alone. The international community has also completely failed to take any meaningful initiative towards environmentally sustainable operation and protection of labour rights in this industry.

2.3.2.2 The principle of prevention

The principle of prevention is a well-recognised principle in environmental law. Its importance derives from scientific and economic reason. It is often impossible to fully remedy environmental damage or harm; even if it is possible, the cost may be prohibitive. As observed by the International Court of Justice in the *Gabčíkovo-Nagymaros Project* case: 'in the field of environmental protection, vigilance and prevention are required on account of the often irreversible character of damage to the environment and of the limitations inherent in the very mechanism of reparation of this type of damage'.[77]

Prevention is related to the established international legal principle of the obligation to not cause significant transboundary harm.[78] However, the principle of prevention is far broader than that and may be applicable in many other contexts irrespective of the degree of transboundary harm. This principle is recognised in many international environmental legal instruments.[79] For example, Article 194 of UNCLOS provides that:

76 Maria Sarraf et al., *The Ship Breaking and Recycling Industry in Bangladesh and Pakistan*, World Bank Report No. 58275-SAS (2010) <http://documents.worldbank.org/curated/en/2010/12/13695952/ship-breaking-recycling-industry-bangladesh-pakistan>.

77 *Gabčíkovo-Nagymaros Project* case, above n 68, para 140.

78 The International Court of Justice (ICJ) held that '[t]he existence of the general obligation of States to ensure that activities within their jurisdiction and control respect the environment of other States or of areas beyond national control is now part of the corpus of international law relating to the environment'. *Legality of the Threat or Use of Nuclear Weapons*, Advisory Opinion, ICJ Reports 1996 (I), 226, para 29.

79 For example, UNCLOS, *Convention on the Prevention of Marine Pollution by Dumping of Wastes and Other Matter*, opened for signature 29 December 1972, 11 ILM 1294 (entered into force 30 August 1975); *United Nations Agreement for the Implementation of the Provisions of the United Nations Convention on the Law of the Sea of 10 December 1982 Relating to the Conservation and Management of Straddling Fish Stocks and Highly Migratory Fish Stocks*, opened for signature 4 December 1995, 34 ILM 1542 (entered into force 11 December 2001); *Vienna Convention for the Protection of the Ozone Layer*, opened for signature 22 March 1985, 1513 UNTS 324 (entered into force 22 September 1988); *Montreal Protocol on Substances that Deplete the Ozone Layer*, opened for signature 16 September 1987, 1522 UNTS 3 (entered into force 1 January 1989); *Basel Convention on the Control*

> States shall take, individually or jointly as appropriate, all measures consistent with this Convention that are necessary to *prevent, reduce and control* pollution of the marine environment from any source, using for this purpose the best practicable means at their disposal and in accordance with their capabilities, and they shall endeavour to harmonize their policies in this connection.[80]

This article is also relevant to marine pollution from the shipbreaking industry. The principle of prevention has been recognised as a principle of international law in the decisions of international judicial and arbitral bodies. The arbitral tribunal in the *Iron Rhine* case held that:

> environmental law and the law on development stand not as alternatives but as mutually reinforcing, integral concepts, which require that where development may cause significant harm to the environment there is a duty to prevent, or at least mitigate, such harm. . . . This duty, in the opinion of the Tribunal, has now become a principle of general international law.[81]

The International Court of Justice held in the *Pulp Mills on the River Uruguay* case that the 'principle of prevention, as a customary rule, has its origins in the due diligence that is required of a State in its territory'.[82] The court held that due diligence 'is an obligation which entails not only the adoption of appropriate rules and measures, but also a certain level of vigilance in their enforcement and the exercise of administrative control applicable to public and private operators, such as the monitoring of activities undertaken by such operators'.[83] The obligation of monitoring is very important in the context of the shipbreaking industry. Despite serious environmental pollution and labour rights violations, there is almost no monitoring from the Bangladeshi government. The successful prosecution or other action by government authorities against the environmental pollution in the shipbreaking industry of their own accord is almost absent. Most legal action taken against the polluting shipbreaking industries is initiated by nongovernmental activist organisations. At the same time, the global community has failed to take any collective or individual action for prevention of pollution in the shipbreaking industry.

---

of Transboundary Movements of Hazardous Wastes and Their Disposal, opened for signature 22 March 1989, 1673 UNTS 126 (entered into force 24 May 1992); *United Nations Framework Convention on Climate Change*, opened for signature 9 May 1992, 1771 UNTS 107 (entered into force 21 March 1994); *Convention on Biological Diversity*, opened for signature 5 June 1992, 1760 UNTS 143 (entered into force 29 December 1993).

80 UNCLOS, art 194 (emphasis added).

81 *Iron Rhine Arbitration (Belgium v. Netherlands)* (2008) 27 RIAA 35, para 59.

82 *Pulp Mills on the River Uruguay (Argentina v. Uruguay)*, Judgment, ICJ Rep 2010, 14, para 101.

83 Ibid., para 197.

2.3.2.3 The polluter pays principle

The shipbreaking industry is an example of how the centrality of world systems allows developed or powerful countries to externalise their hazards or environmental harms to developing and least developed countries seated in the semi-periphery and periphery of the globalised world system.[84] A relevant question is how international environmental law can be used to protect the people and environment of the global south from this externalisation of environmental hazards by developed countries. The polluter pays principle in international environmental law may be relevant in this regard.[85] The core of this principle is that the cost of pollution should be the responsibility of the polluter or the person responsible for creating an environmental hazard.

It may, however, be argued that the polluter pays principle has been included in international environmental law in a more restrictive form, which is reflected in Principle 16 of the *Rio Declaration*, as follows:

> National authorities should endeavour to promote the internalization of environmental costs and the use of economic instruments, taking into account the approach that the polluter should, in principle, bear the cost of pollution, with due regard to the public interest and without distorting international trade and investment.[86]

Although the language of this principle is restrictive, it nevertheless imposes an obligation on the polluter to pay. In the *Rhine Chlorides Arbitration*, the tribunal considered the status of the polluter pays principle in general international law. The arbitral tribunal considered that:

> this principle features in several international instruments, bilateral as well as multilateral, and that it operates at various levels of effectiveness. Without denying its importance in treaty law, the Tribunal does not view this principle as being a part of general international law.[87]

84 R. Scott Frey, 'Breaking Ships in the World-System: An Analysis of Two Ship Breaking Capitals, Alang-Sosiya, India and Chittagong, Bangladesh' (2015) 21 *Journal of World-Systems Research* 25.

85 Nicolas de Sadeleer, *Environmental Principles: From Political Slogans to Legal Rules* (Oxford University Press, 2002) 21–60; Kenneth R. Reed, 'Economic Incentives for Pollution Abatement: Applying Theory to Practice' (1970) 12 *Arizona Law Review* 51; Ursula Kettlewell, 'The Answer to Global Pollution? A Critical Examination of the Problems and Potential of the Polluter-Pays Principle' (1992) 3 *Colorado Journal of International Environmental Law and Policy* 429; Sanford E. Gaines, 'The Polluter-Pays Principle: From Economic Equity to Environmental Ethos' (1991) 26 *Texas International Law Journal* 463; Candice Stevens, 'Interpreting the Polluter Pays Principle in the Trade and Environment Context' (1994) 27 *Cornell International Law Journal* 577.

86 *Rio Declaration on Environment and Development*, UN Doc. A/CONF.151/26 (Vol. I) (12 August 1992).

87 *Netherlands v. France (Rhine Chlorides Arbitration)*, Award, ICGJ 374 (PCA 2004), 12 March 2004, para 103 Unofficial English Translation, <https://www.pcacases.com/web/sendAttach/78>.

This decision was made in the context of a treaty for combating pollution of the Rhine River by chlorides. The tribunal did not provide the reason why it considered the polluter pays principle to not be part of 'general international law'. It did not make clear what it meant by the statement: 'does not view this principle as being a part of general international law.' Is it 'customary international law' or 'international law generally'. There are many examples of states making clear statements that they consider it as a general principle of international environmental law. For example, the preamble to the International Convention on Oil Pollution Preparedness, Response and Cooperation (hereinafter OPRC Convention) of 1990 states that:

> The Parties to the Present Convention Taking Account of the 'polluter pays' principle as a general principle of international environmental law.[88]

At present, 109 states, including all major and emerging economies, are party to this convention.[89] No state has imposed a reservation on the above preamble paragraph, which represents clear evidence of global acceptance of the polluter pays principle as a general principle of international environmental law.[90] Even parties to the *Rhine Chlorides Arbitration*, the Netherlands and France, are also partiers to the OPRC Convention. Ten years after the adoption of the OPRC Convention, state parties made the same statement in the preamble of the Protocol on Preparedness, Response and Co-operation to Pollution Incidents by Hazardous and Noxious Substances, 2000 (hereinafter OPRC-HNS Protocol).[91] Similarly, no parties to the OPRC-HNS Protocol have imposed a reservation on the preamble paragraph accepting the polluter pays principle as a general principle of international environmental law.[92] The observation of the arbitral tribunal in the *Rhine Chlorides Arbitration* is most likely incorrect. The polluter pays principle is undoubtedly a general principle of international environmental law.[93] Needless to say, international environmental law is a part of international law.

88 *International Convention on Oil Pollution Preparedness, Response and Cooperation*, opened for signature 30 November 1990, 1891 UNTS 78 (entry into force 13 May 1995) (hereinafter OPRC Convention).

89 International Maritime Organization (IMO), *Status of Multilateral Conventions and Instruments in Respect of Which the International Maritime Organization or Its Secretary-General Performs Depositary or Other Functions, as at 7 July 2016* (7 July 2016) 446 <www.imo.org/en/About/Conventions/StatusOfConventions/Documents/Status%20-%202016.pdf>.

90 Ibid.

91 *Protocol on Preparedness, Response and Co-Operation to Pollution Incidents by Hazardous and Noxious Substances*, opened for signature 15 March 2000, 2007 ATS 41 (entered into force 14 January 2007) (hereinafter OPRC-HNS Protocol).

92 IMO, above n 89, 468.

93 Organisation for Economic Co-operation and Development (OECD), *The Polluter-Pays Principle: OECD Analyses and Recommendations* (OECD, 1992).

The polluter pays principle was first directly mentioned in a recommendation of the Organization for Economic Co-operation and Development (OECD) in 1972.[94] The OECD recommendation defines the principle as follows:

> The principle to be used for allocating costs of pollution prevention and control measures to encourage rational use of scarce environmental resources and to avoid distortions in international trade and investment is the so-called 'polluter pays principle.' This principle means that the polluter should bear the expenses of carrying out the above-mentioned measures decided by public authorities to ensure that the environment is in an acceptable state. In other worlds, the cost of these measures should be reflected in the cost of goods and services which cause pollution in production and/or consumption. Such measures should not be accompanied by subsidies that would create significant distortions in international trade and investment.[95]

In 1974, the OECD reaffirmed that '[t]he Polluter-Pays Principle constitutes for Member countries a fundamental principle for allocating costs of pollution prevention and control measures introduced by the public authorities in Member countries'.[96] The polluter pays principle is also recognised in EU environmental law.[97] The national laws of many countries have institutionalised this principle and many international environmental conventions have included it in various forms.[98] Among these international conventions is the Stockholm Convention, which deserves special mention as it is applicable to the ship-breaking industry. It lists PCBs as one of the persistent organic pollutants (POPs) that are present in many obsolete ships.[99] The Stockholm Convention clearly recognises the polluter pays principle as defined in Principle 16 of the Rio Declaration.[100]

It is well established that the polluter pays principle is a general principle of international environmental law. However, it is not always easy to identify the

94 *Recommendation of the Council on Guiding Principles concerning International Economic Aspects of Environmental Policies*, OECD Council Recommendation C (72)128 (26 May 1972), 14 ILM 236 (1975).

95 Ibid.

96 *Recommendation of the Council on the Implementation of the Polluter-Pays Principle*, OECD Council Recommendation C (74)223 (14 November 1974), 14 ILM 234 (1975).

97 Nicolas Michel de Sadeleer, 'The Polluter-Pays Principle in EU Law – Bold Case Law and Poor Harmonisation' in Hans Christian Bugge (ed) *Pro Natura* (Universitetsforlaget, 2012) 405.

98 For example: OPRC Convention; OPRC-HNS Protocol; *Convention on Persistent Organic Pollutants*, opened for signature 23 May 2001, 40 ILM 532 (entered into force 17 May 2004) (hereinafter Stockholm Convention); *Convention for the Protection of the Marine Environment of the North-East Atlantic*, opened for signature 22 September 1992, 2354 UNTS 67 (entered into force 25 March 1998).

99 See Chapter 3.

100 Stockholm Convention, preamble.

polluter.[101] Recommendation 75/436 of the European Council provides some guidelines in this regard. It defines a polluter as 'someone who directly or indirectly damages the environment or who creates conditions leading to such damage'.[102] According to this recommendation, 'in the case of pollution chains, costs could be charged at the point at which the number of economic operators is least and control is easiest or else at the point where the most effective contribution is made towards improving the environment, and where distortions to competition are avoided'.[103]

Determination of the polluter may seem even more complex for the shipbreaking industry. Who is the polluter: the ship owner or the owner of the shipbreaking company? However, if we consider obsolete ships as waste (which is the case under the Basel Convention),[104] the polluter is undoubtedly the ship owner. It is the responsibility of the ship owner to dispose of the obsolete ship rather than making profit by selling it. Considering the complexity of the shipbreaking industry, ship ownership is the easiest point of control. Shipbreaking is largely an informal industry in developing countries that is operated through an obscure process in which the operator of the recycling or breaking process for a particular vessel may not be the owner of the shipbreaking yard, and labour management of the yard may be by a third party.

2.3.2.4 The principle of common but differentiated responsibilities

The principle of CBDR is one of the most important principles for ensuring equity and justice between developed and developing nations. This principle is associated with various definitions and applications.[105] Principle 7 of the *Rio Declaration* provides as follows:

> In view of the different contributions to global environmental degradation, States have common but differentiated responsibilities. The developed countries acknowledge the responsibility that they bear in the international pursuit

101 Sadeleer, above n 97, 41.

102 *Council Recommendation of 3 March 1975 Regarding Cost Allocation and Action by Public Authorities on Environmental Matters*, 75/436/Euratom, ECSC, EEC, OJ L 194, 25.7.1975, 1–4.

103 Ibid.

104 See Chapter 3.

105 On different aspects of CBDR Principle, see generally, Christopher D. Stone, 'Common but Differentiated Responsibilities in International Law' (2004) 98 *American Journal of International Law* 276; Duncan French, 'Developing States and International Environmental Law: The Importance of Differentiated Responsibilities' (2000) 49 *International and Comparative Law Quarterly* 35; Tuula Honkonen, *The Common but Differentiated Responsibility Principle in Multilateral Environmental Agreements: Regulatory and Policy Aspects* (Kluwer Law International, 2009); Halina Ward, 'Common but Differentiated Debates: Environment, Labour and the World Trade Organization' (1996) 45 *International and Comparative Law Quarterly* 592; Nina E. Bafundo, 'Compliance with the Ozone Treaty: Weak States and the Principle of Common but Differentiated

> to sustainable development in view of the pressures their societies place on the global environment and of the technologies and financial resources they command.[106]

This principle acknowledges the common responsibility of environmental protection and recognises the differentiated capabilities and circumstances of developed and developing countries. A number of international conventions include this principle. The most prominent is the international climate change legal regime. The United Nations Framework Convention on Climate Change (UNFCC) obliges parties to protect the climate system 'on the basis of equity and in accordance with their common but differentiated responsibilities and respective capabilities'.[107] The UNCLOS also recognises this principle with respect to prevention of marine pollution from land-based sources. Article 207 of UNCLOS provides that while cooperating in the development of regulations governing prevention of marine pollution from land-based sources, the economic capacity of developing states and their need for economic development must be taken into account.[108]

These differential responsibilities may be implemented through various process. They can be implemented by imposing different environmental protection responsibilities, providing technical and financial assistance or providing more time for implementation while imposing similar environmental protection obligations on developing countries. The CBDR principle recognises differential legal obligations considering equity and respective capabilities. However, this principle is not a licence to any country for environmental destruction and exertion of serious environmental harm to its own people. Therefore, the present condition of the Bangladeshi shipbreaking industry cannot be justified by this principle.

2.3.3 Environmental justice and labour rights

Labour rights are a very important component of environmental justice in the context of the shipbreaking industry. As discussed in Chapter 1, violation of labour rights is omnipresent in the shipbreaking industry. This section analyses the international legal framework for safeguarding labour rights in the shipbreaking industry. Over the years, the ILO has developed a body of international labour standards defining basic principles and rights at work, mainly through

---

Responsibility' (2006) 21 *American University International Law Review* 461; Lavanya Rajamani, *Differential Treatment in International Environmental Law* (Oxford University Press, 2006); Philippe Cullet, *Differential Treatment in International Environmental Law* (Ashgate, 2003); Anna Huggins and Md Saiful Karim, 'Shifting Traction: Differential Treatment and Substantive and Procedural Regard in the International Climate Change Regime' (2016) 5 *Transnational Environmental Law* 427.

106 Rio Declaration, Principle 7.

107 *United Nations Framework Convention on Climate Change, Opened for Signature*, 4 June 1992, 1771 UNTS 107, art 3 (entered into force 21 March 1994) (hereinafter UNFCCC).

108 UNCLOS, art 207.

legally binding ILO conventions and non-legally binding ILO recommendations.[109] These legal instruments are developed through a tripartite process, including participation of governments, employers and workers to ensure the goal of decent work.[110]

The ILO has played an important role in shaping social and economic human rights in international human rights discourse.[111] It participated in the drafting process of the ICCPR and ICESCR; both these covenants contain provisions related to labour rights.[112] The ILO's initiative for protection of human rights in the context of labour rights pre-dates the UDHR and other major human rights legal instruments. In 1944, the General Conference of the ILO adopted the Declaration of Philadelphia in its Twenty-sixth Session.[113] This declaration took

109 The International Labour Organization's (ILO) governing body identified eight ILO legal instruments as fundamental for rights at work, including *Convention Concerning Freedom of Association and Protection of the Right to Organise*, opened for signature 17 July 1948, 68 UNTS 17 (entered into force generally 4 July 1950); *Convention Concerning the Application of the Principles of the Right to Organise and to Bargain Collectively*, opened for signature 1 July 1949, 96 UNTS 257 (entered into force generally 18 July 1951); *Convention Concerning Forced or Compulsory Labour*, opened for signature 28 June 1930, 39 UNTS 55 (entered into force 1 May 1932); *Convention Concerning the Abolition of Forced Labour*, opened for signature 25 June 1957, 320 UNTS 291 (entered into force 17 January 1959); *Convention Concerning Minimum Age for Admission to Employment*, opened for signature 26 June 1973, 1015 UNTS 297 (entered into force 19 June 1976); *Convention Concerning the Prohibition and Immediate Action for the Elimination of the Worst Forms of Child Labour*, opened for signature, 17 June 1999, 2133 UNTS 161 (entered into force 19 November 2000); *Convention Concerning Equal Remuneration for Men and Women Workers for Work of Equal Value*, opened for signature 29 June 1951 165 UNTS 303 (entered into force 23 May 1953); *Convention Concerning Discrimination in Respect of Employment and Occupation*, opened for signature 25 June 1958, 362 UNTS 31 (entered into force 15 June 1960).

110 Gerry Rodgers, Eddy Lee, Lee Swepston and Jasmien Van Daele, *The International Labour Organization and the Quest for Social Justice, 1919–2009* (International Labour Office, 2009); Kaushik Basu et al., *International Labour Standards: History, Theory, and Policy Options* (John Wiley & Sons, 2008).

111 Rodgers et al., ibid., 38.

112 Ibid.

113 *Constitution of the International Labour Organization*, opened for signature 28 June 1919, Part XIII of Treaty of Versailles (1919) (hereinafter ILO Constitution), annex. Article 1 of ILO Constitution 'A permanent organization is hereby established for the promotion of the objects set forth in the Preamble to this Constitution and in the *Declaration Concerning the Aims and Purposes of the International Labour Organization Adopted at Philadelphia on 10 May 1944, the Text of Which Is Annexed to This Constitution* (emphasis added). 'The original text of the Constitution, established in 1919, has been modified by the amendment of 1922 which entered into force on 4 June 1934; the Instrument of Amendment of 1945 which entered into force on 26 September 1946; the Instrument of Amendment of 1946 which entered into force on 20 April 1948; the Instrument of Amendment of 1953 which entered into force on 20 May 1954; the Instrument of Amendment of 1962 which entered into force on 22 May 1963; and the Instrument of Amendment of 1972 which entered into force on 1 November 1974'. ILO, Constitution <www.ilo.org/dyn/normlex/en/f?p=1000:62:0::NO:62:P62_LIST_ENTRIE_ID:2453907:NO>; see also, ILO, *Declaration on Fundamental Principles and Rights at Work* (1998) adopted by the International

a right-based approach, and many of the expressions it uses were later adopted by international and regional human rights instruments. This declaration recognises, among others, the need for freedom of expression and of association, freedom and dignity, equal opportunity, social justice, full employment and the raising of standards of living, the right of collective bargaining and protection for the lives and health of workers.[114] Over the years, ILO legal instruments have been developed to regulate various labour rights including freedom of association and collective bargaining,[115] the elimination of forced labour,[116] the abolition of child labour,[117] the elimination of discrimination,[118] OHS and working conditions.[119]

Labour Conference, 86th Session, Geneva, June 1998 <www.ilo.org/dyn/normlex/en/f?p=1000:62:0::NO:62:P62_LIST_ENTRIE_ID:2453911:NO>.

114 Eddy Lee, 'Declaration of Philadelphia: Retrospect and Prospect' (1994) 133 *International Labour Review* 467; Richard A. Melanson, 'Human Rights and the American Withdrawal from the ILO' (1979) 1 *Universal Human Rights* 43; Lammy Betten, 'International Implementation of Economic and Social Rights by ILO' (1988) 6 *Netherlands Quarterly of Human Rights* 29; Francis Wolf, 'ILO Experience in the Implementation of Human Rights' (1975) 10 *Journal of International Law and Economics* 599; Marius Olivier, 'International Labour and Social Security Standards: A Developing Country Critique' (2013) 29 *International Journal of Comparative Labour Law and Industrial Relations* 21.

115 *Convention Concerning Freedom of Association and Protection of the Right to Organise*, opened for signature 17 July 1948, 68 UNTS 17 (entered into force generally 4 July 1950); *Convention Concerning the Application of the Principles of the Right to Organise and to Bargain Collectively*, opened for signature 1 July 1949, 96 UNTS 257 (entered into force 18 July 1951); *Convention Concerning Protection and Facilities to be Afforded to Workers' Representatives in the Undertaking*, opened for signature 23 June 1971, 883 UNTS. 111 (entered into force 30 June 1973).

116 *Convention Concerning Forced or Compulsory Labour*, opened for signature 28 June 1930, 39 UNTS 55 (entered into force 1 May 1932); *Convention Concerning the Abolition of Forced Labour*, opened for signature 25 June 1957, 320 UNTS 291 (entered into force 17 January 1959).

117 *Convention Concerning Minimum Age for Admission to Employment*, opened for signature 26 June 1973, 1015 UNTS 297 (entered into force 19 June 1976); *Convention Concerning the Prohibition and Immediate Action for the Elimination of the Worst Forms of Child Labour*, opened for signature, 17 June 1999, 2133 UNTS 161 (entered into force 19 November 2000).

118 *Convention Concerning Equal Remuneration for Men and Women Workers for Work of Equal Value*, opened for signature 29 June 1951 165 UNTS 303 (entered into force 23 May 1953); *Convention Concerning Discrimination in Respect of Employment and Occupation*, opened for signature 25 June 1958, 362 UNTS 31 (entered into force 15 June 1960).

119 *Convention Concerning Occupational Safety and Health and the Working Environment*, adopted on 22 Jun 1981 ILO Convention 155 (entered into force Aug 1983); *Convention Concerning the Promotional Framework for Occupational Safety and Health*, adopted on 15 June 2006, ILO Convention 187 (entered into force 20 February 2009); *Convention Concerning Occupational Health Services*, adopted on 25 June 1985, ILO Convention 161 (entered into force 17 February 1988); *Convention Concerning the Protection of Workers against Ionising Radiations*, adopted on 22 June 1960, ILO Convention 115 (entered into force 17 June 1962); *Convention Concerning Prevention and Control of Occupational Hazards Caused by Carcinogenic Substances and Agents*, adopted on 24 June 1974, ILO Convention 139 (entered into force 10 June 1976); *Convention Concerning the Protection of Workers against Occupational Hazards in the Working Environment Due to Air Pollution,*

In 2004, the ILO developed its Guidelines for improving safety and health in the shipbreaking industry.[120] These guidelines identify shipbreaking as a hazardous industry and classify the industry as hazardous waste management.[121] They also state that in some cases shipbreaking may not be covered by labour laws and social protection, and that there are difficulties in law enforcement.[122] The ILO Guidelines elaborate detailed provisions for the following:

- 'Occupational safety and health management'
- 'reporting, recording and notification of work-related injuries and diseases, ill health and incident'
- 'operational planning'
- 'general preventive and protective measures'
- 'management of hazardous substances'
- 'measures against physical hazards'
- 'safety requirements for tools, machines and equipment'
- 'competence and training'
- 'contingency and emergency preparedness'
- 'special protection'
- 'welfare'.[123]

However, after more than a decade of adoption of the ILO Guidelines, death remains a regular occurrence in the shipbreaking industry of Bangladesh. It seems that international and national legal frameworks are a paper umbrella that dissolves in the rain. None of these guidelines have been practically implemented in the shipbreaking industry of Bangladesh, despite recent inclusion of some of them in the relevant regulations of Bangladesh.

It is the primary responsibility of the state in which the industry is located to implement labour rights included in the ILO legal instruments and human rights treaties. However, developed countries who allow their shipping companies (or beneficial owners of shipping companies or ships) to sell obsolete ships to shipbreakers in developing country are in flagrant violation of labour rights and cannot escape responsibility for violating internationally recognised human rights.

Noise and Vibration, adopted on 20 June 1977, ILO Convention 148 (entered into force 11 July 1979); *Convention Concerning Safety in the Use of Asbestos*, adopted on 24 June 1986, ILO Convention 162 (entered into force 16 June 1989); *Convention Concerning Safety in the Use of Chemicals at Work*, adopted on 25 June 1990, ILO Convention 170 (entered into force 4 November 1993).

120 ILO, *Safety and Health in Shipbreaking: Guidelines for Asian Countries and Turkey* (2004) <www.ilo.org/public/english/region/asro/beijing/download/ship_breaking.pdf>.

121 Ibid., 4.

122 Ibid.

123 Ibid.

2.3.4 *UNCLOS and protection of the marine environment in a just and equitable way*

UNCLOS as an umbrella convention imposes a general obligation to protect and preserve the marine environment.[124] It also obliges states, individually or jointly, to take measures for prevention, reduction and control of marine pollution.[125] UNCLOS, more particularly, obliges states to take measures to minimise the release of persistent toxic, harmful and noxious substances[126] from land-based sources[127] and dumping[128] as well as minimising pollution from vessels.[129] These general obligations are highly relevant in the shipbreaking industry because pollution from shipbreaking can be treated at the same time as pollution from vessels and land-based sources. Substances may be released into the marine environment from obsolete vessels while beaching or during the breaking and recycling processes. Moreover, many of the substances found in obsolete ships are persistent. Even the pollution from this industry may in some circumstances be treated as dumping waste in the ocean.[130] Unfortunately, this is an industry in which many opportunities for marine pollution are present.

Two particular provisions of UNCLOS are very important with respect to environmental justice in the shipbreaking industry. Article 202 of UNCLOS provides for scientific and technical assistance for developing countries for protection of the marine environment and prevention of marine pollution.[131] Article 203 provides for the preferential treatment of developing countries in allocat-

124 UNCLOS, art 192. UNCLOS defines pollution of the marine environment as 'the introduction by man, directly or indirectly, of substances or energy into the marine environment, including estuaries, which results or is likely to result in such deleterious effects as harm to living resources and marine life, hazards to human health, hindrance to marine activities, including fishing and other legitimate uses of the sea, impairment of quality for use of sea water and reduction of amenities'. UNCLOS, art 1; See generally, Alan E. Boyle, 'Marine Pollution under the Law of the Sea Convention' (1985) 79 *American Journal of International Law* 347; William L. Schachte Jr, 'The Value of the 1982 UN Convention on the Law of the Sea: Preserving Our Freedoms and Protecting the Environment' (1992) 23 *Ocean Development and International Law* 55; Jonathan I. Charney, 'The Marine Environment and the 1982 United Nations Convention on the Law of the Sea' (1994) 28 *International Lawyer* 879; Md Saiful Karim, 'UNCLOS and Regional Action for Protection of the Marine Environment: Perspectives of the South Asian Seas Region' (2008) 29 *Bangladesh Institute of International and Strategic Studies Journal* 415; Moira L. McConnell and Edgar Gold, 'The Modern Law of the Sea: Framework for the Protection and Preservation of Marine Environment?' (1991) 23 *Case Western Reserve Journal of International Law* 23.

125 UNCLOS, art 193.

126 UNCLOS, art 193.

127 UNCLOS, arts 193, 207, 213.

128 UNCLOS, arts 193, 210, 216.

129 UNCLOS, arts 193, 211, 217, 218, 219, 220.

130 UNCOS defines 'dumping' as '(i) any deliberate disposal of wastes or other matter from vessels, aircraft, platforms or other man-made structures at sea; (ii) any deliberate disposal of vessels, aircraft, platforms'. UNCLOS, art 1(5).

131 UNCLOS, art 202.

ing funds, technical assistance and specialised services from relevant international organisations for prevention, reduction and control of marine pollution.[132] Article 202 obliges states directly or through competent international organisations to provide assistance to developing countries for the following:

- 'training of their scientific and technical personnel;
- facilitating their participation in relevant international programmes;
- supplying them with necessary equipment and facilities;
- enhancing their capacity to manufacture such equipment;
- advice on and developing facilities for research, monitoring, educational and other programmes'.[133]

Despite this clear obligation, the developed world as a whole has failed to provide any meaningful assistance to Bangladesh for the equipment and facilities required for environmentally sound operation of its shipbreaking industry. One of the tragedies of international environmental law is the defiance of the obligation of the developed world to provide assistance. In this respect, shipbreaking is not an isolated case; rather, it is an example of global environmental injustice. Shipbreaking is also an example of environmental injustice where developed countries export their environmental hazards to least developed countries and take no responsibility for this. This is a clear violation of the spirit of UNCLOS, which provides that this convention 'will contribute to the strengthening of peace, security, cooperation and friendly relations among all nations in conformity with the principles of justice and equal rights and will *promote the economic and social advancement of all peoples of the world*'.[134] What is happening in the shipbreaking industry is the opposite of UNCLOS's call for justice, equal rights and economic and social advancement of all peoples.

2.4 Environmental justice in the context of Bangladesh

Like many other former British colonies, Bangladesh follows the common law tradition.[135] The country was formerly part of British India and a part of Pakistan after the end of British colonial rule in 1947. In 1971, Bangladesh emerged as an independent nation following a historic struggle and war for independence. The Constitution of Bangladesh follows the principle of separation of power. Bangladesh has a Westminster-type democracy with a prime minister as the head of its government. The country has a unicameral legislature. The judiciary is headed by the Chief Justice of Bangladesh. The Supreme Court is the highest court of the country, having two divisions: the Appellate Division (AD) and the High Court Division (HCD).

132 UNCLOS, art 203.
133 UNCLOS, art 202.
134 UNCLOS, preamble (emphasis added).
135 See generally Kazi Ebadul Hoque, *Administration of Justice in Bangladesh* (Asiatic Society of Bangladesh, 2003).

Bangladesh adopted its constitution in 1972, and it is the supreme law of the land.[136] The Constitution of Bangladesh pledges in its preamble that it shall be a fundamental aim of the state to realise 'a society in which rule of law, fundamental human rights and freedom, equality and justice, political, economic and social, will be secured for all citizens'.[137] Bangladesh began with a very progressive constitution. However, the constitutional journey of the country has been marked by interruptions and downturns.[138]

2.4.1 Environmental justice and socio-economic rights

Part II of the Constitution of Bangladesh lists a number of fundamental principles of state policy as aspirational provisions.[139] Article 14 of this part states that the emancipation of 'the toiling masses, the peasants and workers and backward sections of the people from all forms of exploitation' is a fundamental responsibility of the state.[140] The constitution also embraces a socialist economic system for attaining 'a just and egalitarian society, free from the exploitation of man by man'.[141] The constitution acknowledges as the fundamental principles of state policy the provision of basic necessities,[142] rural development and agricultural revolution,[143] free and compulsory education,[144] public health[145] and equality of opportunity.[146] Through an amendment in 2011, this part now includes a new

136 The Constitution of the People's Republic of Bangladesh, 1972, art 7(2).
137 The Constitution of the People's Republic of Bangladesh, 1972, preamble.
138 The 'constitutional development in Bangladesh has not been very easy and even. The constitution was born healthy, but grew up to become sick and wounded, struggling to gather sufficient strength to stand and move upright. This truly reflects equally unhealthy social, economic and political development of the country'. M. Shah Alam, *Selected Writings on International Law, Constitutional Law and Human Rights* (New Warsi Book Corporation, 2016) 343–344.
139 The Constitution of the People's Republic of Bangladesh, 1972, Part II. On aspirational provisions and socio-economic rights in the Constitution of Bangladesh and other countries, see generally, Kamal Hossain, *Economic and Social Justice Under the Constitution of Bangladesh* (First AK Khan Memorial Law Lecture, University of Chittagong, 27 February 2016); Ellen Wiles, 'Aspirational Principles or Enforceable Rights? Future for Socio-Economic Rights in National Law' (2006) 22 *American University International Law Review* 35; B. Obinna Okere, 'Fundamental Objectives and Directive Principles of State Policy under the Nigerian Constitution' (1983) 32 *International and Comparative Law Quarterly* 214; David Bilchitz, *Poverty and Fundamental Rights: The Justification and Enforcement of Socio-Economic Rights* (Oxford University Press, 2008); Anashri Pillay, 'Revisiting the Indian Experience of Economic and Social Rights Adjudication: The Need for a Principled Approach to Judicial Activism and Restraint' (2014) 63 *International and Comparative Law Quarterly* 385.
140 The Constitution of the People's Republic of Bangladesh, 1972, art 14.
141 The Constitution of the People's Republic of Bangladesh, 1972, art 10.
142 The Constitution of the People's Republic of Bangladesh, 1972, art 15.
143 The Constitution of the People's Republic of Bangladesh, 1972, art 16.
144 The Constitution of the People's Republic of Bangladesh, 1972, art 18.
145 The Constitution of the People's Republic of Bangladesh, 1972, art 18.
146 The Constitution of the People's Republic of Bangladesh, 1972, art 19.

article as follows: 'The State shall endeavour to protect and improve the environment and to preserve and safeguard the natural resources, biodiversity, wetlands, forests and wild life for the present and future citizens'.[147]

Article 8(2) of the constitution states that fundamental principles of state policy 'shall be fundamental to the governance of Bangladesh, shall be applied by the State in the making of laws, shall be a guide to the interpretation of the Constitution and of the other laws of Bangladesh, and shall form the basis of the work of the State and of its citizens, *but shall not be judicially enforceable*'.[148] Thus, these principles are not enforceable by the court.[149] The Supreme Court of Bangladesh has clearly stated in a number of cases that these principles are distinguished from law and are non-enforceable.[150] Nevertheless, the state has an obligation to act on these principles,[151] and in some recent cases the HCD of the Supreme Court has shown a propensity to enforce them.[152] However, according to constitutional law expert Mahmudul Islam, direct enforcement of these principles by the court would be a violation of Article 8(2) of the constitution.[153] As observed by the Appellate Division of the Bangladesh Supreme Court:

> The reason for not making these principles judicially enforceable is obvious. They are in the nature of people's programme for socio-economic development of the country in a peaceful manner, not overnight, but gradually. Implementation of these programmes require resources, technical know-how and many other things including mass-education. Whether all these pre-requisites for a peaceful socio-economic revolution exist is for the State to decide.[154]

The fundamental principles of the state policy part of the Constitution of Bangladesh mainly relate to economic and social rights without creating the room for immediate judicial enforcement. This is sensible considering the economic situation of a newly emerged country that was subject to colonial oppression for several centuries.[155] Nevertheless, it should be noted that inclusion of these

147 The Constitution of the People's Republic of Bangladesh, 1972, art 18A.

148 The Constitution of the People's Republic of Bangladesh, 1972, art 8(2) (emphasis added).

149 The Constitution of the People's Republic of Bangladesh, 1972, art 8(2).

150 *Kudrat-E-Elahi Panir v. Bangladesh* (1992) 44 DLR (AD) 319; *M Saleem Ullah v. Justice M A Quddus Chowdhury* (1994) 46 DLR (HCD) 691; *Aftab Uddin v. Bangladesh* (1996) 48 DLR (HCD) 1; Mahmudaul Islam, *Constitutional Law of Bangladesh* (Mullick Brothers, 2012) 74–75.

151 *Wahab v. Secretary Ministry of Land* (1996) 1 MLR (HC) 338.

152 *Major-General KM Safiullah v. Bangladesh* (2010) 18 BLT (Special Issue – 01) 1 (cited in Islam, above n 150); *Human Rights for Peace for Bangladesh v. Bangladesh* (2011) 19 BLT (HCD) 107.

153 Islam, above n 150, 75.

154 *Kudrat-E-Elahi Panir v. Bangladesh*, above n 150, 331.

155 Fazle Kaderi Mohammad Abdul Munim, 'The Challenges of Social Justice' (1984) 7 *Law and International Affairs* 1. See also, Fazle Kaderi Mohammad Abdul Munim, *Rights of the Citizen under the Constitution and Law* (Bangladesh Institute of Law and International Affairs, 1975)

principles in the constitution was directly linked with the aspiration to establish an independent state based on the rule of law and justice after British and Pakistani oppression ended. Treating these principals as fully non-enforceable after 45 years of independence is against the spirit of the constitution. In many ways, Bangladesh has achieved remarkable success in a range of sectors, and the country is progressing towards rapid industrialisation and economic development. It would not be unreasonable for the Supreme Court, on a case-by-case basis, to draw the attention of the government to implementation of these principles where it is practically possible. As stated above, it is the fundamental objective of the Constitution of Bangladesh that the state shall take all possible endeavours to create a society based on political, economic and social justice.[156] The inclusion of a provision in the constitution indicating that these fundamental principles are not judicially enforceable was justified considering the new state's inability to immediately ensure socio-economic rights for everyone. The reason for inclusion of this provision was mainly the economic inability of the newly independent state to provide these socio-economic rights.

It is difficult to believe that the drafters of the constitution imagined that basic necessities would be unrealisable after 45 years of independence and that these would be unenforceable rights forever if the state attained the capacity to provide some of these rights in many instances. However, what would be the interpretation of this enforceability related provision in cases where the state has clearly achieved the ability to provide some of these socio-economic rights? Socio-economic rights are generally treated as positive rights, unlike civil and political rights, which are generally negative rights. However, some so-called socio-economic rights may have an aspect of negative rights: for example, environmental rights. Article 18A of the Constitution of Bangladesh, which obliges the state to endeavour to protect environment and biodiversity, has an aspect of negative rights. On many occasions, the government itself is the polluter or permits pollution by private entities by violating legal requirements.[157] If the gov-

156 India's constitution has provisions similar to Bangladesh's fundamental principles of state policy, called *directive principles of state policy*. The Supreme Court of India said the following to illustrate the importance of these principles: 'The significance of the perception that Parts III [Fundamental Rights] and IV [Directive Principles of State Policy] together constitute the core of commitment to social revolution and they, together, are the conscience of the Constitution is to be traced to a deep understanding of the scheme of the Indian Constitution. Parts III and IV are like two wheels of a chariot, one no less important than the other. Snap one and the other will lose its efficacy. They are like a twin formula for achieving the social revolution which is the ideal which the visionary founders of the Constitution set before themselves. In other words, the Indian Constitution is founded on the bed-rock of the balance between Parts III and IV'. *Minerva Mills v. Union of India* (1980) AIR (SC) 1789.

157 As observed by former Chief Justice of Bangladesh ATM Afzal, 'It is worth noting that many sectoral laws explicitly contain provisions to inform local people about projects and to both invite and resolve objections raised. For example, the 1927 Forest Act requires the inquiry and settlement of all private claims when restrictions are to be imposed when the status of a public forest is changed through re-classifying as a Reserved or Protected

ernment simply refrained from establishing an environmentally harmful industry (e.g. the Bangladesh government is planning to establish a shipbreaking yard near the world's largest mangrove forest) or did not provide environmental clearance for a highly polluting industry, the environmental rights of nearby people would be ensured without taking any positive steps, but rather by taking a negative step.[158] We are living in an increasingly changing world. Something which was an aspiration 45 years ago may no longer be aspirational. A constitution is a living document. In interpreting the Constitution of Bangladesh, the Supreme Court cannot totally ignore the historical background and current realities.[159]

As observed earlier, justice will require emancipation of people from various unfreedoms. Realisation of economic and social rights is essential for ensuring the freedom of choice, but people facing extreme poverty may have very little choice.[160] The failure of Bangladesh to realise the fundamental principles of its state policy, particularly those related to poverty alleviation and the emancipation of 'the toiling masses the peasants and workers and backward sections of the people from all forms of exploitation', is responsible for gross injustices in the country's shipbreaking industry. Poverty remains the central contributing

---

Forest. The 1920 Agricultural and Sanitary Improvement Act and the 1952 Embankment and Drainage Act explicitly guarantee the rights of local populations and interest-holding parties in proposed project areas to examine and raise objections to the project being considered. Furthermore, neither legal rights nor interests can be extinguished without appropriate compensation. Many of the adverse local, social and environmental impacts induced by development projects could be avoided or minimised if the procedures of law were followed. Some laws contain inter sectoral restrictions on development projects which are neither followed nor enforced. An example of this is the Conservation of Fish Act, 1950 which provides in the schedule a long list of rivers and their segments where no water control measure can be undertaken, so that natural spawning and feeding grounds of fish remain undisturbed. These examples prove that it is a tragedy when public agencies flout their own laws and then chase the people for violating the law to justify the failures of their so called development projects. In such situations, judicial review of administrative action would be effective in upholding rule of law'. ATM Afzal, *Country Statement – Bangladesh*, presented at the Regional Symposium on the Role of Judiciary in Promoting the Rule of Law in the Area of Sustainable Development, Colombo, Sri Lanka, 4–6 July 1997. Cited in *Dr Mohiuddin Farooque v. Bangladesh and Others* (1998) 50 DLR (HCD) 84 (FAP 20 Case Merits).

158 See, for example, Heather Plumridge Bedi, 'Right to Food, Right to Mine? Competing Human Rights Claims in Bangladesh' (2015) 59 *Geoforum* 248.

159 As noted by Justice Latifur Rahman, 'Part II of our Constitution relates to fundamental principles of State Policy . . . . A Constitution of a country is a document of social evolution and it is dynamic in nature. It should encompass in itself the growing demands, needs of people and change of time. A Constitution cannot be morbid at all. The language used by the framers of the Constitution must be given a meaningful interpretation with the evolution and growth of our society. An obligation is cast on the Constitutional Court which is the apex court of the Country to interpret the Constitution in a manner in which social, economic and political justice can be advanced for the welfare of the state and its citizens'. FAP 20 Case (Standing), above n 56.

160 David Begg, 'Poverty and Human Rights in Bangladesh' (2000) 1 *Melbourne Journal of International Law* 149.

factor in many aspects of injustice in Bangladesh, particularly environmental injustice.[161]

The civil and political rights included as fundamental rights in the constitution will be meaningless, or at least will fail to ensure justice, if a lack of implementation of socio-economic rights limits the decision making power of marginalised segments of society. Constitutional interpretation should not lose sight of the reality on the ground. As discussed later, the Constitution of Bangladesh clearly prohibits forced labour and includes this provision in its fundamental rights section.[162] However, this is meaningless if poor people are compelled to perform hazardous work like shipbreaking due to their extreme poverty. Similarly, everyone has the same right to seek recourse in the court. However, litigation in a common law country is a highly expensive business. Equal access to justice is a paper tiger when a victim of environmental pollution does not have money. The emancipation of people from poverty and hunger cannot be just an aspiration after 45 years of independence. As the guardian of the constitution, the highest court of the country should not turn a blind eye to reality. Therefore, a progressive interpretation of the economic and social rights included in Part II of the Constitution of Bangladesh is desirable if it can be proven that the government has the capacity to take certain measures to eliminate inequality. Otherwise, it may create a serious disturbance in society.

As noted by former Chief Justice of Bangladesh Justice Badrul Haider Chowdhury in his *Kamini Kumar Dutta memorial law lecture*:

> The future constitutional policy of this nation will depend to a large extent upon the work of the Supreme Court and its decisions. It has to keep balance between the seemingly contradictory forces. In doing so, it cannot ignore the social, economic and political tendencies of the time.[163]

In interpreting the constitution, the Supreme Court must consider the interests of the people, particularly those belonging to marginalised segments of society.[164]

161 'There are at least two prominent "evils" behind environmental degradation, namely, "affluence" and "poverty". Both of these factors expose two extremes and diametrically opposite facts and qualities of life. Affluence represents the height of the existence or use of the benefits of so-called "development" while poverty indicates either the absence or the inadequacy of "development". Therefore, both the existence and non-existence of development equally threaten the environment'. Mohiuddin Farooque, 'Institutional and Legal Aspects in Resolving Conflicts of Development and Environment in Bangladesh' in Ock-Kyung Kim and James Ypsilantis (eds) *People, Development and Environment: Complex Interlinkages in Bangladesh* (IUCN, 1993) 141, 142.

162 The Constitution of the People's Republic of Bangladesh, 1972, art 34.

163 Badrul Haider Chowdhury, *Evolution of the Supreme Court of Bangladesh* (University of Dhaka, 1990) 169.

164 'This Constitution of ours is not the outcome of a negotiated settlement with a former colonial power. It was not drawn upon the consent, concurrence or approval of any external sovereign power. Nor is it the last of an oft-replaced and oft-substituted Constitution after several Constitutions were tried and failed, although as many as 13 [now 16] amendments have so far been made to it. It is the fruit of a historic war of independence, achieved with

Another former Chief Justice of Bangladesh, Justice Mustafa Kamal in his *Kamini Kumar Dutta memorial law lecture*, similarly observed that

> [c]onstitutional development is no doubt an evolution of the constitution through judicial decisions, but judicial decisions on the Constitution are the outcome of dedicated lawyering backed by intensive academic studies. A purposive and articulate academic community and an ever persistent lawyer community magnify the *patent and latent in the Constitution* in all its facts and phases and it is they who by their continuous constitutional quests keep the torch of the Constitution burning . . .[165]

There is a lack of research on the true meaning and status of the fundamental principles of state policy listed in the Constitution of Bangladesh in light of its drafting history.[166]

2.4.2 Fundamental rights and environmental justice in the shipbreaking industry

Part III of the Constitution of Bangladesh includes some fundamental human rights. Articles 31 and 32 safeguard the right to life as a fundamental right. Article 31 ensures the legal protection of right to life, liberty, body, property and reputation. Article 32 also guarantees the protection of right to life and personal liberty. The Bangladesh Supreme Court expanded the scope of the right to life from civil and political aspects to socio-economic aspects. The court in Bangladesh is highly influenced by developments in the neighbouring country of India. Indian courts have interpreted a similar provision in the Indian Constitution (Article 21 of the Indian Constitution) very liberally.[167] In *Olga Tellis v. Bombay Municipal Corporation* the court held the following:

> These Writ Petitions portray the plight of lakhs of persons who live on pavements and in slums in the city of Bombay . . . . Those who have made

the lives and sacrifice of a telling number of people for a common cause making it a class part from other Constitutions of comparable description. It is a Constitution in which the people features as the dominant actor. It was the people of Bangladesh who in exercise of their own self-proclaimed native power made a clean break from the past unshackling the bondage of a past statehood and adopted a Constitution of its own choosing. The Constitution, historically and in real terms, is a manifestation of what is called "the People's Power" The people of Bangladesh, therefore, are central, as opposed to ornamental, to the framing of the Constitution'. FAP 20 Case (Standing), above n 56.

165 Mustafa Kamal, *Bangladesh Constitution: Trends and Issues* (University of Dhaka, 1994) v (emphasis added).

166 For one exception, see the judicial enforceability of economic, social and cultural rights contained in the Constitution of Bangladesh: Muhammad Ekramul Haque, *Protection of Economic, Social and Cultural Rights: A Critical Analysis of the Fundamental Principles of State Policy in the Constitution of Bangladesh* (PhD thesis, Monash University, 2012).

167 See cases cited in above n 56.

> pavements their homes exist in the midst of filth and squalor, which has to be seen to believed . . . It is these men and women who have come to this Court to ask for a judgment that they cannot be evicted from their squalid shelters without being offered alternative accommodation. They rely for their rights on Article 21 of the Constitution which guarantees that no person shall be deprived of his life except according to procedure established by law. They do not contend that they have a right to live on the pavements. Their contention is that they have a right to live, a right which cannot be exercised without the means of livelihood.[168]

In *Subhash Kumar v. State of Bihar*, the Indian Supreme Court held that the right to life guaranteed by article 21 'includes the right of enjoyment of pollution-free water and air for full enjoyment of life'.[169]

The wider meaning of the right to life was considered by the Bangladesh Supreme Court in *Dr. Mohiuddin Farooque v. Bangladesh and others*, where the court held the following:

> [R]ight to life is not only limited to the protection of life and limbs but extends to the protection of health and strength of the workers, their means of livelihood, enjoyment of pollution-free water and air, bare necessaries of life, facilities for education, development of children, maternity benefit, free movement, maintenance and improvement of public health by creating and sustaining conditions congenial to good health and ensuring quality of life consistent with human dignity.[170]

Similarly, Justice Bimalendu Bikash Roy Chowdhury said in the FAP 20 case:

> Although we do not have any provision like article 48-A [Bangladesh now has a similar provision, article 18A] of the Indian Constitution for protection and improvement of environment, articles 31 and 32 of our Constitution protect right to life as a fundamental right. It encompasses within its ambit, the protection and preservation of environment, ecological balance free from pollution of air and water, sanitation without which life can hardly be enjoyed. Any act or omission contrary thereto will be violative of the said right to life.[171]

Justice A.B.M. Khairul Haque held in another case that the right to life means 'qualitative life among others, free from environmental hazards'.[172] Justice Md

168 *Olga Tellis v. Bombay Municipal Corporation*, above n 56.
169 *Subhash Kumar v. State of Bihar*, above n 56.
170 *Radiated Milk Case*, above n 56, 442.
171 *FAP 20 Case* (Standing), above n 56, 25.
172 *Industrial Pollution Case*, above n 56, 79.

Tafazzul Islam, citing and applying the decision of the Supreme Court of India in *Virender Gaur v. State of Haryana*,[173] held the following:

> [H]ygienic environment is an integral facet of right to healthy life and it will be impossible to live with human dignity without a humane and healthy environmental protection. Therefore, it has now become a matter of grave concern for human existence. Promoting environment protection implies maintenance of environment as a whole comprising the man-made and natural environment. Therefore, there is a constitutional imperative of the State government and the municipalities not only to ensure and safeguard proper environment but also an imperative duty to take adequate measures to promote, protect, and improve both the man-made and the natural environment.[174]

Violation of labour rights is a major issue in the shipbreaking industry of Bangladesh. Article 34 of the Constitution of Bangladesh prohibits all forms of forced labour. Article 37 ensures freedom of assembly, Article 38 guarantees the freedom of association and Article 40 safeguards the freedom of profession and occupation. However, these rights are mostly included as negative rights, which means that the government will not impose unreasonable or unlawful restrictions for these rights. The problem in shipbreaking is mainly that poor workers are forced to work in a hazardous industry because their economic condition compels them to do so despite the serious risks. In many situations, these workers face a modern form of economic slavery, deprived of all legal rights.[175] This is totally against the spirit of Article 34 of the constitution and is a gross violation of the right to life under Articles 31 and 32. In a case related to the release of bonded labourers, Justice P. N. Bhagwati of the Indian Supreme Court held that:

> it is not enough merely to identify and release bonded labourers but it is equally, perhaps more, important that after identification and release, they must be rehabilitated, because without rehabilitation, they would be driven by poverty, helplessness and despair into serfdom once again . . . We, who have not experienced poverty and hunger, want and destitution, talk platitudinous of freedom and liberty but these words have no meaning for a person who has not even a square meal per day, hardly a roof over his head and scarcely one piece of cloth to cover his shame . . . It is therefore imperative that neither the Government nor the Court should be content with merely

173 *Virender Gaur v. State of Haryana*, above n 56.

174 *Rabia Bhuiyan, MP v. Ministry of LGRD*, above n 56, 184.

175 Md Saiful Karim, 'Violation of Labour Rights in the Ship-Breaking Yards of Bangladesh: Legal Norms and Reality' (2009) 25 *The International Journal of Comparative Labour Law and Industrial Relations* 379.

> securing identification and release of bonded labourers but every effort must be made by them to see that the freed bonded labourers are properly and suitably rehabilitated after identification and release.[176]

This is equally true for the shipbreaking industry of Bangladesh. If the industry is closed or workers are released, the plight of these workers will not end. Either the workers should be introduced to other sectors or the shipbreaking industry must operate in a safe and environmentally sound way. Only in this way can we ensure complete justice.

The Constitution of Bangladesh provides a right to 'any person aggrieved' to seek recourse to the High Court Division of the Supreme Court for the enforcement of the fundamental rights conferred by Part III of the constitution.[177] The Supreme Court of Bangladesh liberally interpreted the term 'any person aggrieved' in the early stage of the constitutional journey of the country. In *Kazi Mukhlesur Rahman v. Bangladesh*, two years after the adoption of the constitution, the Supreme Court considered the question of *locus standi* liberally and granted standing to the applicant due to a constitutional issue of grave importance.[178] However, the development of public interest litigation has been slow in Bangladesh, mainly 'owing to frequent interruptions with the working of the Constitution and owing to intermittent de-clothing of the Constitutional jurisdiction of the Superior Courts'.[179] The Bangladesh Supreme Court has shown a restrictive approach in some cases, particularly where the applicant failed to show that they are representing a downtrodden or deprived segment of society who are not able to represent themselves.[180] The Supreme Court specifically recognised the *locus standi* of environmental activist organisations in the *FAP 20 Case* when it allowed standing to the Bangladesh Environmental Lawyers Association (BELA) to challenge a government development project upholding the rights of local people.[181] Following this decision, the Supreme Court was flooded with

176 *Neeraja Chaudhary v. State of MP* (1984) AIR (SC) 1099.

177 'The High Court Division on the application of any person aggrieved, may give such directions or orders to any person or authority, including any person performing any function in connection with the affairs of the Republic, as may be appropriate for the enforcement of any of the fundamental rights conferred by Part III of this Constitution'. The Constitution of the People's Republic of Bangladesh, 1972, art 102(1).

178 *Kazi Mukhlesur Rahman v. Bangladesh* (1974) 26 DLR (AD) 44 (Berubari Case).

179 *FAP 20 Case* (Standing), above n 56, 12, per Mustafa Kamal J.

180 Ibid, per ATM Afzal J, 4; See *Bangladesh Sangbadpatra Parishad v. Bangladesh* (1991) 43 DLR (AD) 126; *Dada Match Workers Union v. Government of Bangladesh* (1977) 29 DLR (HCD) 188.

181 *FAP 20 Case* (Standing), above 56. On public interest litigation in Bangladesh, see generally, Jona Razzaque, 'Access to Environmental Justice: Role of the Judiciary in Bangladesh' (2000) 4 *Bangladesh Journal of Law* 1; Jona Razzaque, *Public Interest Environmental Litigation in India, Pakistan and Bangladesh* (Kluwer, 2004); Naim Ahmed, *Public Interest Litigation: Constitutional Issues and Remedies* (Bangladesh Legal Aid and Services Trust, 1999); Ridwanul Hoque, *Judicial Activism in Bangladesh: A Golden Mean Approach* (Cambridge Scholars Publishing, 2011).

public interest litigations (PILs). These PILs played an instrumental role in the development of environmental jurisprudence in Bangladesh.[182] However, despite repeated interventions by the court, the government on many occasions has been reluctant to implement decisions.[183]

Despite supporting a broader role of the court, we must acknowledge the limitation of courts as a policy making forum and the lack of effectiveness of PIL in many respects.[184] As discussed later in this book, the jurisprudential development of the right to life and legislative development for regulation of shipbreaking due to the activism and intervention of the Bangladesh Supreme Court did very little to bring meaningful change to the lives of shipbreaking workers.

2.5 Conclusion

The concepts of environmental rights and environmental justice have witnessed rapid development in the last few decades at both the conceptual and practical levels. International and national legal systems increasingly recognise these concepts. However, despite these developments, almost every month someone dies in the Bangladesh shipbreaking industry. This brings us back to the conceptual framework of realisation-based justice and the concepts of *niti*, *nyaya* and *matsyanyaya*. We need a society based on *nyaya* or a realisation-based justice system to eliminate *matsyanyaya*. As observed earlier, without implementation of socio-economic rights and without removing economic unfreedoms, regulatory changes will not work. Development must be established as a freedom, giving people the opportunity of choice. Using this fundamental conceptual understanding, the subsequent chapters of this book examine the challenges in realising environmental justice in the shipbreaking industry of Bangladesh.

182 Md Saiful Karim, Okechukwu Benjamin Vincents and Mia Mahmudur Rahim, 'Legal Activism for Ensuring Environmental Justice' (2012) 7 *Asian Journal of Comparative Law* 346.

183 Awal Hossain Mollah, 'Judicial Activism and Human Rights in Bangladesh: A Critique' (2014) 56 *International Journal of Law and Management* 494.

184 Lavanya Rajamani, 'Public Interest Environmental Litigation in India: Exploring Issues of Access, Participation, Equity, Effectiveness and Sustainability' (2007) 19 *Journal of Environmental Law* 293; Lavanya Rajamani, 'The Right to Environmental Protection in India: Many a Slip between the Cup and the Lip?' (2007) 16 *Review of European Community and International Environmental Law* 274; Karim, Vincents and Rahim, above n 182; Jona Razzaque, 'Linking Human Rights, Development and Environment: Experiences from Litigation in South Asia' (2007) 18 *Fordham Environmental Law Review*, 587, 605; Abdullah Al Faruque and Md Saiful Karim, 'Environmental Law of Bangladesh' in Nicholas A. Robinson, Elizabeth Burleson and Lin-Heng Lye (eds), *Comparative Environmental Law and Regulation* (Thomson Reuters, 2016) 7A:1.

3 Existing international environmental conventions – relevance in ensuring environmental justice in the shipbreaking industry

3.1 Introduction

This chapter examines the role that major international environmental conventions may play in ensuring environmentally sustainable operation of the shipbreaking industry. A number of international environmental conventions may be directly or indirectly relevant to the shipbreaking industry. These legal instruments can be divided into two groups: IMO marine environmental conventions, and international conventions for transboundary movement and environmentally sound disposal of hazardous wastes and other hazardous substances.

Section 3.2 presents an overview of some IMO marine environmental conventions that may be relevant to the shipbreaking industry. Transboundary movement and environmentally sound disposal of hazardous wastes has become a major issue in international environmental law in recent decades. A number of international and regional conventions have been developed for control of transboundary movement and environmentally sound disposal of hazardous wastes. Most prominent of these is the Basel Convention.[1] Section 3.3 presents a critical analysis of this international convention related to hazardous wastes, which is highly relevant for the prevention of environmental pollution from the shipbreaking industry. Apart from international conventions regulating transboundary movement and environmentally sound management of hazardous wastes, international legal instruments dealing with POPs and hazardous chemicals may be relevant to the shipbreaking industry as many obsolete ships contains these substances.[2] Section 3.4 and 3.5 examine the applicability of the Stockholm Convention[3] and the Rotterdam Convention[4] to the shipbreaking industry.

1 *Basel Convention on the Control of Transboundary Movements of Hazardous Wastes and Their Disposal*, opened for signature 22 March 1989, 1673 UNTS 126 (entered into force 24 May 1992).

2 Zada Marie Lipman, 'International Regulation of Hazardous Chemicals and Its Efficacy in Promoting Sustainability for Developing Countries' (2006) 2 *International Journal of Environmental, Cultural, Economic and Social Sustainability* 85.

3 *Stockholm Convention on Persistent Organic Pollutants*, opened for signature 22 May 2001, 2256 UNTS 119 (entered into force 17 May 2004) (hereinafter Stockholm Convention).

4 *Rotterdam Convention on the Prior Informed Consent Procedure for Certain Hazardous Chemicals and Pesticides in International Trade*, opened for signature 10 September 1998, 2244 UNTS 337 (entered into force 24 February 2004) (hereinafter Rotterdam Convention).

This chapter argues that although many international conventions are relevant for environmentally sustainable operation of the shipbreaking industry, practical implementation of these international legal instruments is very difficult largely due to the unwillingness of state parties to implement international legal instruments and the practical realities of the international shipping sector, including the culture of flags of convenience, which allows ship owners and shipbreaking business owners to circumvent legal requirements.[5]

3.2 Shipbreaking and International Maritime Organization marine environmental conventions

UNCLOS established a framework for the development of international rules and regulations for prevention of marine pollution from vessels.[6] It elaborated on the jurisdiction of flag, port and coastal state for prevention of marine pollution.[7] By reference it includes regulations developed by competent international organisations as generally accepted international rules and standards.[8] Prevention of pollution to the environment from vessels is a complex area of international environmental law.[9] To cover many aspects of marine pollution from vessels, a large

5 On implementation, see generally, Md Saiful Karim, 'Implementation of the MARPOL Convention in Developing Countries' (2010) 79 *Nordic Journal of International Law* 303; Md Saiful Karim, 'Implementation of the MARPOL Convention in Bangladesh' (2009) 5 *Macquarie Journal of International and Comparative Environmental Law* 51; Md Saiful Karim, 'Environmental Pollution from Shipbreaking Industry: International Law and National Legal Response' (2010) 22 *Georgetown International Environmental Law Review* 185.

6 *United Nations Convention on the Law of the Sea*, opened for signature 10 December 1982, 1833 UNTS 3 (entered into force 16 November 1994), (hereinafter UNCLOS) art 211.

7 UNCLOS, arts 211, 217, 218, 219, 220, 221, 224, 225, 226, 227 228, 229, 230, 231, 232 and 233. Daniel Bodansky, 'Protecting the Marine Environment from Vessel-Source Pollution: UNCLOS III and Beyond' (1991) 18 *Ecology Law Quarterly* 719; John Warren Kindt, 'Vessel-Source Pollution and the Law of the Sea' (1984) 17 *Vanderbilt Journal of Transnational Law* 287.

8 Bernard H. Oxman, 'The Duty to Respect Generally Accepted International Standards' (1991) 24 *New York University Journal of International Law and Politics* 110; Louis B. Sohn 'Generally Accepted International Rules' (1986) 61 *Washington Law Review* 1073. 'Although IMO is explicitly mentioned in only one of the articles of UNCLOS (article 2 of Annex VIII), several provisions in the Convention refer to the "competent international Organization" in connection with the adoption of international shipping rules and standards in matters concerning maritime safety efficiency of navigation and the prevention and control of marine pollution from vessels and by dumping . . . In such cases, the expression "competent international organization", when used in the singular in UNCLOS, applies exclusively to IMO, bearing in mind the global mandate of the Organization as a specialized agency within the United Nations system established by the Convention on the International Maritime Organization.' IMO, *Implications of the United Nations Convention on the Law of the Sea for the International Maritime Organization*, IMO Doc. LEG/MISC.7 (19 January 2012).

9 Md Saiful Karim, *Prevention of Pollution of the Marine Environment from Vessels: The Potential and Limits of the International Maritime Organisation* (Springer, 2015); Alan Khee-Jin Tan, *Vessel-Source Marine Pollution: The Law and Politics of International Regulation* (Cambridge University Press, 2006).

number of international legal instruments have been adopted.[10] Many of these legal instruments are highly technical, and deal with a range of issues including, inter alia, oil pollution from ships, chemical pollution from ships, sewage from ships, garbage from ships, air pollution from ships, greenhouse gas emissions from ships, pollution preparedness and response, ballast water management, biofouling and anti-fouling systems. Some of these issues and legal instruments may be relevant for the shipbreaking industry, as examined in this section.

MARPOL 73/78 is the most important international convention for prevention of pollution from vessels.[11] As discussed later in this chapter, an obsolete vessel during its final voyage can be treated simultaneously as a ship and as waste. The MARPOL Convention was adopted in 1973 following the Torrey Canyon incident in 1967, which demonstrated the inadequacy of the previously operational 1954 International Convention for the Prevention of Pollution of the Sea by Oil.[12] The MARPOL Convention has been amended on many occasions and currently includes provisions for different aspects of marine pollution covered in six annexes. Annex I deals with oil pollution, Annex II is related to noxious liquid substances in bulk, Annex III covers harmful substances carried by sea in packaged form, Annex IV is related to sewage from ships, Annex V regulates garbage from ships and Annex VI regulates air pollution from ships.

The most relevant provision of the MARPOL Convention for shipbreaking is the provision related to oil pollution prevention, particularly criteria for oil discharge. The MARPOL Convention prohibits any discharge into the sea of oil or oily mixtures from the cargo area of an oil tanker within 50 nautical miles of the nearest land. The convention also prohibits discharge into the sea of oil or oily mixtures from ships of 400 gross tonnage unless certain conditions are fulfilled, including, inter alia, that the oil content of the effluent without dilution

10 Some of these conventions are *International Convention Relating to Intervention on the High Seas in Cases of Oil Pollution Casualties*, opened for signature 29 November 1969, 9 ILM 25 (entered into force 6 May 1975) as amended by the 1973 *Protocol Relating to Intervention on the High Seas in Cases of Marine Pollution by Substances Other Than Oil*, opened for signature 2 November 1973, 13 ILM 650 (entered into force 30 March 1983); *International Convention for the Prevention of Pollution from Ships*, opened for signature 2 November 1973, 1340 UNTS 184 as modified by the Protocol of 1978 to the 1973 Convention, opened for signature 17 February 1978, 1341 UNTS 3 (entered into force 2 October 1983) (hereinafter MARPOL 73/78); *International Convention on Oil Pollution Preparedness, Response and Cooperation*, opened for signature 30 November 1990, 30 ILM 733 (entered into force 13 May 1995); *International Convention for the Control and Management of Ship's Ballast Water and Sediments*, IMO Doc. BWM/CONF/36 (16 February 2004) (entered into force 8 September 2017) (hereinafter BWM Convention); *International Convention on the Control of Harmful Anti-Fouling Systems on Ships 2001*, IMO Doc. AFS/CONF/26 (5 October 2001) (entered into force 17 September 2008) (hereinafter AFS Convention).

11 Andrew Griffin, 'MARPOL 73/78 and Vessel Pollution: A Glass Half Full or Half Empty' (1994) 1 *Indiana Journal of Global Legal Studies* 489.

12 *International Convention for the Prevention of Pollution of the Sea by Oil*, opened for signature 12 May 1954, 327 UNTS 3 (entered into force 26 July 1958).

does not exceed 15 parts per million. If cargo or fuel oil from an obsolete ship is discharged into the sea, it is a clear violation of the MARPOL Convention. According to the Port Reception Facility Database of the IMO Global Integrated Shipping Information System, Bangladesh does not have any port reception facilities for oily waste.[13] It is thus likely that shipbreakers are discharging oil into the territorial waters of Bangladesh, clearly violating the MARPOL Convention. Similar observations can be made for some other aspects of vessel-source pollution including the control of pollution by noxious substances (Annex II), the prevention of pollution by sewage (Annex IV) and the prevention of pollution by garbage (Annex V).

The applicability of the MARPOL Convention in the shipbreaking industry is dependent on the following determination: 'when does a ship cease to be a ship'.[14] The MARPOL Convention may be applicable until beaching, after which the applicability of this convention is doubtful. Therefore, whether the MARPOL Convention is violated largely depends on when the discharge is occurring.[15]

The shipbreaking industry may impose a serious threat to Bangladesh marine biodiversity due to the discharge of ballast waters. Ships use ballast water to stabilise vessels at sea. It is reasonable to assume that ships contain ballast water on their final voyage to the shipbreaking yards to maintain stability.[16] This ballast water is discharged at sea prior to beaching as part of the cleaning process.[17] In many parts of the world ballast water is recognised as being responsible for destruction of biodiversity thorough the introduction of alien species and spreading of pathogenic microorganisms.[18]

13 International Maritime Organization (IMO), *GISIS: Port Reception Facilities* (2016) <https://gisis.imo.org/Public/PRF/SearchPort.aspx>.

14 *Recycling of Ships: Report of the Correspondence Group (Submitted by the Coordinator of the Correspondence Group)*, IMO Doc MEPC 46/7 (18 January 2001), 6.

15 Ibid.

16 'The final voyage of a ship to a scrapping facility will almost always be with the ship in ballast for the same operational reasons for which a ship requires to carry ballast water in service. It is also universally accepted and documented that such ballast water and entrained sediment contains harmful, non-indigenous, alien or unwanted aquatic organisms and pathogens. Therefore management measures are essential to minimise the environmental effects of these harmful species in ballast water and sediment when it is discharged or released, particularly within coastal maritime zones'. *Potential Environmental Effects of Ships Ballast Water Discharges in Considering the Involvement of IMO in Regulating the Scrapping of Ships (Submitted by Friends of the Earth International)*, IMO Doc. MEPC 44/16 (3 December 1999).

17 NGO Shipbreaking Platform, *Why Ships Are Toxic* (2017) <www.shipbreakingplatform.org/main-aspects/why-ships-are-toxic/>.

18 Sarah A. Baileya, 'An Overview of Thirty Years of Research on Ballast Water as a Vector for Aquatic Invasive Species to Freshwater and Marine Environments' (2015) 18 *Aquatic Ecosystem Health and Management* 261; Nicholas Bax et al., 'Marine Invasive Alien Species: A Threat to Global Biodiversity' (2003) 27 *Marine Policy* 313; James T. Carlton, 'Transoceanic and Interoceanic Dispersal of Coastal Organisms: The Biology of Ballast Water' (1985) 23 *Oceanography and Marine Biology Annual Review* 313; James T. Carlton, 'Patterns of

Article 196 of UNCLOS imposes an obligation on states to take all measures necessary to prevent, reduce and control intentional or accidental introduction of alien or new species that may cause significant and harmful changes to a particular marine environment.[19] Similarly, the Convention on Biological Diversity obliges state parties to 'prevent the introduction of, control or eradicate those alien species which threaten ecosystems, habitats or species'.[20] In 2004, the International Convention for the Control and Management of Ships' Ballast Water and Sediments was adopted under the auspices of the IMO.[21] This convention imposes a number of general obligations and also introduces a ballast water management plan and standards.[22]

Paints are used both above and below the waterline of vessels. Paint used below the waterline is called anti-fouling paint, which is used to stop growth of marine life such as algae and molluscs on the hull because attachment of marine organism slows down the ship. Anti-fouling paint may contain the organotin tributylin (TBT). Paint used in ships may also contain a number of other hazardous substances including lead carbonate, cadmium, other organotins (such as tributyltin

---

Transoceanic Marine Biological Invasions in the Pacific Ocean' (1987) 41 *Bulletin of Marine Science* 452; Matej David and Marko Perkovič, 'Ballast Water Sampling as a Critical Component of Biological Invasions Risk Management' (2004) 49 *Marine Pollution Bulletin* 313; Susan A. McCarthy and Farukh M. Khabaty, 'International Dissemination of Epidemic *Vibrio cholerae* by Cargo Ship Ballast and Other Nonpotable Waters' (1994) 60 *Applied and Environmental Microbiology* 2597; Gustaaf M. Hallegraeff and Christopher J. Bolch, 'Transport of Toxic Dinoflagellate Cysts via Ships' Ballast Water' (1991) 22 *Marine Pollution Bulletin* 27; Keith R. Hayes and Cathryn Sliwa, 'Identifying Potential Marine Pests – a Deductive Approach Applied to Australia' (2003) 46 *Marine Pollution Bulletin* 91; R.J. Williams et al., 'Cargo Vessel Ballast Water as a Vector for the Transport of Non-Indigenous Marine Species' (1988) 26 *Estuarine, Coastal and Shelf Science* 409; Ian C. Davidson and Christina Simkanin, 'The Biology of Ballast Water 25 Years Later' (2012) 14 *Biological Invasions* 9; C.K. Takahashi et al., 'Ballast Water: A Review of the Impact on the World Public Health' (2008) 14 *Journal of Venomous Animals and Toxins Including Tropical Diseases* 395; Sharonne O'Shea and Allegra Cangelosi, 'Trojan Horses in Our Harbors: Biological Contamination from Ballast Water Discharge' (1996) 27 *University of Toledo Law Review* 381.

19 UNCLOS, art 196.

20 *Convention on Biological Diversity*, opened for signature 5 June 1992, 1760 UNTS 79 (entered into force 29 December 1993) art 8(h).

21 BWM Convention, above n 10.

22 See generally, David Ciesla, 'Developments in Vessel-Based Pollution: The International Maritime Organization's Ballast Water Convention and the European Union's Regulation to Phase out Single-Hull Oil Tankers' (2004) 15 *Colorado Journal of International Environmental Law and Policy* 107; Patrick Donner, 'Ballast Water Treatment Ashore – Better for the Environment and for Seafarers' (2010) 9 *WMU Journal of Maritime Affairs* 191; Jeremy Firestone and James J. Corbett, 'Coastal and Port Environments: International Legal and Policy Responses to Reduce Ballast Water Introductions of Potentially Invasive Species' (2006) 7 *Sustainable Development Law and Policy* 45; Stephan Gollasch et al., 'Critical Review of the IMO International Convention on the Management of Ships' Ballast Water and Sediments' (2007) 6 *Harmful Algae* 585; Michael Tsimplis, 'Alien Species Stay Home: The International Convention for the Control and Management of Ships' Ballast Water and Sediments 2004' (2005) 19 *International Journal of Marine and Coastal Law* 411.

oxide), arsenic, zinc chromate and lead chromate.[23] In shipbreaking yards workers cut ships into pieces using oxy-acetylene torches. During this process toxic fumes are released from paint.[24] These substances thus pose a threat to shipbreaking workers and people in nearby areas, as well as creating a serious threat to the marine and coastal environment.[25]

In 2001, the IMO member states adopted the International Convention on the Control of Harmful Anti-fouling Systems on Ships (AFS Convention). This convention prohibits application or re-application of organotin compounds, which act as biocides in anti-fouling systems.[26] The convention also provides that no ship shall bear these compounds on its hull or external parts or surfaces. However, the convention provides an alternative way of compliance whereby a ship can bear these prohibited compounds if it uses a coating to form a barrier to stop the prohibited compounds from leaching from underlying noncompliant anti-fouling systems.[27] This convention thus is not very effective from the perspective of the shipbreaking industry because many existing ships arriving in shipbreaking yards will have hazardous substances concealed under the acceptable substances. Hazardous substances covered by a non-hazardous substance will ultimately be released during the shipbreaking process. As observed by India in a submission to IMO:

> in the matter of phasing out of TBT paint, provision for application of sealer coat should not be encouraged as such over-painting with eco-friendly paint would make handling of the bottom layer of TBT paint at the recycling yard almost impossible. The responsibility of phasing out should not be shifted from ship owner to ship recycler. Thus, one IMO Convention for protection of environment should not be at the cost of another measure for the protection of the same environment . . . We strongly feel that AFS Convention should be reviewed in this regard.[28]

Another convention administered by the IMO that may be relevant for the shipbreaking industry is the Convention on the Prevention of Marine Pollution by Dumping of Wastes and Other Matter 1972 (hereinafter London Dumping Convention).[29] This convention was adopted in 1972 and amended by a protocol

23 Correspondence Group Report, above 14, 13–14.
24 Ibid.
25 Ibid.
26 AFS Convention, Annex 1.
27 AFS Convention, Annex 1.
28 *Recycling of Ships: Comments on Document MEPC 48/3 (Submitted by India)*, IMO Doc. MEPC 48/3/2 (9 August 2002).
29 *Convention on the Prevention of Marine Pollution by Dumping of Wastes and Other Matter*, opened for signature 29 December 1972, 11 ILM 1294 (entered into force 30 August 1975).

in 1996 (hereinafter London Dumping Protocol).[30] The convention as amended by the London Dumping Protocol defines as dumping any 'deliberate disposal into the sea of vessels, aircraft, platforms or other man-made structures at sea' as well as 'abandonment or toppling at site of platforms or other man-made structures at sea, for the sole purpose of deliberate disposal'.[31] However, dumping of 'vessels and platforms or other man-made structures at sea' is allowed by the London Dumping Convention and Protocol.[32] The IMO adopted specific guidelines for national authorities in the assessment of applications to dump obsolete vessels in a manner consistent with the provisions of the London Dumping Convention and Protocol.[33] However, dumping obsolete commercial vessels is not very common, so the practical outcome of this convention in the global shipbreaking industry is not significant. Similarly, another IMO convention that may be relevant but that has very limited practical significance for the shipbreaking industry in developing countries is the 2007 Nairobi International Convention on the Removal of Wrecks.[34]

Although some of the IMO marine environmental conventions may be relevant to the shipbreaking industry, their practical implications are not noticeable. The role of these conventions in ensuring environmental justice in the Bangladeshi shipbreaking industries is absolutely minimal. None of the above mentioned conventions have been adopted for the shipbreaking industry. Nevertheless, non-implementation of these conventions where applicable is a clear violation of them.

3.3 The Basel Convention

This section introduces the Basel Convention and critically examines the major legal issues relating to the application of this convention in the shipbreaking industry. The Basel Convention is the most important international treaty for regulation of transboundary movement of hazardous wastes and their environmentally sound disposal.[35] The main aims of the convention are (i) reducing

30 *Protocol to the Convention on the Prevention of Marine Pollution by Dumping of Wastes and Other Matter*, opened for signature 7 November 1996, 36 ILM 1 (entered into force 24 March 2006) (hereinafter London Dumping Protocol).

31 London Dumping Protocol, art 1(4).

32 London Dumping Protocol, Annex 1.

33 *Revised Specific Guidelines for the Assessment of Vessels*, IMO Doc. LC 38/16 (18 October 2016). Annex 7. According to these guidelines, 'A permit to dump a vessel at sea shall be refused if the permitting authority determines that appropriate opportunities exist to reuse, recycle or treat the vessel without undue risks to human health or the environment or disproportionate costs'.

34 *Nairobi International Convention on the Removal of Wrecks*, opened for signature 18 May 2007, IMO Doc LEG/CONF.16/19 (entered into force 14 April 2015).

35 See generally, Cristina A. Lucier and Brian J. Gareau, 'Obstacles to Preserving Precaution and Equity in Global Hazardous Waste Regulation: An Analysis of Contested Knowledge in the Basel Convention' (2016) 16 *International Environmental Agreements: Politics, Law and*

the generation of hazardous wastes; (ii) limiting transboundary movement of hazardous wastes; and (iii) establishing a framework of regulation for permissible transboundary movement of hazardous wastes.[36]

The Basel Convention requires that transboundary movements of hazardous wastes that are permissible be carried out in accordance with the procedure prescribed by the convention.[37] This procedure is referred to as prior informed consent (PIC), although this term is not used in the Basel Convention. Parties are required to appoint a competent authority to administer the PIC procedure.[38] It is a duty of '[t]he State of export [to] notify, or [to] require the generator or exporter to notify', all concerned states 'of any proposed transboundary movement of [wastes]'.[39] Such notification must contain information about the hazardous wastes as prescribed by the convention.[40] In turn, the 'State of import shall respond to the notifier in writing, consenting to the movement with or without conditions, denying permission for the movement, or requesting additional information'.[41] At the same time, before permitting the export, the state of export must obtain written consent from all transit states.[42]

How far the Basel Convention will be applicable to all aspects of transboundary movement of end-of-life ships remains, at least in the view of some scholars, a dilemma in international law.[43] Application of the Basel Convention to the shipbreaking industry involves some legal questions. These include whether a ship can be considered a hazardous waste; how to determine the 'state of export'; and how the flag state can take action if a ship decides to depart for the graveyard from a port in another country.[44]

The Conference of Parties (CoP) of the Basel Convention first considered the legal aspect of ship dismantling at its fifth meeting held in December 1999, almost

---

Economics 493; David P. Hackett, 'An Assessment of the Basel Convention on the Control of Transboundary Movements of Hazardous Wastes and Their Disposal' (1990) 5 *American University International Law Review* 291; Katharina Kummer, 'The International Regulation of Transboundary Traffic in Hazardous Wastes: The 1989 Basel Convention' (1992) 41 *International and Comparative Law Quarterly* 530; Marguerite M. Cusack, 'International Law and the Transboundary Shipment of Hazardous Waste to the Third World: Will the Basel Convention Make a Difference?' (1990) 5 *American University International Law Review* 393.

36 Iwona Rummel-Bulska, 'The Basel Convention and the UN Convention on the Law of the Sea' in Henrik Ringbom (ed) *Competing Norms in the Law of Marine Environmental Protection* (Kluwer Law International, 1997) 83, 83–84.

37 Basel Convention, arts 4(1), 4(2).

38 Basel Convention, art 5.

39 Basel Convention, arts 6(1), 2(10).

40 Basel Convention, art 6(1).

41 Basel Convention, arts 6(2), 2(11).

42 Basel Convention, arts 6(4), 2(12).

43 Geir Ulfstein, *Legal Aspects of Scrapping of Vessels, a Study for the Norwegian Ministry of Environment* (9 March 1999) 3–4 <www.shipbreakingplatform.org/shipbrea_wp2011/wp-content/uploads/2011/11/MD1999dismantling-ships-academic-survey.pdf>.

44 Ibid., 3.

a decade after the adoption of the convention.[45] At this meeting, a representative of the IMO stated that there is a lack of internationally agreed procedure involving the flag state, the state of reception and international organisations, and that there were loopholes in the Basel Convention and IMO conventions (existing at the time) because none of these legal instruments were specifically designed for dealing with the issue of ship dismantling.[46] The CoP adopted a decision at this meeting to request the Technical Working Group and the Legal Working Group to discuss the legal aspects of ship dismantling and to collaborate with the IMO on this matter.[47] The sixth meeting of the CoP, held in 2003, adopted the Technical Guidelines for the Environmentally Sound Management of the Full and Partial Dismantling of Ships (hereinafter Basel Guidelines).[48] These guidelines are discussed later in this section.

Although over the years initiatives have been taken to make the Basel Convention operational in the shipbreaking sector, the global community has not yet been successful in ensuring environmentally sound disposal of obsolete ships. The substantive obligations of PIC and environmentally sound disposal of obsolete ships under the Basel Convention would be difficult to enforce against ship owners and shipbreaking companies using existing international mechanisms. However, there is no barrier to taking national action on the part of any shipbreaking nation to apply these substantive obligations in their territory. As discussed later in this book, the Bangladesh Supreme Court unsuccessfully took a proactive role for implementation of the Basel Convention in the Bangladeshi shipbreaking industry.

The following sections briefly discuss three critical legal issues pertaining to the application of the Basel Convention in the shipbreaking industry: whether an end-of-life ship can be treated as waste; the Basel Ban amendment's effect on the export of end-of-life ships to developing countries;[49] and determination of the country of export. Section 3.3.4 addresses issues related to problems in enforcement of the Basel Convention in the shipbreaking industry. Section 3.3.5 introduces the Basel Guidelines adopted by the CoP of the Basel Convention and their role in the environmentally sound management of the shipbreaking industry.

3.3.1 *Whether an end-of-life ship can be treated as waste*

The Basel Convention defines 'wastes' as 'substances or objects which are disposed of or are intended to be disposed of or are required to be disposed of by the provisions of national law'.[50] With some minor exceptions, the convention

45 *Report of the Fifth Meeting of the Conference of the Parties to the Basel Convention*, UNEP Doc. UNEP/CHW.5/29 (10 December 1999)
46 Ibid., 110.
47 Ibid., 56.
48 *Report of the Conference of the Parties to the Basel Convention on the Control of Transboundary Movements of Hazardous Wastes and Their Disposal*, UNEP Doc. UNEP/CHW.6/40 (10 February 2003) 138.
49 *Decisions Adopted by the Third Meeting of the Conference of the Parties to the Basel Convention*, Dec. III/1, U.N. Doc. UNEP/CHW.3/35 (28 November 1995).
50 Basel Convention, art 2(1).

is equally applicable to wastes to be recycled and wastes marked for other forms of disposal.[51] Annex I of the convention elaborates on a number of categories of 'hazardous wastes'.[52] Many substances present in ships including asbestos, PCBs, lead and arsenic are listed as hazardous wastes under the Basel Convention.[53] Wastes that are considered to be hazardous wastes by the domestic legislation of the countries of export, import and transit are also treated as hazardous wastes.[54]

Whether an obsolete ship can be considered as waste was long a burning issue that was apparently resolved by a 2003 decision of a Working Group Meeting of the Basel Convention. The working group agreed that 'a ship may become waste, in accordance with Article 2 of the Basel Convention, and that at the same time it may be defined as a ship under other international rules'.[55] In the same decision the working group invited comments from the parties on when should a ship become waste and when should it cease to be a ship.[56] These questions generated diversified responses. The IMO stated that the MARPOL Convention defines a ship as 'a vessel of any type whatsoever operating in the marine environment and includes hydrofoil boats, air-cushion vehicles, submersibles, floating craft and fixed or floating platforms'.[57] The IMO was of the opinion that IMO legal instruments, particularly the MARPOL Convention, do not use specific criteria to determine when a ship ceases to be a ship, other than providing the above definition of ship.[58] Similarly, the UN Division for Ocean Affairs and Law of the Sea commented that 'UNCLOS does not contain any provisions on the dismantling of ships' and 'does not specifically address when a ship ceases to be a ship'.[59] After considering different views, the CoP of the Basel Convention declared that 'many ships and other floating structures are known to contain hazardous materials and that such hazardous materials may become hazardous wastes as listed in the annexes to the Basel Convention'.[60]

51 Basel Convention, art 2(4), Annex IV.

52 Basel Convention, art 1(1)(a), Annex I. 'These categories of wastes will be subject to this convention if they possess any of the hazardous characteristics contained in Annex III, which includes, inter alia, explosive and flammable substances or wastes liable to spontaneous combustion; oxidising agents; organic peroxides; poisonous (acute) or infectious substances; corrosives; liberation of toxic gases in contact with air or water; and toxic and ecotoxic substances'. Basel Convention, art 1(1)(a), Annex III.

53 Basel Convention, Annex I.

54 Basel Convention, art 1(1)(b).

55 *Report of the Open-Ended Working Group of the Basel Convention on the Work of Its Second Session*, UN Doc. UNEP/CHW/OEWG/2/12 (16 December 2003), 17 (hereinafter Basel Convention Open-ended Working Group Report).

56 Ibid.

57 MARPOL 73/78, art 2(4).

58 *Report of the Marine Environment Protection Committee on Its Forty-Seventh Session*, IMO Doc. MEPC 47/20 (18 March 2002) 20.

59 *Legal Aspects of the Full and Partial Dismantling of Ships: Comments Provided by Parties and Others*, UNEP Doc. UNEP/CHW/OEWG/3/INF/5 (24 February 2004) 32.

60 *Report of the Conference of the Parties to the Basel Convention on the Control of Transboundary Movements of Hazardous Wastes and Their Disposal*, 63, UN Doc. UNEP/CHW.7/33 (25 January 2005).

However, loopholes still exist. If the owner of a ship hides the information that the ship is on its final voyage, the ship may be treated as a ship and not as waste.[61] Nevertheless, if the importing state sincerely wants to comply with its obligations under the Basel Convention, this problem can be solved. For example, under existing laws in Bangladesh, if a ship is not imported under a Letter of Credit declaring that the ship will be scrapped in a shipbreaking yard, it cannot be beached in the shipbreaking yards.[62] The ship can be imported only after payment of the prescribed import tax for scrapping in Bangladesh.[63]

3.3.2 Export of end-of-life ships to developing countries and the Basel Ban amendment

The Basel Convention does not prohibit the export of wastes from developed countries to developing countries. However, there are certain provisions that have significance in the north – south trade in hazardous wastes.[64] If any developing country prohibits import of certain wastes, other countries cannot export such wastes to that country.[65] In its second meeting, the CoP of the Basel Convention agreed to an immediate ban on the export of hazardous wastes from the OECD to developing countries.[66] However, as this decision was not incorporated as an amendment to the convention, there was some doubt as to whether it was legally binding. In light of this uncertainty, at the third meeting of the CoP the ban was adopted as an amendment to the Basel Convention. This amendment prohibits export of hazardous wastes from the OECD, European Community and Liechtenstein to other countries. However, the amendment has not yet come into force.[67]

It is not clear whether there is presently any international legal barrier to the export of hazardous wastes from developed to developing countries. From the outset, it has been a debatable question whether the CoP decision of March 1994 is a legally binding instrument.[68] The incorporation of the 1994 decision as an

61 Ulfstein, above n 43, 8, 10.

62 Government of the Peoples Republic of Bangladesh, Custom House, Chittagong, General Notification 15 (20 April 1987).

63 Ibid.

64 See generally David A. Wirth, 'Trade Implication of the Basel Convention Amendment Banning North-South Trade in Hazardous Wastes' (1998) 7 *Review of European Community and International Environmental Law* 237, 243.

65 Basel Convention, art 4(1)(b).

66 *Report of the Second Meeting of the Conference of the Parties to the Basel Convention*, 19–20, UN Doc. UNEP/CHW.2/30 (25 March 1994).

67 The amendment requires ratification by at least three-quarters of the parties. At present, 88 countries have ratified the amendment. Secretariat of the Basel Convention, *Amendment to the Basel Convention on the Control of Transboundary Movements of Hazardous Wastes and Their Disposal* (2017) <www.basel.int/Countries/StatusofRatifications/BanAmendment/tabid/1344/Default.aspx>.

68 As Zada Lipman said, '[u]ntil recently, this decision was persuasive, but not binding under international law'. Zada Lipman, 'Transboundary Movement of Hazardous Waste: Environmental Justice Issues for Developing Countries' (1999) *Acta Juridica* 266, 276.

amendment in 1995 itself indicates that parties to the convention consider this decision persuasive and not legally binding.[69]

The above discussion suggests that until the Basel Ban comes into effect, there is no direct legal ban on exporting hazardous wastes from developed to developing countries. Nevertheless, the amendment has the potential to influence regional and national legislation relating to waste management. For example, the EU has adopted Regulations on Waste Shipments to implement the Basel Ban even before it enters into force.[70] Moreover, states that have ratified or signed the Basel Ban amendment have the obligation to not defeat its object and purpose prior to its entry into force under customary international law, as codified by the Vienna Convention on the Law of Treaties.[71]

The Basel Convention allows transboundary movement of wastes if they are 'required as a raw material for recycling or recovery industries in the State of import'.[72] In most shipbreaking countries, shipbreaking purports to be a recycling industry, and obsolete ships are dismantled for the recovery of iron and steel. Thus, in that sense, the export of obsolete ships to developing countries from developed countries may arguably not be illegal under the Basel Convention; however, in another sense, the export of obsolete ships to developing countries must be illegal, as it is an obligation of the parties to the Basel Convention to ensure 'that hazardous wastes or other wastes, to be exported, are managed in an environmentally sound manner in the State of import'.[73] Shipbreaking operations in developing countries are known to lack the proper facilities for environmentally sound management of hazardous wastes.[74]

Exporting obsolete ships from developed to developing countries for recycling is considered illegal only if the exporting country knows that the importing country will not recycle the obsolete ship in an environmentally sound manner and does not have the capacity to handle hazardous substances therein in an environmentally sound manner. Whether or not a country is able to handle particular types of hazardous wastes is not dependent on the economic condition

69 As observed by Kathrina Kummer, 'The legal value of such a decision is not clearly defined. In the strictest sense, it is not legally binding on the parties to the Convention. On the other hand, it is clearly intended to be more than a mere non-binding recommendation'. Katharina Kummer, *International Management of Hazardous Wastes: The Basel Convention and Related Legal Rules* (Oxford University Press, 1995) 64.

70 *Council Regulation 120/97 of 20 January 1997, Amending Regulation (EC) No. 259/93 on the Supervision and Control of Shipments of Waste within, into and Out of the European Community*, 1997 O.J. (L 22) 14. This regulation was replaced in 2006. *Regulation (EC) No. 1013/2006 of the European Parliament and of the Council of 14 June 2006 on Shipments of Waste, Council Regulation 1013/2006*, 2006 OJ (L 190) 1. In 2013, the European Union adopted a separate regulation for ship recycling.

71 *Vienna Convention on the Law of Treaties*, opened for signature 23 May 1969, 1155 UNTS 331 (entered into force 27 January 1980) art 18.

72 Basel Convention, art 4(9)(b).

73 Basel Convention, arts 4(8), 4(2)(d).

74 Peter Rousmaniere and Nikhil Raj, 'Shipbreaking in the Developing World: Problems and Prospects' (2007) 13 *International Journal of Occupational and Environmental Health* 359.

of that country. If necessary, any country could establish the facilities necessary to handle certain types of hazardous wastes with the help of international donor agencies or wealthy economies. For this reason alone, it is not necessary to relocate shipbreaking industries from developing countries to developed countries, as some NGOs have suggested.[75] However, under any circumstances, the current state of a shipbreaking industry that is responsible for regular casualties of its workers is unacceptable. Nevertheless, exporting obsolete ships with hazardous substances to developing shipbreaking countries is undoubtedly illegal because the shipbreaking industries in these countries do not have the capacity for environmentally sound management of hazardous substances or wastes.

3.3.3 Debate on the country of export and transboundary movement

The Basel Convention defines 'State of export' as the state 'from which a transboundary movement of waste is planned to be initiated or is initiated'.[76] According to Geir Ulfstein, in practice, this definition does not hold flag states accountable under the convention for their vessels leaving as wastes from overseas ports to another country, and the port states have no jurisdiction over such vessels.[77] However, lawyers for the Basel Action Network (BAN) have taken the opposite view. They 'disagree with [Ulfstein's] conclusion that port states have no jurisdiction over vessels destined for scrapping with regard to scrapping in other states; or that flag states are not responsible for the activities of their vessels'.[78] According to BAN, '[i]ndeed it is clear that many of the Basel obligations will apply to Parties holding jurisdiction over owners, brokers, captains, crew, etc.'.[79]

If flag states are sincere about their obligation under the Basel Convention, they may take action against the owner of the ship or people responsible for unauthorised transboundary movement. It is an international obligation of the Basel parties to prohibit unauthorised transportation or disposal of hazardous wastes.[80] Parties to the Basel Convention also have an obligation to take appropriate legal and administrative measures to prevent contravention of the convention.[81] Moreover, it is an obligation of all parties to require that hazardous wastes are accompanied by a movement document from the exporter.[82] However, the application of these requirements is not an easy task because a ship can start its journey to the

75 Greenpeace, *No More Ships for Scrap to India or Bangladesh: Green Groups Expose* (11 July 2005) <www.greenpeace.org/india/en/news/no-more-ships-for-scrap-to-ind/>.
76 Basel Convention, art 2(10).
77 Ulfstein, above n 43, 12–13.
78 *Legal Aspects of the Full and Partial Dismantling of Ships* (submitted by Basel Action Network & Greenpeace International) 1, UN Doc. UNEP/CHW/LWG/5/4/Add.1 (21 May 2002).
79 Ibid.
80 Basel Convention, art 4(7)(a).
81 Basel Convention, art 4(4).
82 Basel Convention, art 4(7)(c).

shipbreaking yard as a ship and not as waste. In that case, the issue of who should administer the procedure of movement documents and PIC is problematic.

Even EU countries, which are willing to implement the Basel Ban before it enters into force, intend to apply the Basel Convention only if their flagged ships leave for a recycling facility from their ports. According to the United Kingdom (UK) ship recycling strategy, '[w]here a *UK-flagged vessel is being exported from a UK port* for recycling, it is likely to fall within the definition of waste and thus be subject to the EC WSR [European Commission Waste Shipment Regulation]'.[83] It is clear from this statement that the UK will be treated as an exporting state under the Basel Convention or its regional implementing law, the EC WSR, only if a ship leaves for a recycling facility from a UK port. This leaves open the reasonable question of why a country should take action against its nationals if it is not regarded as the country of export under international law.

As mentioned earlier, according to Ulfstein, flag states have no accountability under the present framework of the Basel Convention for their vessels leaving as waste from overseas ports to another country.[84] The points raised by Ulfstein cannot be denied simply on the basis that states have an international obligation to take action against their citizens if they contravene the Basel Convention. If both importing and exporting countries allowed the movement, another country may not take action on the grounds that the ship owner is a citizen of that particular country. It may take action against an owner of one of its flagged ships if the movement is not allowed. If a ship owner decides to send a ship to a shipbreaking yard from the high seas, there will be no exporting country at all. Nevertheless, the flag state has a general obligation to ensure that the ship owner follows the procedure of the Basel Convention and ensures environmentally sound disposal of their ships.

3.3.4 Problems in enforcement of the Basel Convention in the shipbreaking industry

Due to some inherent problems, it is difficult to enforce the Basel Convention in the field of shipbreaking.[85] The convention was adopted to control transboundary movement of hazardous wastes without considering complicated issues, such as shipbreaking. There is little reason to be optimistic about the future success of the Basel Ban because it still has not come into effect after 22 years. Even if it comes into effect in the future, it will not be able to prevent the north – south trade of obsolete ships because ship owners have many ways to evade the convention. A huge number of ships operate under flags of convenience, which allow ship owners

83 Department for Environment, Food and Rural Affairs, *UK Ship Recycling Strategy* (February 2007) 6 <http://webarchive.nationalarchives.gov.uk/20081105144808/www.defra.gov.uk/environment/waste/strategy/pdf/shiprecycle-strategy.pdf> (emphasis added).

84 Ulfstein, above n 43, 12–13.

85 John F. Sawyer, 'Shipbreaking and the North – South Debate: Economic Development or Environmental and Labor Catastrophe?' (2002) 20 *Penn State International Law Review* 535, 562; Matt Cohen, 'U.S. Shipbreaking Exports: Balancing Safe Disposal with Economic Realities' (2005) 28 *Environs: Environmental Law and Policy Journal* 237.

from developed countries to easily hide their identities. A study has shown that almost 73% of the world's merchant fleet operates under flags of convenience or 'flagged in a country other than that of the vessels beneficial ownership'.[86] Further, to bypass the law, if a ship owner transfers ownership to someone from a developing country who then decides to send the ship for scrapping, and the ship begins its last voyage from a developing country's port, the voyage cannot be treated as transboundary movement of wastes from a developed to a developing country.

The dispute between India and Denmark regarding the Danish vessel *Riky* is a clear example of how easily the EC WSR – the implementing law of the Basel Ban in the EU – can be evaded without consequence. This dispute involved a ferry originally named *Kong Frederik IX*, and then renamed *Frederik* and finally, *Riky*.[87] The ferry was registered in St. Vincent and the Grenadines, but when sold, it was docked in Denmark.[88] The ferry contained asbestos.[89] When departing Denmark, the owner of the ship informed Danish authorities that the ship had been sold for service in the Middle East as a cargo ship, and the ship left Denmark on 16 March 2005.[90] After bypassing Danish law and leaving Danish waters, the ship sailed directly to India to be dismantled, violating relevant principles of the Basel Convention.[91] On 22 April 2005 the ship reached India.[92] Although Denmark considered itself the state of export, it could not re-import the ship, as India did not agree.[93]

A discussion on the overall implementation of the Basel Convention is not within the scope of the present book. Its implementation in the shipbreaking industry is a difficult issue, not only for developing countries but for developed countries as well. Even India, one of the world's largest shipbreaking countries, has on occasion expressed serious reservations about the applicability of the Basel Convention in the field of shipbreaking. In a communication with the Danish Minister for Environment regarding the controversy of transboundary movement of the ship *Riky*, the then-Indian Minister for Environment said that his country did not recognise the obsolete ship as waste.[94]

Although in the case of *Riky* the Indian Minister claimed that the ship could not be classified as waste, developing shipbreaking nations have not rejected

86 Patrizia Heidegger et al., *What a Difference a Flag Makes: Why Ship Owners' Responsibility to Ensure Sustainable Ship Recycling Needs to go beyond Flag State Jurisdiction* (NGO Shipbreaking Platform, 2015), 1.

87 *Recycling of Ships: Proposal for an Enforceable Legally Binding System for the Recycling of Ships*, para 3, IMO Doc. MEPC 53/3/7 (13 May 2005), (submitted by Denmark).

88 Ibid.

89 Ibid.

90 Ibid., paras 4–5.

91 Ibid., paras 6–7.

92 Ibid., para 8.

93 Ibid.

94 The minister said '[w]e have determined that the ship cannot be classified as "Wastes" within the scope of Act 2.1 [sic] of the Basel Convention'. Basel Action Network, *Legal Analysis of Letter from Mr Raja to Ms Hedegaard Regarding the Legal Application of the Basel Convention to the Kong Frederik IX (aka Riky)* (3 May 2005) <http://archive.ban.org/library/BAN_analysis_Ricky.pdf>.

outright the applicability of the Basel Convention to the shipbreaking industry.[95] Nevertheless, no developing shipbreaking country has implemented the Basel Convention in its domestic legal framework in a practical sense. In some countries, laws relating to the management of wastes reflect the Basel Convention to some extent, but most of the time governments of these countries are reluctant to apply them to the shipbreaking industry.

Against this backdrop, national courts, influenced by environmental activists, have come forward and taken a proactive role in implementing the Basel Convention in domestic arenas. In India, the Supreme Court issued a decision that detailed general requirements for ship recycling facilities.[96] These general requirements, if implemented properly, may ensure compliance in India with both the Basel Convention and the Hong Kong Convention on ship recycling.[97] However, this judgment failed to satisfy environmentalists in some aspects. In its decision, the Supreme Court rejected the petitioner's claim that all ships must be decontaminated before importation into India.[98] Here, Justice Arijit Pasayat observed, '[i]t is suggested that before leaving port in a foreign country a certificate that it is totally de-contaminated should be obtained. We find many practical difficulties in accepting this suggestion'.[99] In two cases, the Bangladesh Supreme Court provided a number of directives to the government, including an order to frame rules to prevent entry of hazardous ships into Bangladesh and for the safe and environmentally

95 When a Working Group Meeting of the Basel Convention adopted the decision OEWG-II/4, deciding that a ship can be treated as waste under the convention, the developing shipbreaking countries, including Bangladesh, China, India, Pakistan and Turkey, did not oppose the decision. Basel Convention Open-ended Working Group Report, above n 55.

96 *Research Foundation for Science v. Union of India*, Writ Petition No. 657 of 1995 (Unreported judgment delivered on 6 September 2007, India) <www.legalservicesindia.com/judgments/sep/case_6a_9_07.htm>.

97 In a statement, Dr Nikos Mikelis of the IMO observed,

> From the limited review of the initial decision of the Supreme Court of India in the case of the dismantling of the *Blue Lady*, it appeared that the new regime governing ship recycling in India is surprisingly similar to the draft text of the new convention. If the requirements imposed by the decision of the Supreme Court of India are aligned with the draft requirements of the new convention as understood and described, and if they can be further aligned if necessary to the final requirements of the adopted convention then there would be no serious impediments in the way of India ratifying the new convention nor would there appear to be any major requirements for recycling in excess of what is being already required by the decision of the Supreme Court. TNN, 'India Ahead of IMO on Ship Recycling Norms.

The Economic Times (online) 28 January 2008 <http://economictimes.indiatimes.com/rssarticleshow/msid-2736359,prtpage-1.cms>. See generally, David Dodds, 'Breaking Up Is Hard to Do: Environmental Effects of Shipwrecking and Possible Solutions under India's Environmental Regime' (2007) 20 *Pacific McGeorge Global Business and Development Law Journal* 207.

98 *Research Foundation for Science v. Union of India*, above n 96.

99 Ibid.

sound management of the shipbreaking industry.[100] However, the directions of the Supreme Court have not been followed properly by the government or industry.[101]

Nevertheless, whether these countries are able to implement the Basel Convention and the Hong Kong Convention on Ship Recycling cannot be ascertained from just a few judgments because the history of environmental activism in these countries is littered with scores of examples where the ambitious judgments of higher courts on environmental issues have not been implemented at all.[102]

The present state of shipbreaking yards in developing countries is contrary to the Basel Convention principle of environmentally sound management. More importantly, the convention provision of PIC has never been properly implemented in the shipbreaking industry by either exporting or importing countries.[103] Further, the Basel Convention obligation to minimise hazardous wastes generation has not been followed by developed countries with large shipping interests.[104]

The main downside of the situation is the serious violation of the obligation to minimise hazardous waste generation.[105] In the case of ships, this obligation can only be satisfied by building ships without using hazardous substances, or at least by keeping the amount of hazardous substances to a minimal level. In that case, the question of containing hazardous substances would not arise when these ships are sent to scrapping yards at the end of their lives.

3.3.5 Environmentally sound management and the Basel Convention guidelines

As mentioned above, the Basel Convention imposes an obligation on state parities for environmentally sound management of all types of waste. According to this convention:

> Environmentally sound management of hazardous wastes or other wastes' means taking all practicable steps to ensure that hazardous wastes or other wastes are managed in a manner which will protect human health and the environment against the adverse effects which may result from such waste.[106]

100 *Bangladesh Environmental Lawyers Association v. Bangladesh*, Writ Petition No. 3916 of 2006 (Unreported judgment delivered 6 July 2006, Bangladesh Supreme Court High Court Division); *Bangladesh Environmental Lawyers Association v. Ministry of Shipping*, Writ Petition No. 7260 of 2008 (Unreported judgment dated 17 March 2009).

101 See Chapter 5.

102 Md Saiful Karim, Okechukwu Benjamin Vincents and Mia Mahmudur Rahim 'Legal Activism for Ensuring Environmental Justice' (2012) 7 *Asian Journal of Comparative Law* 346; Jona Razzaque, 'Linking Human Rights, Development and Environment: Experiences from Litigation in South Asia' (2007) 18 *Fordham Environmental Law Review* 587, 605; Abdullah Al Faruque and Md Saiful Karim, 'Environmental Law of Bangladesh' in Nicholas A. Robinson, Elizabeth Burleson and Lin-Heng Lye (eds) *Comparative Environmental Law and Regulation* (Thomson Reuters, 2016) 7A:1.

103 Basel Convention, art 6(2).

104 Basel Convention, 4(2)(a).

105 Basel Convention, 4(2)(a).

106 Basel Convention, art 2(8).

Article 4(2) of the Basel Convention also lists a number of general obligations for ensuring environmentally sound management of hazardous wastes. In December 2002, the Basel parties adopted the Basel Guidelines.[107] The intention of these guidelines is to provide guidance to shipbreaking countries and to enable ship dismantling facilities to attain environmentally sound management.[108] The guidelines provide recommendations regarding the implementation of the recommended procedures, processes and practices, and for monitoring and verification of performance.[109] The guidelines identify that the fulfilment of the following legal, institutional and technical conditions are essential for achieving environmentally sound management:

- 'a regulatory and enforcement infrastructure ensuring compliance with applicable regulations
- authorisation of sites or facilities ensuring an adequate standard of technology and pollution control to deal with hazardous wastes
- monitoring of environmental performance at sites or facilities at which hazardous wastes are handled
- enforcement capability ensuring appropriate action taken in cases where monitoring reveals noncompliant management of hazardous wastes or resulting unacceptable emissions
- training and awareness of personnel involved in the dismantling process'.[110]

Although the guidelines are advisory in nature, they have at least the status of international soft law.[111] The Basel Guidelines could be used as a benchmark to identify whether a country is able to dispose of obsolete ships with hazardous substances in an environmentally sound manner. If properly implemented, the Basel Guidelines

107 *Technical Guidelines for the Environmentally Sound Management of the Full and Partial Dismantling of Ships*, UN Doc. UNEP/CHW/6/23 (8 August 2002) (hereinafter Basel Guidelines).

108 Ibid., 7.

109 Ibid.

110 Ibid., 84.

111 The Basel Convention under article 4(8) and article 15(4) confers power to the Conference of Parties to make guidelines for environmentally sound management of hazardous waste. Basel Convention, arts. 4(8), 15(4). According to article 4(8), '[t]echnical guidelines for the environmentally sound management of wastes subject to this Convention shall be decided by the Parties at their first meeting'. Basel Convention, art 4(8). Again, as per article 15(4), '[t]he Parties at their first meeting shall consider any additional measures needed to assist them in fulfilling their responsibilities with respect to the protection and the preservation of the marine environment in the context of this Convention'. Basel Convention, art 15(4). These articles confer power to the conference of parties to frame guidelines for environmentally sound management of hazardous wastes, and any such guideline if framed under the Basel Convention may impose a quasi-legal obligation on the parties to the convention. Although it has not been explicitly mentioned in the guidelines that the guidelines have been adopted under article 4(8), giving the name technical guidelines indicates that the conference of parties adopted these guidelines under the power vested upon it by the article 4(8) of the convention.

may ensure environmentally sound management of the shipbreaking industry; however, effective initiative has not been taken by the Bangladesh government, the United Nations Environment Programme (UNEP) or the Basel Secretariat to properly implement the guidelines in developing countries. Fifteen years after the adoption of the Basel Guidelines, their implementation is yet to be achieved in the practical sense. The scenario of the shipbreaking industry in Bangladesh is no less abhorrent than it was in 2002 when the guidelines were adopted.

To ensure environmentally sound disposal of obsolete ships, which is the ultimate goal of the global community, banning the export of obsolete ships from developed to developing countries is not a solution. It is also not wise to think that this problem can be solved primarily by introducing a new international legal instrument for 'green' shipbuilding. Even under the existing international legal framework, green shipbuilding is required. The Basel Convention provision relating to the minimisation of hazardous wastes obviously imposes an obligation for green shipbuilding.[112] The new instrument should, in clear language, ban the use of hazardous substances such as asbestos, PCBs, TBT and polycyclic aromatic hydrocarbons (PAHs) in ship manufacturing and encourage research to find suitable alternatives to these substances. This is the aim of the Hong Kong Convention, which is discussed in the next chapter. Nonetheless, problems will remain as any new legal instrument for green shipbuilding may not be able to adequately deal with existing ships. Creating environmentally sound ship disposal facilities is arguably a solution to this problem. The global community should make a concerted effort to help governments and shipbreaking yard owners in developing countries to improve existing shipbreaking facilities and ensure the environmentally sound disposal of obsolete ships.

3.4 The Stockholm Convention

POPs are a type of hazardous substance that persist in the atmosphere; they are scattered in nature and bio-accumulate in humans as well as wildlife.[113] To protect human health and the environment from POPs, the Stockholm Convention

112 According to Greenpeace International and the International Confederation of Free Trade Unions (ICFTU), 'the Basel Convention is not best placed to address the "up-stream" design of ships, nor the owners' relevant responsibilities prior to a ship's designation as a waste. Lastly, the issue of international standards in the ship-breaking industry for workers and the environment needs to be addressed jointly by the IMO, the International Labour Organization (ILO), the Basel Convention, UNEP and other relevant bodies'. *Work Programme of the Committee and Subsidiary Bodies: Scrapping of Ships (Submitted by Greenpeace International and the ICFTU)*, IMO Doc. MEPC 43/18/6 (2 April 1999).

113 'Specific effects of POPs can include cancer, allergies and hypersensitivity, damage to the central and peripheral nervous systems, reproductive disorders, and disruption of the immune system. Some POPs are also considered to be endocrine disrupters, which, by altering the hormonal system, can damage the reproductive and immune systems of exposed individuals as well as their offspring; they can also have developmental and carcinogenic effects'. Secretariat of the Stockholm Convention, *What Are POPs?* (2008) <http://chm.pops.int/TheConvention/ThePOPs/tabid/673/Default.aspx>.

was adopted in 2001.[114] This convention lists PCBs as a POP.[115] PCBs are used in many ships, particularly war ships.[116] The Stockholm Convention limits the scope of export of POPs, including PCBs without the PIC of the importing country.[117] Moreover, a party can export POPs only for the purpose of environmentally sound disposal.[118] Accordingly, before exporting a ship containing PCBs, exporting countries must consider the Stockholm Convention. However, like other international legal instruments, practical application of this convention in the shipbreaking industry is not evident.

3.5 The Rotterdam Convention

The Rotterdam Convention was adopted in 1998.[119] This convention lists a number of chemicals for which receiving informed consent from the importing country prior to export is compulsory.[120] Annex III of the convention lists certain chemicals, such as polybrominated biphenyls (PBBs), PCBs and polychlorinated terphenyls[121] that may be found in the structure of many ships. This convention applies to '[b]anned or severely restricted chemicals' and '[s]everely hazardous pesticide formulations', but it does not apply to wastes.[122] However, this omission does not necessarily impose any restriction on the application of the convention in the shipbreaking industry. A Working Group Meeting of the

114 Paul E. Hagen and Michael P. Walls, 'The Stockholm Convention on Persistent Organic Pollutants' (2005) 19 *Natural Resources and Environment* 49; Joel A. Mintz, 'Two Cheers for Global POPs: A Summary and Assessment of the Stockholm Convention on Persistent Organic Pollutants' (2002) 14 *Georgetown International Environmental Law Review* 319; Peter L. Lallas, 'The Stockholm Convention on Persistent Organic Pollutants' (2001) 95 *American Journal of International Law* 692; Hayley Hung, Athanasios A. Katsoyiannis and Ramon Guardans, 'Ten Years of Global Monitoring under the Stockholm Convention on Persistent Organic Pollutants (POPs): Trends, Sources and Transport Modelling' (2016) 217 *Environmental Pollution* 1.

115 Stockholm Convention, Annex A.

116 Basel Action Network (BAN), *The French Deception: PCBs and the Clemenceau* (1 February 2006) 4 <http://archive.ban.org/library/the_french_deception.pdf>.

117 Stockholm Convention, art 3(2).

118 Stockholm Convention, art 3(2).

119 See generally, Paula Barrios, 'The Rotterdam Convention on Hazardous Chemicals: A Meaningful Step toward Environmental Protection?' (2004) 16 *Georgetown International Environmental Law Review* 679; Nancy S. Zahedi, 'Implementing the Rotterdam Convention: The Challenges of Transforming Aspirational Goals into Effective Controls on Hazardous Pesticide Exports to Developing Countries' (1999) 11 *Georgetown International Environmental Law Review* 707; Ted L. McDorman, 'The Rotterdam Convention on the Prior Informed Consent Procedure for Certain Hazardous Chemicals and Pesticides in International Trade: Some Legal Notes' (2004) 13 *Review of European Community and International Environmental Law* 187; Katharina Kummer, 'Prior Informed Consent for Chemicals In International Trade: The 1998 Rotterdam Convention' (1999) 8 *Review of European Community and International Environmental Law* 323.

120 Rotterdam Convention, art 12, annex III.

121 Rotterdam Convention, annex III.

122 Rotterdam Convention, art 3.

Basel Convention observed that 'a ship may become waste, in accordance with Article 2 of the Basel Convention, and that at the same time it may be defined as a ship under other international rules'.[123] If a ship contains any of the hazardous chemicals listed in the Rotterdam Convention, 'prior informed consent' from the country of import will be necessary. Nevertheless, any practical application of this convention in the shipbreaking industry is unknown.

3.6 Conclusion

Although the above-mentioned conventions are relevant to the shipbreaking industry, this industry was not in the minds of the drafters of these conventions. Therefore, despite their general applicability, practical use of these conventions in the shipbreaking industry is limited.

The main issue related to the conventions discussed here is their failure to acknowledge environmental justice aspects. These highly technical international legal instruments fail to make any meaningful change in developing countries. In many instances, due to increasing pressure from the developed world, the gross environmental injustice inflicted on a marginalised segment of society in the global south has not been considered at all. For example, movement of hazardous wastes to the global south is a serious cause of injustice, but the Basel Convention does not use the terms justice, equity or fairness.[124] Rather than ensuring internalisation of cost of waste management by the generator of wastes, the conventions deal with anecdotal technical issues. They also fail to implement, in any practical sense or meaningful way, the polluter pays principle and the principle of prevention. These conventions also fail to provide remedies for the disproportionate burden the global south bears in the management of hazardous wastes and are silent with respect to the rampant violation of the fundamental human rights of the most marginalised segment of the global south, in order to uphold developed countries' business interests. Failure of the international legal system in ensuring environmental justice in shipbreaking and other ultra-hazardous industries is almost inevitable because the very structure of these legal instruments is fundamentally flawed, being developed through an institutional system in which the developed world sets the ground rules in their own terms.

Although most international marine environmental conventions acknowledge the need for technical assistance in developing countries, provisions related to technical assistance are largely ineffective or are not operationalised in a meaningful sense.[125] Due to the growing awareness for environmental protection, the developed world has adopted these technical legal instruments, but their policy of using the global south as a repository for their hazardous wastes remains active. Despite obligations under various conventions, practical initiatives for environmentally sound management of the shipbreaking industry are seriously lacking.

123 Basel Convention Open-Ended Working Group Report, above n 55.

124 Chukwumerije Okereke, *Global Justice and Neoliberal Environmental Governance: Ethics, Sustainable Development and International Co-Operation* (Routledge, 2008) 82.

125 Karim (2009), above n 5; Karim (2010), above n 5; Karim, above n 9.

4 Development of an international legal framework for ship recycling

Whither environmental justice

4.1 Introduction

The shipbreaking industry is partially regulated by international law relating to transboundary movement of hazardous wastes and their environmentally sound disposal. The international legal obligation for green shipbuilding, if it exists, is also important for environmentally sound disposal of end-of-life ships.

This chapter is dedicated to international regulatory development for safe and environmentally sound disposal of obsolete ships. It introduces the salient features of the Hong Kong Convention[1] and discusses the critical legal debates presently surrounding this convention. Given its paramount importance, the Hong Kong Convention deserves an elaborate and critical discussion in this book. This chapter also concisely analyses the 2013 EU SRR.[2] It particularly examines whether these new legal instruments will be able to play a meaningful role in ensuring environmental justice in the shipbreaking yards of developing countries.

4.2 International Maritime Organization initiatives for regulation of shipbreaking

The first known discussion on shipbreaking in the IMO Marine Environment Protection Committee (MEPC) occurred – albeit incidentally – in 1992 when the MEPC adopted Resolution MEPC.53(32): Development of the Capacity of Ship Scrapping for the Smooth Implementation of the Amendments to Annex I of MARPOL 73/78. An amendment to Annex I of the MARPOL Convention requires the use of a double hull in certain types of new and existing oil tankers, ultimately resulting in the gradual phasing out of existing single-hull tankers. This requirement was later amended in the wake of each of two incidents involving the ships the *Erika* and *Prestige*, to accelerate the phasing out of single-hull tankers.

1 *Hong Kong International Convention for the Safe and Environmentally Sound Recycling of Ships*, opened for signature 1 September 2009, IMO Doc. SR/CONF/45 (19 May 2009) (not yet in force) (hereinafter Hong Kong Convention).

2 *Regulation (EU) No. 1257/2013 of the European Parliament and of the Council of 20 November 2013 on Ship Recycling and Amending Regulation (EC) No. 1013/2006 and Directive 2009/16/EC*, 2013, OJ (L 330) 1 (hereinafter EU SRR).

This action created an unprecedented supply of decommissioned oil tankers with ultra-hazardous materials in developing country shipbreaking yards, particularly those in Bangladesh.[3] According to *Resolution MEPC.53(32)* of 1992 the demand for scrapping facilities may increase due to this amendment. Through this resolution, the MEPC urged IMO member states to undertake research and development to increase ship scrapping capacity. It also clearly urged developed countries to provide technical assistance and technology transfer to developing countries for the development of ship scrapping facilities.[4] However, no practical initiatives have been taken to implement the technical assistance and technology transfer-related provisions of this resolution.

The IMO began considering the issue of shipbreaking in 1998 when a delegation from Norway drew the attention of the MEPC at its 42nd meeting to problems associated with the 'dismantling of ships'. Norway proposed to include this issue in the MEPC's work programme. The committee asked Norway to submit a proposal to the 43rd meeting of the MEPC to include this issue in its work programme.[5] Following the MEPC's request at its 42nd meeting, Norway submitted a formal proposal to include the issue of 'scrapping of ships' on the MEPC agenda for its 43rd meeting held from 28 June to 2 July 1999, highlighting the safety and environmental problems associated with dismantling of ships.[6]

The Norwegian proposal to include this issue in the MEPC work programme was hotly debated at MEPC 43, particularly considering the scope of the IMO in relation to this issue. A number of delegations supported the inclusion of this matter in the MEPC work programme on the basis that 'the matter is within IMO's scope since the matter is related to ships and scrapping of ships presents an issue of concern with regard to the pollution of the environment by ships and, therefore, IMO should consider to develop necessary measures'.[7] However,

3 Hasan Muhammad Abdullah et al., 'Monitoring the Drastic Growth of Ship Breaking Yards in Sitakunda: A Threat to the Coastal Environment of Bangladesh' (2013) 185 *Environmental Monitoring and Assessment* 3839, 3843–3844; Greenpeace, *Oil Tanker Phase Out Threatens Asian Workers and Environment* (4 April 2005) <www.greenpeace.org/international/en/press/releases/shipbreak/>.

4 *Development of the Capacity of Ship Scrapping for the Smooth Implementation of the Amendments to Annex I of MARPOL 73/78, Resolution MEPC. (53) 32*, adopted on 6 March 1992, IMO Doc. MEPC 32/20 (6 March 1992), Annex 7.

5 *Report of the Marine Environment Protection Committee on Its Forty-Second Session*, IMO Doc. MEPC 42/22 (16 November 1998) 58.

6 *Work Programme of the Committee and Subsidiary Bodies: Scrapping of Ships (Submitted by Norway)*, IMO Doc. MEPC 43/18/1 (12 February 1999). Also see: *Work Programme of the Committee and Subsidiary Bodies: Scrapping of Ships (Submitted by Greenpeace International and the ICFTU)*, IMO Doc. MEPC 43/18/6 (2 April 1999); *Work Programme of the Committee and Subsidiary Bodies: Scrapping of Ships (Submitted by Denmark)*, IMO Doc. MEPC 43/18/9 (14 May 1999); *Work Programme of the Committee and Subsidiary Bodies: Scrapping of Ships (Note by the International Chamber of Shipping (ICS))*, IMO Doc. MEPC 43/18/10 (14 May 1999).

7 *Report of the Marine Environment Protection Committee on Its Forty-Third Session*, IMO Doc. MEPC 43/21 (6 July 1999), 56.

some delegates opposed inclusion of this matter on the work programme of the MEPC, expressing the view that 'when a ship is taken out of service and removed from the register, it is no longer a "ship". Besides, ship scrapping is basically an industry on shore with the main concern being shipbreaking workers' health and safety, which, in their view, are outside the purview of IMO'.[8] *Resolution MEPC.53(32)* on the development of the capacity of ship scrapping was also brought to the attention of the committee.[9] Ultimately, the majority of delegates supported the inclusion of a new agenda item for the MEPC work programme, calling it 'ship recycling'; thus, the committee decided to include this new agenda item in MEPC 44.[10] Accordingly, ship recycling was included in the agenda of MEPC 44 held in March 2000.

At MEPC 44, Norway submitted a proposal for a future work plan for the IMO regarding ship recycling, and proposed a cradle-to-grave perspective recognising that the shipping industry has responsibility for environmentally friendly waste management. Norway also proposed that a binding international regime should be developed to ensure universally acceptable environmental and safety standards of ship recycling activities.[11] It proposed a stepwise approach and proposed to develop guidelines or a code of practice as an intermediate step.[12] The Norwegian proposal stated that the future international regime should address the measures to be taken before a ship enters a scrap yard, including a ship inventory dossier documenting the environmental status of the ship; waste removal guidelines; development of an international framework for standards, reporting, control and certification of recycling sites; definition of decommissioning procedures for obsolete ships; and specification of the roles of the flag state, the port (receiving) state and the IMO in the ship's decommissioning.[13] The Netherlands, although not advocating for adoption of a legal instrument, supported the idea of international guidelines under the auspices of the IMO and proposed the establishment of a ship recycling fund.[14]

IMO competence with respect to shipbreaking was again questioned by some parties at the meeting. Brazil made a submission that the competent forum for this matter should be the same as that for the Basel Convention and that IMO activities should be limited in so far as they relate to the London Dumping Convention.[15] However, Norway was of the opinion that the IMO should lead the

8 Ibid.
9 Ibid.
10 Ibid., 57.
11 *Recycling of Ships Proposal for an IMO Work Plan (Submitted by Norway)*, IMO Doc. MEPC 44/16/2 (24 December 1999) (hereinafter Submission of Norway in MEPC 44).
12 Ibid.
13 Ibid.
14 *Report of the Marine Environment Protection Committee on Its Forty-Fourth Session*, IMO Doc. MEPC 44/20 (12 April 2000) 59 (hereinafter MEPC 44 Report); *Recycling of Ships: Additional Information Related to Ship Scrapping (Submitted by the Netherlands)*, IMO Doc. MEPC 44/16/1 (23 December 1999).
15 *Recycling of Ships (Submitted by Brazil)*, IMO Doc. MEPC 44/16/3 (24 December 1999).

activities regarding ship recalling because ship recycling is well within the purposes of the organisation listed in Article 1 of the Convention on the International Maritime Organization.[16] Norway also suggested that recycling of ships falls into the ship – shore interface and that shore-based requirements and the ship – shore interface are not new for the IMO: for example, the MARPOL Convention has shore-based requirements.[17] At the meeting, representatives from India and Bangladesh attempted to demonstrate that the industry is safer than generally reported.[18] This illustrates how the opinion of these countries' governments is aligned with the view of shipbreaking companies that shamelessly deny the appalling working conditions in the shipbreaking yards. Finally, the committee agreed to consider the matter further and decided to establish a correspondence group with a mandate to submit a report to MEPC 46.

Accordingly, the correspondence group submitted its report to MEPC 46 outlining current practices in the shipbreaking industry; safety and environmental risks associated with current practices; existing government and industry procedures; activities of other international forums, particularly the ILO and the Basel Convention; and views about the IMO's future role in reducing environmental and safety risks.[19] The scope of future IMO work again was hotly debated at the meeting. Several parties supported the Indian view that shipbreaking is a land-based industry and that the 'IMO should limit its action to providing internationally binding guidelines for preparing a vessel before it goes for recycling and IMO's role should end once the ship is de-registered on reaching the breaker's yard'.[20] The issues around interagency conflict and cooperation between the ILO, IMO and Basel Convention were discussed again.[21] Against this backdrop, the MEPC reconstituted the correspondence group and asked it to submit a report to MEPC 47 that had the following aims:

1 to identify all stakeholders and their perceived roles during the life-cycle of a ship
2 to identify and elaborate on the perceived role of IMO in ship recycling
3 to identify the existing international, national and additional industry and/or other relevant standards/guidelines, possibly applicable to ship recycling within the perceived role of IMO as indicated in paragraph 2
4 to recommend possible courses of action for further consideration by the Committee, and to identify the pros and cons associated with each option.[22]

16 *Convention on the International Maritime Organization*, opened for signature 6 March 1948, 289 UNTS 48 (entered into force 17 March 1958), art 1 (hereinafter the IMO Convention).
17 Submission of Norway in MEPC 44, above n 11.
18 MEPC 44 Report, above n 14.
19 *Report of the Correspondence Group (Submitted by the Coordinator of the Correspondence Group)*, IMO Doc. MEPC 46/7 (18 January 2001).
20 *Report of the Marine Environment Protection Committee on Its Forty-Sixth Session*, IMO Doc. MEPC 46/23 (16 May 2001) 46; *Recycling of Ships (Submitted by India)*, IMO Doc. MEPC 46/7/1 (14 February 2001).
21 Ibid.
22 Ibid., annex 12.

MEPC 47 considered the report of the correspondence group[23] and again debated the precise nature of a future IMO instrument, the role of the IMO and inter-agency cooperation with other UN processes.[24] The MEPC report stated the following about the overlaps, gaps and conflicts between international conventions:

> The complexity of the issues relating to the recycling of ships goes beyond the individual scope of multilateral agreements such as the London Convention, UNCLOS, IMO instruments, ILO and the Basel Convention. Each multilateral agreement needs to clarify its requirements. It is imperative that the co-operative efforts of the secretariats and the Parties to these instruments, and other stakeholders, continue in such a manner as to reduce environmental and safety risks and health and welfare concerns for the environment . . . Each convention needs to assess its requirements and develop, in co-operation with others, mechanisms for addressing its responsibilities.[25]

A number of delegates proposed a legally binding instrument under the auspices of the IMO. However, parties had divergent opinions about the scope of the instrument. For example, India was of the opinion that the IMO should add a new and separate annex to the MARPOL Convention on ship recycling, including a system for recording hazardous materials and potentially including guidelines for recycling.[26] Greenpeace International proposed a comprehensive legal instrument covering all aspects of ship recycling complementing 'existing relevant international, regional, national and local legal instruments'.[27] At this meeting, the Industry Working Party on Ship Recycling submitted an Industry Code of Practice on Ship Recycling for IMO recognition and further development.[28]

23 *Report of the Correspondence Group (Submitted by the Coordinator of the Correspondence Group)*, IMO Doc. MEPC 47/3/3 (30 November 2001).

24 *Report of the Marine Environment Protection Committee on Its Forty-Seventh Session*, IMO Doc. MEPC 47/20 (18 March 2002) 16–21 (hereinafter MEPC Report 47).

25 Ibid., 20.

26 *Proposal for Consideration of the Committee for Developing a New Annex under MARPOL 73/78 for Ship Recycling (Submitted by India)*, IMO Doc. MEPC 47/3/4 (7 January 2002).

27 In this meeting, Greenpeace International stated that

> IMO should develop an internationally legally-binding instrument addressing the recycling of ships. This instrument should be designed so as to complement existing relevant international, regional, national and local legal instruments in order to ensure that a truly comprehensive and enforceable international regime governing the recycling of ships may be realised. Specifically, Greenpeace considers that IMO should establish formal requirements for the presentation of ships for recycling. In this respect, it is our view that the legal responsibility for compliance with the requirements should rest with the shipowners.
>
> Comments on the Report of the Correspondence Group (Submitted by Greenpeace International), IMO Doc. MEPC 47/3/5 (11 January 2002)

28 *Recycling of Ships (Submitted by the International Chamber of Shipping (ICS) on behalf of the Industry Working Party on Ship Recycling)*, IMO Doc. MEPC 47/3/2 (30 November 2001). The following organisations were involved with this Code of Practice: Baltic and International Maritime Council (BIMCO); International Association of Dry Cargo

MEPC 47 decided to develop a guidelines for ship recycling and reconstituted the correspondence group to prepare a draft[29] and that was submitted at MEPC 48.[30] The MEPC considered the draft and reconstituted the correspondence group for further development of the guidelines.[31] MEPC 49, held in 2003, considered the revised draft of the guidelines prepared by the correspondence group[32] and approved it for consideration by the IMO Assembly.[33]

The IMO Assembly in 2003 adopted the IMO Guidelines on Ship Recycling (hereinafter IMO Guidelines).[34] These guidelines have a quasi-legal status because they were adopted by an IMO Assembly resolution.[35] Moreover, they may be treated as generally accepted international rules and standards by a competent international organisation.[36] There is at least a moral obligation for all parties at the Convention on the International Maritime Organization to follow these guidelines. If we read the IMO Guidelines together with the Basel Convention, the failure of any country to comply with the guidelines may constitute strong evidence of that country's inability to conduct environmentally sound disposal of hazardous substances.

The guidelines seek to encourage recycling as the best means for disposal of ships. They provided guidance on how to prepare ships for recycling and to minimise both the use of potentially hazardous materials and the generation of wastes during a ship's operating life.[37] The IMO Guidelines introduce a new system called the Green Passport, which is an inventory of potentially hazardous

Shipowners (INTERCARGO); International Association of Independent Tanker Owners (INTERTANKO); International Chamber of Shipping (ICS); International Tanker Owners Pollution Federation; International Transport Workers Federation; Oil Companies' International Marine Forum (OCIMF); European Community Shipowners' Associations (ECSA); and International Association of Classification Societies.

29 MEPC Report 47, above n 24, annex 9.

30 *Recycling of Ships: Report of the Correspondence Group (Submitted by the Coordinator of the Correspondence Group)*, IMO Doc. MEPC 48/3 (3 July 2002).

31 *Report of the Marine Environment Protection Committee on Its Forty-Eighth Session*, IMO Doc. MEPC 48/21 (24 October 2002) 22.

32 *Recycling of Ships: Report of the Correspondence Group (Submitted by the Coordinator of the Correspondence Group)*, IMO Doc. MEPC 49/3/1 (28 March 2003).

33 *Report of the Marine Environment Protection Committee on Its Forty-Ninth Session*, IMO Doc. MEPC 49/22 (8 August 2003) 31.

34 *IMO Guidelines on Ship Recycling*, IMO Doc. A23/Res.962 (4 March 2004) (hereinafter IMO Guidelines).

35 Patricia Birnie, 'The Status of Environmental "Soft Law": Trends and Examples with Special Focus on IMO Norms' in Henrik Ringbom (ed) *Competing Norms in the Law of Marine Environmental Protection* (Kluwer Law International, 1997) 31, 47–48.

36 See generally, Bernard H. Oxman, 'The Duty to Respect Generally Accepted International Standards' (1991) 24 *New York University Journal of International Law and Politics* 110; Louis B. Sohn, 'Generally Accepted International Rules' (1986) 61 *Washington Law Review* 1073; *Implications of the United Nations Convention on the Law of the Sea for the International Maritime Organization*, IMO Doc. LEG/MISC.7 (19 January 2012).

37 IMO Guidelines, above n 34, at para 1.6.2.

substances on the ship that will accompany the ship throughout its lifespan.[38] Successive owners of the ship must maintain the accuracy of the Green Passport by incorporating information regarding all relevant changes.[39] The final owner of the ship must deliver these documents to the recycling facility.[40] Obviously, there are some benefits to having accurate information about a ship's hazardous materials. However, giving this document the title 'Green Passport' may be viewed as little more than a mockery of the concept; it may be a passport, but it is certainly not green. The Green Passport is effectively an inventory of hazardous materials and does not necessarily impose any obligation to decontaminate a ship before sending it to a developing world recycling facility.

Environmentalists have voiced serious reservations about the effectiveness of the IMO Guidelines. Greenpeace indicated that the IMO Guidelines will not be able to change the current state of the ship recycling facilities.[41] This prediction has been borne out, as the guidelines have failed to bring any considerable change to developing countries' shipbreaking industries. The main loophole in the IMO Guidelines is that they shift the primary responsibility of environmentally sound disposal of obsolete ships to developing countries hosting the shipbreaking industry. It was stated in the guidelines that:

> In general, these Guidelines accept that the obligation for environmental and worker protection in ship recycling facilities must rest with the recycling facility itself and with the regulatory authorities of the country in which the recycling facility operates. Nevertheless, it is acknowledged that shipowners and other stakeholders have a responsibility to address the issues involved.[42]

Making an unnecessary reference that developing countries have the primary responsibility clearly indicates the ill-intention to externalise the developed

38 Ibid., at para 5.1.
39 Ibid.
40 Ibid.
41 'Greenpeace and BAN believe that the IMO Guidelines, while containing some excellent provisions, pose an effort to deflect responsibility away from the shipping industry (the polluter in this case) to its victims (developing countries and communities). The Basel Convention on the other hand, is a legally binding instrument that has sought to do precisely the opposite, namely to hold waste generators accountable through State action to prevent the exploitation of developing countries. It is time for the IMO to recognize the established principles of international law with respect to environmental justice and producer responsibilities. Only through such acknowledgement can the gap of inconsistency between the existing IMO Guidelines and the Basel Convention and its Guidelines be closed and we can achieve a coherent set of international instruments to solve the shipbreaking crisis'. *Analysis of Inconsistencies between the IMO Guidelines on Ship Recycling and the Basel Convention (Submitted by Greenpeace International)*, IMO Doc. MEPC 51/INF.11 (6 February 2004) (hereinafter Greenpeace International).
42 IMO Guidelines, above n 34.

world's shipping companies' environmental responsibilities. Deliberately omitting reference to the global environmental injustice and responsibilities of developed country shipping companies and the state of the beneficial owners of those companies – thereby placing the main responsibility on the shoulders of the victims of pollution – will clearly promote environmental injustice. This approach is in clear violation of the polluter pays principle.

The IMO Guidelines also refrain from classifying obsolete vessels as waste, taking the totally opposite position from the Basel Convention. The guidelines define hazardous materials as those 'posing harm to human health or the environment identified in the IMDG (International Maritime Dangerous Goods) Code, the Basel Convention, or other international authorities or instruments'.[43] Interestingly, the Basel Convention does not define hazardous materials; rather, it defines hazardous wastes and other wastes.[44] This hypocritical approach clearly makes the very foundation of the IMO Guidelines questionable. Moreover, the guidelines totally fail to address the issue of environmental justice, particularly the global environmental injustice aspect of the shipbreaking industry. Unsurprisingly, the guidelines fail to play any role in ensuring environmental sustainability and worker safety in this ultra-hazardous industry.

Against this backdrop, the Hong Kong Convention has been adopted under the auspices of the IMO. The following section analyses the provisions of this convention.

4.3 The Hong Kong Convention

An Intersessional working group meeting of the MEPC held 13–15 July 2005 agreed that the IMO should develop a legally binding instrument addressing the following:

- 'the design, construction, operation and preparation of ships so as to facilitate safe and environmentally sound recycling, without compromising the safety and operational efficiency of ships;
- the operation of recycling facilities in a safe and environmentally sound manner; and
- the establishment of an appropriate enforcement mechanism for ship recycling (certification/reporting requirements)'.[45]

MEPC 53, held in July 2005, considered this recommendation. The parties debated whether the IMO should regulate this land-based industry and whether the Basel Convention should be the appropriate forum for this.[46] Nevertheless,

43 Ibid.

44 Greenpeace International, above n 41.

45 *Report of the Marine Environment Protection Committee on Its Fifty-Third Session*, IMO Doc. MEPC 53/24 (25 July 2005) 18.

46 Ibid., 18–21.

MEPC 53 decided to endorse the working group's recommendation for a legally binding instrument under the auspices of the IMO.[47] Subsequently, the IMO Assembly requested the MEPC to develop a new legally binding instrument on ship recycling.[48] At MEPC 54, held in December 2005, Norway submitted a draft for an international convention for the safe and environmentally sound recycling of ships.[49] After almost four years of negotiation and discussion in MEPC meetings as well as in a number of intersessional and correspondence group meetings, the Hong Kong Convention was adopted on 15 May 2009 at a Diplomatic Conference held in Hong Kong.

4.3.1 The main features of the convention

The Hong Kong Convention includes a general obligation on each party to undertake to give full and complete effect to the provisions of the convention 'in order to prevent, reduce, minimize and, to the extent practicable, eliminate accidents, injuries and other adverse effects on human health and the environment caused by Ship Recycling, and enhance ship safety, protection of human health and the environment throughout a ship's operating life'.[50] Although the convention obliges parties to implement its provisions, it specifically mentions that parties are free to take more stringent measures for ensuring safe and environmentally sound ship recycling. However, during the negotiation process this issue was hotly debated. IMO's Legal Office provided the opinion that the provision 'is unclear and may raise concerns in suggesting that a coastal State could consider imposing more stringent requirements on foreign flagships. Since a State can always impose more stringent requirements on ships entitled to fly its own flag and on recycling facilities located in its territory it was suggested to delete this paragraph'.[51] However, after extensive debate the parties decided to include this provision.[52] This particular provision may provide the coastal state power to impose more stringent requirements for foreign ship. However, a coastal state's jurisdiction over this matter is quite limited. Under Article 21 of UNCLOS, a coastal state has the right to adopt laws and regulations relating to innocent passage in the territorial sea with respect to safety of navigation, protection of marine

47 Ibid.

48 *New Legally Binding Instrument on Ship Recycling*, IMO Doc. A24/Res.981 (6 February 2006) [hereinafter IMO Resolution].

49 *Proposal for a New Legally-Binding Instrument on Recycling of Ships (Submitted by Norway)*, IMO Doc. MEPC 54/3 (5 December 2005) (hereinafter Draft Convention Submitted by Norway).

50 Hong Kong Convention, art 1(1).

51 *Report of the Second Intersessional Meeting of the Working Group on Ship Recycling*, IMO Doc. MEPC 56/3 (11 May 2007) 4 (hereinafter Second Intersessional Meeting Report).

52 *Report of the Third Intersessional Meeting of the Working Group on Ship Recycling*, IMO Doc. MEPC 57/3 (25 January 2008) 3 (hereinafter Third Intersessional Meeting Report).

environment and prevention pollution.[53] However, the coastal state's 'laws and regulations shall not apply to the design, construction, manning or equipment of foreign ships unless they are giving effect to generally accepted international rules or standards'.[54] IMO conventions are regarded as generally accepted international rules.[55] Therefore, it can be assumed that a coastal state's ability to impose anything more restrictive then the Hong Kong Convention provision is very limited unless this is allowed by another convention, such as the Basel Convention. A coastal state's jurisdiction in the Exclusive Economic Zone is also restricted.[56] Therefore, the possibility of a coastal state's abuse of this provision is very limited. However, a port state may impose stringent requirements on vessels voluntarily visiting its ports.[57] A related issue is the application of this convention to non-party ships. According to Article 3(4) of the Hong Kong Convention, parties are required to apply the requirement of this convention to ensure that non-party ships do not receive favourable treatment.[58] Moreover, Article 6 of the convention obliges parties to ensure the application of regulations introduced by this convention while recycling ships entitled to fly the flag of non-parties.[59]

In its preamble, the Hong Kong Convention recognises the parallel role of the Basel Convention 'in protecting human health and the environment against the adverse effects which may result from' hazardous wastes, and the role of the ILO 'in protecting the occupational safety and health of workers involved in ship recycling'.[60] The convention takes a cradle-to-grave approach and is applicable to ships flying the flag or operating under the authority of a party to this convention.[61] It is also applicable to ship recycling facilities operating under the jurisdiction of a party to the convention.[62] Although the convention recognises the role of the Basel Convention with respect to hazardous wastes, it refrains from defining the term hazardous wastes; it defines only hazardous materials in

53 *United Nations Convention on the Law of the Sea*, opened for signature 10 December 1982, 1833 UNTS 3 (entered into force 16 November 1994), (hereinafter UNCLOS), art 21(1).
54 UNCLOS, art 21(2).
55 Md Saiful Karim, *Prevention of Pollution of the Marine Environment from Vessels: The Potential and Limits of the International Maritime Organisation* (Springer, 2015) 31–36; Bernard H. Oxman, 'The Duty to Respect Generally Accepted International Standards' (1991) 24 *New York University Journal of International Law and Politics* 109; Louis B. Sohn, '"Generally Accepted" International Rules' (1986) 61 *Washington Law Review* 1073.
56 Karim, ibid.; Erik Jaap Molenaar, *Coastal State Jurisdiction over Vessel-Source Pollution* (Kluwer Law International, 1998).
57 Karim, ibid.; Richard A. Legatski, 'Port State Jurisdiction over Vessel-Source Marine Pollution' (1977) 2 *Harvard Environmental Law Review* 448; Tatjana Keselj, 'Port State Jurisdiction in Respect of Pollution from Ships: The 1982 United Nations Convention on the Law of the Sea and the Memoranda of Understanding' (1999) 30 *Ocean Development and International Law* 127.
58 Hong Kong Convention, art 3(4).
59 Hong Kong Convention, art 6.
60 Hong Kong Convention, preamble.
61 Hong Kong Convention, art 3(1)(1).
62 Hong Kong Convention, art 3(1)(2).

its definition article. As mentioned in the previous chapter, there was resistance from the IMO to consider an obsolete ship as waste at any stage. However, as discussed, ships can and should be treated as waste when they are 'disposed of or are intended to be disposed', and if a ship contains hazardous substances it should be treated as hazardous waste. Nevertheless, the Hong Kong Convention avoids defining obsolete ships as waste and deals with this issue in an alternative way – it uses a different term, 'hazardous material', which it defines as 'any material or substance which is liable to create hazards to human health and/or the environment'.[63]

The Hong Kong Convention obliges each party to require vessels operating with its flag and ship recycling facilities under its jurisdiction to comply with the provision of this convention.[64] Like many other IMO conventions, the Hong Kong Convention includes articles listing the basic principles followed by an annex consisting of technical regulations. The convention includes 21 articles, 25 regulations in the annex and seven appendices. The convention is supported by a number of guidelines. The provisions of this convention may be broadly divided into two main sections: requirements for ships and requirements for ship recycling facilities. Some provisions may have effects for both ships and ship recycling facilities. The two main aims of the convention are limiting the use of hazardous materials in ships and promoting environmentally sound management of ship recycling facilities. As elaborated in the following sections, the convention's effectiveness for ensuring environmentally sound disposal of existing ships is very limited.

4.3.1.1 Design, construction, operation and maintenance of ships

The Hong Kong Convention introduces some restrictions on the installation or use of hazardous materials in ships. Appendix 1 of the convention lists a number of substances as hazardous materials, including asbestos, ozone-depleting substances, PCBs and prohibited anti-fouling compounds under the AFS Convention.[65] The Hong Kong Convention imposes an obligation on the parties to prohibit and/or restrict the installation or use of these materials on their ships.[66] The parties are also obliged to 'prohibit and/or restrict the installation or use of such materials on ships, whilst in its ports, shipyards, ship repair yards, or offshore terminals'.[67] The convention also introduces procedures to amend the list of hazardous materials included in Appendix 1. Therefore, there is scope for adding new materials to the list if needed.

The Hong Kong Convention also requires new ships to have on board an inventory of hazardous materials identifying any hazardous materials listed in Appendices 1

63 Hong Kong Convention, art 2(9).
64 Hong Kong Convention, art 4.
65 Hong Kong Convention, appendix 1.
66 Hong Kong Convention, reg 4(1).
67 Hong Kong Convention, reg 4(2).

and 2 of the convention that are contained in the ship's structure or equipment, along with their location and approximate quantities. Existing ships are also required to comply with this provision. Appendix 2 of the convention introduces a minimum list of items to be included in the inventory of hazardous materials. In 2011, the IMO's MEPC adopted Guidelines for the Development of the Inventory of Hazardous Materials.[68] In 2015, this was replaced by revised guidelines.[69]

4.3.1.2 Controls, authorisation and environmentally sound management of ship recycling facilities

The Hong Kong Convention obliges each party to establish the necessary regulatory framework for authorisation of ship recycling facilities with appropriate conditions to comply with the Hong Kong Convention and for safe and environmentally sound design, construction and operation of ship recycling facilities within its jurisdiction.[70] It also obliges parties to establish proper mechanisms for inspection, monitoring, enforcement, entry and sampling, and an audit scheme for ship recycling facilities taking into consideration the guidelines developed by the IMO.[71] The convention also elaborates on provisions for authorisation of ship recycling facilities, taking into account the guidelines developed by the IMO.[72] Ship recycling facilities are required to have a management system, procedure and technique for the prevention of health risks to workers and local people and for prevention, reduction, minimisation and (to the extent practicable) elimination of adverse effects on the environment, taking into account the guidelines developed by the IMO.[73] Ship recycling facilities are allowed to accept ships that comply or meet the requirements of the Hong Kong Convention.[74] The convention elaborates on provisions for ship recycling facility plans; prevention of adverse effects on human health and the environment; safe and environmentally sound management of hazardous materials; emergency preparedness and response; worker safety and training; and reporting on incidents, accidents, occupational diseases and chronic effects.[75] These provisions are further elaborated in the Guidelines for Safe and Environmentally Sound Ship Recycling adopted in 2012.[76]

68 *Guidelines for the Development of the Inventory of Hazardous Materials*, 2011 (Resolution MEPC.197(62)), IMO Doc. MEPC 62/24 (26 July 2011) Annex 3.

69 *Guidelines for the Development of the Inventory of Hazardous Materials*, 2015 (Resolution MEPC.269(68)), IMO Doc. MEPC 68/21/Add.1 (29 May 2015) Annex 17.

70 Hong Kong Convention, reg 15.

71 Hong Kong Convention, reg 15.

72 Hong Kong Convention, reg 16, *Guidelines for the Authorization of Ship Recycling Facilities*, 2012 (Resolution MEPC.211(63)), IMO Doc. MEPC 63/23 (14 March 2012) Annex 5.

73 Hong Kong Convention, reg 17(1).

74 Hong Kong Convention, reg 17(2)

75 Hong Kong Convention, regs 18, 19, 20, 21, 22 and 23.

76 *Guidelines for Safe and Environmentally Sound Ship Recycling*, 2012 (Resolution MEPC. 210(63)), IMO Doc. MEPC 63/23 (14 March 2012) Annex 4.

4.3.1.3 Preparation and reporting for ship recycling

Both ship owners and ship recycling facilities have a role in the preparation of ships for recycling. Ship recycling facilities are required to prepare and submit a ship-specific recycling plan for each ship to the competent authority of the state authorising the ship recycling facility, prior to any recycling of a ship, taking into account the guidelines developed by the IMO.[77] This plan will be developed taking into account the information provided by the ship's owner in a language acceptable to the state authorising the ship recycling facility.[78] The plan shall 'include information concerning, inter alia, the establishment, maintenance, and monitoring of Safe-for-entry and Safe-for-hot-work conditions and how the type and amount of materials including those identified in the Inventory of Hazardous Materials will be managed'.[79] The competent authority of the authorising state may require the explicit or tacit approval of this ship recycling plan (SRP).[80] In 2011, the IMO adopted the Guidelines for the Development of the Ship Recycling Plan.[81] The guidelines elaborate on the framework for SRPs including, inter alia, pre-arrival elements, arrival of the ship, management of hazardous materials, Safe-for-entry and Safe-for-hot-work procedures, the dismantling sequence and other necessary elements.[82]

4.3.1.4 Surveys, certification, detection of violation and communication of information

Like many other IMO conventions, the Hong Kong Convention introduces a survey and certification system.[83] Ships are required to carry an International Certificate on Inventory of Hazardous Materials issued by either the flag state or by any person authorised by the flag state.[84] The convention also introduces the International Ready for Recycling Certificate to be issued after the final survey of a ship prior to commencement of its recycling.[85] The convention requires four different surveys. The first, or initial survey, must be conducted before the ship is put into service or before an International Certificate on Inventory of Hazardous Materials is issued.[86] The main aim of this survey is to verify the inventory of hazardous materials. After the initial survey there should be a renewal survey no later than every five years.[87] An additional survey may be conducted at the

77 Hong Kong Convention, reg 9(1).
78 Hong Kong Convention, regs 9(1), 9(2).
79 Hong Kong Convention, reg 9(3).
80 Hong Kong Convention, reg 9(4).
81 *Guidelines for the Development of the Ship Recycling Plan (SRP)*, 2011, IMO Doc. MEPC 62/24 (26 July 2011) Annex 2.
82 Ibid.
83 Hong Kong Convention, art 5.
84 Hong Kong Convention, reg 11(1).
85 Hong Kong Convention, reg 11(11).
86 Hong Kong Convention, reg 10(1).
87 Hong Kong Convention, reg 10(2).

request of the ship owner if there is 'a change, replacement, or significant repair of the structure, equipment, systems, fittings, arrangements and material'.[88] Last, a final survey must be conducted before the ship is taken out of service and before the commencement of ship recycling. Surveys are to be carried out by the flag state or surveyor/organisation nominated by the flag state.[89]

The Hong Kong Convention creates an inspection regime very similar to other IMO conventions. It provides jurisdiction to port states for inspection of ships to determine whether the ship is carrying either a valid International Certificate on Inventory of Hazardous Materials or International Ready for Recycling Certificate.[90] The port state is allowed to carry out a detailed inspection if the ship does not carry a valid certificate; if the condition of the ship or its equipment does not substantially correspond with the certificate; or if the ship fails to implement a procedure for Part 1 of the Inventory of Hazardous Materials.[91] The convention also introduces a violation detection procedure similar to other IMO conventions where parties to the convention have an obligation to cooperate for the detection of violations and enforcement of the convention.[92] A party can request a port state to investigate if it holds evidence that a ship is operating, has operated or is about to operate in violation of any provision of the Hong Kong Convention.[93] The port state shall communicate the results of the investigation to the requesting state, the flag state and the IMO for appropriate action.[94] Like other IMO conventions, this convention provides the port state the jurisdiction to warn, detain, dismiss or exclude the ship from its ports. If this occurs, the port state must immediately communicate this action to the flag state and the IMO.[95]

With respect to the ship, the Hong Kong Convention primarily grants prescriptive and enforcement jurisdiction to the flag state. However, any violation of the requirements of the Hong Kong Convention within the jurisdiction of any party can be prohibited, and sanctions can be established under the law of that party. Like other IMO conventions, this provision in fact creates room for action mainly by the port state. The scope of taking action by a coastal state may be very limited considering the jurisdictional limitations of coastal states under UNCLOS.[96] The Hong Kong Convention explicitly mentions that this convention shall not prejudice the rights and obligations under UNCLOS and customary international laws of the sea.[97]

88 Hong Kong Convention, reg 10(3).
89 Hong Kong Convention, reg 10(4).
90 Hong Kong Convention, art 8(1).
91 Hong Kong Convention, art 8(2).
92 Hong Kong Convention, art 9(1).
93 Hong Kong Convention, art 9(2).
94 Hong Kong Convention, art 9(3).
95 Hong Kong Convention, art 9(3).
96 On coastal state jurisdiction, see generally, Karim, above n 55, 31–36; Erik Jaap Molenaar, *Coastal State Jurisdiction over Vessel-Source Pollution* (Kluwer Law International, 1998).
97 Hong Kong Convention, 15(1).

Similarly, a party to the Hong Kong Convention – if it has sufficient evidence that a ship recycling facility is operating, has operated or is about to operate in violation of any provision of this convention – can request the host state to investigate.[98] The host state has an obligation under this convention to send a report to the requesting state with information on action taken or to be taken. Prescriptive and enforcement jurisdiction over ship recycling facilities is presumably granted to the host state.[99] However, the convention introduces a system in which other parties can report violations to the host state and the host state is to investigate the matter.[100] The host state has an obligation to inform the requesting state and the IMO about the action taken.[101]

4.3.2 Major limitations of the Hong Kong Convention

The Hong Kong Convention has several limitations that create some doubt about its future success. This section highlights some of the most critical limitations of the convention, including ambiguity in ensuring standards of shipbreaking facilitates, lack of provision for pre-cleaning of ships, lack of provision for downstream management of hazardous materials, lack of effective provision for Safe-for-hot work and Safe-for-entry certificates, and disregarding of international environmental law principles, human rights and global environmental justice.[102]

4.3.2.1 Standards of shipbreaking facilitates

Shipbreaking can be done in a number of ways including dry-dock shipbreaking, pier breaking, slipway recycling and beach shipbreaking or beaching.[103] Three major shipbreaking countries, Bangladesh, India and Pakistan, employ the beaching method, which is responsible for serious pollution and hazardous working conditions. There is no agreed definition of beaching. One organisation defines it as the 'dismantling of ships without the use of . . . fixed installations for collection and handling of dangerous and polluting waste'.[104] In this process 'the ship is sailed "full steam onto a tidal flat at spring tide" on sites with a large tidal gauge'.[105] In many situations, the beaching method renders impossible the use of heavy lifting equipment or basic safety equipment such as safety boots on a mudflat, creating hazardous working conditions and increasing the chance of

98 Hong Kong Convention, 9(4).
99 Hong Kong Convention, 9(4).
100 Hong Kong Convention, 9(4).
101 Hong Kong Convention, 9(4).
102 Karim, above n 55, 85–102.
103 International Law and Policy Institute, *Shipbreaking Practices in Bangladesh, India and Pakistan: An Investor Perspective on the Human Rights and Environmental Impacts of Beaching* (International Law and Policy Institute, 2016) 7.
104 Ibid.
105 Ibid.

coastal and marine pollution by contaminants from ships.[106] In a submission by Greenpeace International and Friends of the Earth International (FOEI), which was also signed by other NGOs, it was stated that the beaching system is flawed as it makes it impossible to:

- 'contain oils and toxic contaminants from entering the marine environment;
- bring lifting cranes alongside ships to lift heavy cut pieces or to rescue workers;
- bring emergency equipment (ambulances, fire trucks) to the workers or the ships; and
- protect the fragile intertidal coastal zone from the hazardous wastes on ships'.[107]

This beaching issue was unresolved for a long time in the negotiation process and was debated even at the conference that adopted the convention.[108] However, the Hong Kong Convention does not expressly prohibit current beaching practice because parties were not supportive of this proposal. India, one of the major shipbreaking countries, took a strong position in favour of beaching and made the following statement at the conference:

> There are apprehensions and incorrect perceptions by a few countries in the developed world and an NGO about the environmental friendliness of the beaching method as followed at Alang in India for ship recycling. The beaching method has been in successful existence for several years for ship recycling in India at Alang and this has posed no threat to the environment. Furthermore, this method is the most efficient and cost effective method for recycling of ships from the smallest to the largest sizes, as the natural slope of the beach and the necessary tidal variations at Alang contribute to the easy and environmentally friendly way of ship recycling. It is also well known that about 90% of the global ship recycling has been undertaken over the years by the beaching method.[109]

Although it is true that 90% of ships globally are dismantled using the beaching method, India's claim regarding environmental friendliness of the method is

106 NGO Shipbreaking Platform, *Substandard Shipbreaking: A Global Challenge* (February 2016) <www.shipbreakingplatform.org/shipbrea_wp2011/wp-content/uploads/2016/04/Worldwide-overview_FINAL.pdf>.

107 *Consideration of the Draft International Convention for the Safe and Environmentally Sound Recycling of Ships: Statement of Concern (Submitted by Greenpeace International and FOEI)*, IMO Doc. SR/CONF/CW/INF.1 (14 May 2009).

108 *Opening Address by Mr EE Mitropoulos Secretary-General International Maritime Organization*, IMO Doc. SR/CONF/INF.3 (11 May 2009).

109 *Environmental Comparison of the Beaching Method with other Methods of Recycling of Ships* (Submitted by India), IMO Doc. SR/CONF/36 (1 May 2009).

highly questionable and most likely unfounded considering the current situation in the Indian shipbreaking industry.[110] Against this backdrop, in the final stages of the negotiation, Greenpeace International and FOEI proposed that the following should be added to Regulation 19 of the convention:

> Ship Recycling Facilities authorized by a Party shall establish and utilize procedures to . . . ensure that ship recycling operations taking place on intertidal flats, or ocean beaches or other working platforms which prevent: rapid access to ships by emergency equipment; the ability to utilize cranes and lifting equipment at all times alongside vessels; and the possibility of full containment of pollutants during all cutting and stripping operations, are prohibited.[111]

However, this proposal was not accepted by the parties. As a result, the Hong Kong Convention does not directly prohibit use of the beaching method. However, as noted earlier, Regulation 15 of the convention obliges parties to establish 'standards that are necessary to ensure that Ship Recycling Facilities are designed, constructed, and operated in a safe and environmentally sound manner in accordance with the regulations of this Convention'.[112] How far these obligations can be implemented if the beaching method is used is highly questionable.

4.3.2.2 Pre-cleaning

During negotiations around the Hong Kong Convention, there was a proposal to include a provision for pre-cleaning of obsolete vessels before sending them to the shipbreaking yards of developing countries. Greenpeace submitted the following during the negotiations:

> Due to the transient nature of ships as waste, and the difficulty of identifying the equivalent of a responsible 'exporting State', this most important

110 On environmental condition of Indian shipbreaking industry, see generally, inter alia, the following scientific articles: Vilas Patel et al., 'Taxonomic Profiling of Bacterial Community Structure from Coastal Sediment of Alang–Sosiya Shipbreaking Yard Near Bhavnagar, India' (2015) 101 *Marine Pollution Bulletin* 736; Vilas Patel et al., 'Response of Bacterial Community Structure to Seasonal Fluctuation and Anthropogenic Pollution on Coastal Water of Alang–Sosiya Ship Breaking Yard, Bhavnagar, India' (2014) 161 *Bioresource Technology* 362; M. Srinivasa Reddy et al., 'Distribution, Enrichment and Accumulation of Heavy Metals in Coastal Sediments of Alang–Sosiya Ship Scrapping Yard, India' (2004) 48 *Marine Pollution Bulletin* 1055. On working conditions in the Indian shipbreaking industry, see generally, Geetanjoy Sahu, 'Workers of Alang-Sosiya: A Survey of Working Conditions in a Ship-Breaking Yard, 1983–2013' (2014) 49 *Economic and Political Weekly* 52.

111 *Ensuring Sustainable Green and Safe Ship Dismantling–Concerning Beaching and the Establishment of a Mandatory Fund (Submitted by Greenpeace International and FOEI)*, IMO Doc. SR/CONF/14 (9 February 2009).

112 Hong Kong Convention, reg 15.

> concern can best be addressed in the draft Convention by requiring ship pre-cleaning in developed countries during the life of a ship and prior to its final voyage. Indeed already the shipbreaking State governments of India, Bangladesh, Turkey and Pakistan have endorsed the concept of pre-cleaning or pre-decontamination prior to movement for recycling.[113]

However, this proposal received opposition based on the claim that compulsory pre-cleaning in a developed country may create problems regarding the seaworthiness of ships on their final voyage to the shipbreaking yard. There was a proposal from a number of organisations representing shipping-related companies that if a hazardous material is listed in the inventory of hazardous materials, but the selected ship recycling facility does not have the ability to deal with such materials when cleaning ships, then pre-cleaning will be required and the SRP must, in this instance, show details concerning prior removal of hazardous materials.[114] However, the convention includes an even more dilute provision that reads as follows: 'Ships destined to be recycled shall . . . conduct operations in the period prior to entering the Ship Recycling Facility in order to minimize the amount of cargo residues, remaining fuel oil, and wastes remaining on board'.[115] This provision simply imposes an obligation for limited pre-cleaning of cargo residues, remaining fuel oil and wastes remaining on board but not any hazardous materials that are part of the structure of ships. The Indian Ship Recycling Industries Association submitted that a mechanism should be developed whereby the flag state bears the cost of cleaning hazardous materials if pre-cleaning is not possible.[116] However, no provision along this line was added to the Hong Kong Convention; hence, the burden of hazardous materials disposal is placed squarely on the shoulders of the developing world's shipbreaking yards. This is another example of environmental injustice: rather than internalising environmental pollution costs to shipping companies, they have been externalised to developing shipbreaking countries.

4.3.2.3 Downstream management of hazardous materials

One of the major problems with the Hong Kong Convention is its ambiguous provisions about downstream management of hazardous materials. The convention's

113 *Urgent Considerations for Correcting Deficiencies in the Draft Convention on the Safe and Environmentally Sound Recycling of Ships (Submitted by Greenpeace)*, IMO Doc. MEPC 55/3/7 (10 August 2006) 3.

114 *Proposals for Ship Recycling Plan, Ready for Recycling and Final Surveys (Submitted by the International Chamber of Shipping [ICS], International Parcel Tankers Association [IPTA], International Association of Dry Cargo Shipowners [INTERCARGO], International Association of Independent Tanker Owners [INTERTANKO], and Oil Companies International Marine Forum [OCIMF])*, IMO Doc. MEPC 57/3/18 (8 February 2008) 2.

115 Hong Kong Convention, reg 8(2).

116 *National Workshop on the Development of the International Convention for the Safe and Environmentally Sound Recycling of Ships (Submitted by India)*, IMO Doc. MEPC 57/3/5 (25 January 2008) 4.

definition of 'ship recycling' *excludes further processing or disposal in separate facilities*.[117] It defines a 'ship recycling facility' as 'a defined area that is a site, yard or facility used for the recycling of ships'.[118] This definition creates ambiguity about downstream management of hazardous materials because the convention is only applicable for 'ships entitled to fly the flag of a Party or operating under its authority' and 'Ship Recycling Facilities operating under the jurisdiction of a Party'.[119]

Nevertheless, Regulation 20(3) of the convention requires ship recycling facilities to 'ensure safe and environmentally sound management of all Hazardous Materials and wastes removed from the ship recycled at that Ship Recycling Facility'.[120] The convention also requires that wastes generated from recycling activities shall only be 'transferred to a waste management facility authorized to deal with their treatment and disposal in a safe and environmentally sound manner'.[121] However, the convention does not make any explicit provision about who will authorise downstream waste treatment facilities and the required standard for those downstream facilities.[122] As observed by the Special Rapporteur of the United Nations Human Rights Council:

> The new Convention stipulates that wastes generated from recycling activities should only be transferred to a waste-management facility authorised to deal with their treatment and disposal in an environmentally sound manner. However, there are no provisions in the Convention to ensure that waste dispatched to downstream facilities is traceable, thereby enabling verification of its proper handling, treatment and ultimate disposal.[123]

In response to this, the IMO submitted that Regulation 20(3) of the convention, cited above, covers the issue and that more explicit provisions for the traceability of wastes are included in the 2012 Guidelines for Safe and Environmentally Sound Ship Recycling, one of the six guidelines adopted under the Hong Kong

117 '"Ship Recycling" means the activity of complete or partial dismantling of a ship at a Ship Recycling Facility in order to recover components and materials for reprocessing and re-use, whilst taking care of hazardous and other materials, and includes associated operations such as storage and treatment of components and materials on site, but not their further processing or disposal in separate facilities'. Hong Kong Convention, art 2(10).

118 Hong Kong Convention, art 2(11).

119 Hong Kong Convention, art 3(1).

120 Hong Kong Convention, reg 20(3).

121 Hong Kong Convention, reg 20(4).

122 Marcos A. Orellana et al., *Shipbreaking and the Basel Convention: Analysis of the Level of Control Established Under the Hong Kong Convention* (Centre for International Environmental Law, 2011) 45.

123 Special Rapporteur on the adverse effects of the movement and dumping of toxic and dangerous products and wastes on the enjoyment of human rights, *Preliminary Assessment of Whether the Hong Kong Convention Establishes an Equivalent Level of Control and Enforcement as that Established under the Basel Convention* <www.shipbreakingplatform.org/shipbrea_wp2011/wp-content/uploads/2011/12/UN-special-rapporateur-on-Basel-IMO-conventions-comparison.doc> (hereinafter UNHRC Special Rapporteur Comment).

Convention.[124] Paragraph 3.4.2.6 of these guidelines provides that:

> In situations where the Hazardous Materials and wastes are sent off site, the SRFP [ship recycling facility plan] should describe procedures to ensure that they are transferred only to a facility authorized to deal with their safe and environmentally sound treatment and disposal . . . The SRFP should identify all off-site management and disposal facilities, describe how the materials will be managed at those facilities and identify all authorizations, permits, certificates, approvals and licences required by national and other agencies authorizing the facilities to manage the wastes. The SRFP should include procedures for tracking Hazardous Materials and wastes as they are transported from the Ship Recycling Facility to their ultimate destination, and for managing and storing documentation, including that of subcontractors . . . The final waste management facilities should adhere to national standards and requirements which should take into account applicable international standards and requirements.[125]

Although the guidelines themselves may not be a legally binding instrument, there is explicit mention of the guidelines in Regulations 17.1, 18, 19, 20(2) and 22 of the Hong Kong Convention. Therefore, parties are bound to take the guidelines into consideration to ensure environmentally sound management of ship recycling facilities. In this respect, the IMO also stated that '[i]t is also paramount to underline that Party [sic] obligations arising under the Basel Convention for the environmentally sound management of wastes, would continue to apply after the entry into force of the Hong Kong Convention. So, in this respect, the regulations of the Hong Kong Convention stop where the Basel Convention takes over'.[126] It is clear from this statement that obligations under the Basel Convention for environmentally sound management of hazardous wastes will exist alongside obligations under the Hong Kong Convention.

Nevertheless, the Hong Kong Convention and its associated guidelines suffer from the same fundamental lacuna discussed in the earlier sections of this chapter – shifting of the financial and environmental burden of hazardous wastes management to developing countries' shipbreaking yards without creating any financial obligation for the developed world's shipping companies – thereby blatantly disregarding the polluter pays principle. Use of many of the hazardous substances in older vessels is now prohibited by relevant international legal instruments. Ironically, the shipping industry is profiting by selling obsolete ships with these hazardous materials rather than spending money on environmentally sound disposal of these hazardous substances, while other industries may be spending money to properly dispose of similar substances.

124 IMO, *The Hong Kong Convention and IMO's Position in Relation to the Preliminary Assessment by the UNHRC Special Rapporteur* <archive.basel.int/ships/oewg-vii12-comments/comments/imo.doc>.

125 Guidelines for Safe and Environmentally Sound Ship Recycling, above n 76.

126 IMO, above n 124.

4.3.2.4 *Safe-for-hot-work and Safe-for-entry certificates*

As discussed in Chapter 1, fire and explosions due to unsafe conditions for hot work are the main killers in the Bangladeshi shipbreaking industry. Safe-for-hot-work and Safe-for-entry procedures are two essential elements of safety of workers in the shipbreaking industry.[127] The Hong Kong Convention fails miserably to create an international regulation for issuance of Safe-for-hot work and Safe-for-entry Certificates before sending an obsolete ship to a developing country's shipbreaking yard.

This issue was hotly debated during the negotiations. Norway's first draft of the Hong Kong Convention initially included a provision that the final survey of the ship shall verify 'that the ship is prepared for gas-free-for-hot-work'.[128] This provision received serious opposition from the shipping industry, which made a submission to MEPC 54 proposing that the mandatory requirement for gas-freeing should be dealt with in regulations for readying for recycling, and the SRP.[129] Due to pressure from the industry, this provision was seriously diluted in the final version of the convention, which provides that the final survey simply verifies that the SRP prepared by the ship recycling facility 'contains information concerning the establishment, maintenance and monitoring of Safe-for-entry and Safe-for-hot work conditions'.[130] Presumably this provision does not require obtaining a Safe-for-hot work and Safe-for-entry Certificate prior to sending the ship to a developing country shipbreaking yard. This is another example of shifting the burden to developing countries' shipbreaking yards.

India raised the issue of the Safe-for-hot work Certificate several times during the negotiations. At MEPC 55, India made the following submission:

> It was accepted that this essential measure has the greatest impact on safety in recycling facilities and this should be made mandatory. Cargo tanks, slop tanks and all other hazardous liquid tanks and spaces (except for the fuel oil tanks and sludge tanks in machinery spaces which are needed for the final voyage) should be gas-freed for man-entry and hot-work prior to or during the final voyage to the recycling yard and the vessel needs to be handed over in this condition to the recycling yard.[131]

At the Second Intersessional Meeting of the Working Group on Ship Recycling, India proposed that gas-free-for-hot-work certification should be addressed in the

127 See generally, *Proposal for Providing Clarity in the Convention and Reaffirming the Importance of Safe-for-Hot-work and Safe-for-Entry Conditions During Recycling (Submitted by the United States)*, IMO Doc. SR/CONF/33 (29 April 2009).
128 Draft Convention Submitted by Norway, above n 49.
129 *Proposal for a New Legally Binding Instrument on Recycling of Ships: Industry Comments (Submitted by ICS, BIMCO, INTERTANKO, INTERCARGO, IPTA, WNTI)*, IMO Doc. MEPC 54/3/11 (27 January 2006).
130 Hong Kong Convention, reg 10(4)(2).
131 *Development of the Draft International Convention for the Safe and Environmentally Sound Recycling of Ships (Submitted by India)*, IMO Doc. MEPC 55/3/12 (17 August 2006).

convention itself, not just in the non-mandatory guidelines.[132] There was an agreement that relevant regulation of the convention will reflect this matter.[133] However, the working group was of the opinion that the issue of gas-free for hot work is covered in Regulation 9 of the convention.[134] This regulation deals with the SRP for each ship developed by the ship recycling facilities. It also provides that the SRP shall include information about Safe-for-entry and Safe-for-hot-work conditions. However, this provision does not necessarily introduce a prior Safe-for-hot-work certification requirement before sending the ship to a developing country shipbreaking yard.

This issue remained unresolved until the Hong Kong Conference. India took a very robust position for a prior gas-freeing-for-hot-work provision, particularly in the case of tankers. India made a written submission to the conference stating that it has repeatedly requested inclusion of 'a requirement for gas-free-for-hot-work certification. Stipulating the condition of gas-free-for-hot-work is meant to make compulsory for the shipowners the preparation of oil tankers for recycling by cleaning their cargo and slop tanks and cargo pipes prior to their arrival at the Ship Recycling Facility'.[135] It also expressed the concern that 'one may be tempted to deduce that there is a bias in favour of the shipowner in the draft text of the Convention'.[136] India proposed that the following paragraph should be added to Regulation 8 of the convention: 'Ships destined to be recycled shall . . . in the case of tankers certified to carry oil or chemicals, arrive at the Ship Recycling Facility with clean cargo and slop tanks and cargo pipes and in gas-free-for-hot-work condition'.[137] Although the conference agreed to include a similar provision, it did this with a dangerous modification to the Indian proposal[138] and agreed to add the following paragraph to Regulation 8 of the convention:

> in the case of a tanker, arrive at the Ship Recycling Facility with cargo tanks and pump room(s) in a condition that is ready for certification as Safe-for-entry, or Safe-for-hot work, or both, according to national laws, regulations and policies of the Party under whose jurisdiction the Ship Recycling Facility operates.[139]

Although this paragraph apparently looks similar to India's proposal, there is a marked difference: by referring to the 'national laws, regulations and policies', it most likely creates room for double standards and the creation of pollution

132 Second Intersessional Meeting Report, above n 51, 8.
133 Ibid.
134 Ibid.
135 *Preparation of Oil Tankers for Ship Recycling (Submitted by India)*, IMO Doc. SR/CONF/26 (2 April 2009).
136 Ibid.
137 Ibid.
138 *Consideration of the Draft Text of the International Convention for the Safe and Environmentally Sound Recycling of Ships: Texts Approved on Thursday, 14 May 2009, for Consideration by the Drafting Committee*, IMO Doc. SR/CONF/CW/5 (14 May 2009).
139 Hong Kong Convention, reg 8(3).

havens. Some shipbreaking nations may decide to have lax legal standards to be more competitive in the shipbreaking market.

4.3.2.5 Disregard of international environmental law principles, human rights and global environmental justice

Although in its preamble the Hong Kong Convention makes mention of the precautionary principle, it blatantly disregards a cardinal principle of international and comparative environmental law – the polluter pays principle. The shipping industry should be responsible for the pollution occurring from shipbreaking because shipbreaking is the disposal or management of the shipping industry's waste, namely obsolete ships. This convention fails to establish a mechanism to stop ship owners from profiting from their waste, that is, an obsolete ship. The current international legal framework allows a ship owner to profit from, rather than take responsibility for, the environmentally sound disposal of an obsolete ship. Mentioning only the precautionary principle and not mentioning any other international environmental law principles is rather ironic; the precautionary principle is more relevant in a situation where scientific evidence of a certain type of pollution is somewhat uncertain or inconclusive. However, the detrimental effects of the shipbreaking industry have been demonstrated in much scientific research. Therefore, the more relevant international environmental law principles applicable to the shipbreaking industry are the principle of sustainable development, the principle of prevention, the polluter pays principle and the principle of CBDR. However, none of these principle is explicitly mentioned as a guiding principle of the Hong Kong Convention. Rather than mentioning these international environmental law principles – particularly the polluter pays principle – the convention provides in its preamble that parties should take 'into account the particular characteristics of maritime transport and the need to secure the smooth withdrawal of ships that have reached the end of their operating lives'.[140] However, the industry's need for smooth withdrawal of obsolete ships certainly is not sufficient cause to ignore international environmental law principles, such as the polluter pays principle.

The Hong Kong Convention also fails to consider the issue of environmental justice and violation of human rights in this industry. The convention considers the environmentally sound and safe management of the shipbreaking industry as simply a technical issue. The convention and its negotiation process failed to acknowledge the human side of the problem. As observed by civil society stakeholders at the end of the Hong Kong Conference that adopted the convention, 'When the world cried for help, we threw paper rather than a life ring'.[141] This is probably a correct manifestation of the highly biased negotiation process that adopted this convention.

140 Hong Kong Convention, preamble.

141 *Statements by Delegations and Observers at the Closing Session of the Conference Friday, 15 May 2009*, IMO Doc. SR/CONF/INF.8 (21 May 2009).

It is pertinent to examine how this blatant disregard of the principles of international environmental law and environmental justice was possible. This convention reflects the long-standing influence of developed countries and the international shipping lobby in the IMO negotiations. Moreover, it is an open secret that the interests of some least developed 'flag of convenience' countries may be more aligned to those of shipping companies than to environmental and human rights. The situation is further complicated by the influence of shipbreaking company owners on the governments of developing shipbreaking countries. A revealing example is that Bangladesh was represented in a meeting by a consultant appointed by the Bangladesh Ship Breakers Association (BSBA) along with government officials.[142] Bangladeshi official delegations never include an environmental activist or a workers' representative. Participation of a consultant to the BSBA as part of the government delegation clearly indicates the influence of the organisation within the Bangladeshi government. More troubling is that, unlike other country delegations, the consultant to the BSBA was not included only as an advisor to the Bangladeshi delegation – in some meetings he participated as a representative of Bangladesh. Despite the gross violations of human rights and global environmental justice in this industry, the Bangladeshi delegation and delegations from other developing shipbreaking countries never raised these issues. Presumably the developed country delegations were there mainly to uphold their national interest rather than environmental justice or labour rights in developing shipbreaking countries. Although the Hong Kong Convention directly relates to workers' rights, participation and representation of shipbreaking workers from developing countries in the negotiation process was very limited.

Against this backdrop, human rights and environmental justice issues were raised mainly by observer organisations that have very limited participation rights and no voting rights. Unsurprisingly, numerous submissions and MEPC meeting reports related to the negotiation process reveal that the human rights of workers and local people and the issue of environmental justice was not highly regarded in the agenda. The shipbreaking industry is a glaring example of global environmental injustice. The violation of the human rights of workers is disgraceful. Despite the gross violation of human rights in this industry, the Hong Kong Convention does not make a single reference to international human rights treaties, not even in its preamble, even though it is common to make reference to relevant international legal instruments and global initiatives in a preamble. As mentioned earlier, the IMO negotiation process treated shipbreaking as just a technical issue, blatantly ignoring the human face of the problem.

142 *Marine Environment Protection Committee 60th Session, 22–26 March 2010, List of Participants*, IMO Doc. MEPC 60/INF.1 (26 March 2010); *Marine Environment Protection Committee, 55th Session, 9–13 October 2006, List of Participants*, IMO Doc. MEPC 55/INF.1 (15 November 2006).

4.3.3 Funding and technology transfer

The Hong Kong Convention in practice shifts the main responsibility for environmentally sound disposal of obsolete ships to developing country shipbreaking yards. However, the convention fails to go beyond the generalised approach for technical assistance and cooperation stipulated in other IMO marine environmental conventions. According to Article 13 of the convention, the parties undertake to provide technical assistance in relation to:

- 'training personnel
- technology, equipment and facilities
- joint research and development programmes
- other activities relating to the effective implementation'.[143]

However, similar technology transfer provisions in other IMO conventions are not very successful.[144] Like other IMO conventions, the Hong Kong Convention makes cooperation regarding transfer of management systems and technology subject to national laws and policy.[145] The reluctance of international organisations and state parties to implement funding and technology transfers related to provisions of the convention may be an obstacle to implementation of the convention. If developed countries or regional organisations were to provide state-of-the-art technology and financial assistance to countries like Bangladesh for establishing modern ship recycling facilitates with hazardous-wastes-cleaning and gas-freeing plants, it might be possible to operate shipbreaking in an environmentally sound way. The establishment of plants for removal and treatment of hazardous substances with modern facilities could partially solve the problem. Alternatively, multinational companies could invest in environmentally sound ship recycling facilities in Bangladesh while taking advantage of cheap labour and the ever-increasing demand for iron. Unfortunately, these avenues of solving the problem have not been fully explored. The global community, including intergovernmental organisations and NGOs, is preoccupied with conferences and meetings while failing to take any practical steps to solve the problem in a just and equitable manner.

The IMO, to some extent, seems to appreciate developing countries' need for financial assistance, establishing the International Ship Recycling Trust Fund on 1 May 2006.[146] The fund is primarily dedicated to helping developing countries with training and policy development.[147] For example, the IMO and the

143 Hong Kong Convention, art 13(1).

144 Md Saiful Karim, 'Implementation of the MARPOL Convention in Developing Countries' (2010) 79 *Nordic Journal of International Law* 303.

145 Hong Kong Convention, art 13(2).

146 Nikos Mikelis, *Developments and Issues on Recycling of Ships* (2006) <www.imo.org/includes/blastDataOnly.asp/data_id%3D17980/Developments.pdf>.

147 *Establishment of an International Ship Recycling Trust Fund*, IMO Doc. Circular Letter No. 2703 (20 April 2006).

Bangladesh government are currently implementing a project named *Safe and Environmentally Sound Ship Recycling in Bangladesh*.[148] This project is mainly funded by the Norwegian Agency for Development Cooperation with total funding of US$1,516,275.[149] This amount also includes some funding mobilised by the Secretariat of the Basel, Rotterdam and Stockholm Conventions.[150] The project website lists a number of objectives including economic and environmental impact assessment; assessment of existing hazardous wastes management systems; selection of a suitable site for a hazardous waste storage, treatment and disposal facility; review and upgrading of existing training courses; recommendations for improving government services for the ship recycling industry; and proposals for future projects to implement recommendations arising from the project.[151]

Some of the aims of the project may be useful. However, the economic and environmental impacts of the shipbreaking industry in Bangladesh are already well-documented. What value further analysis will add is not entirely clear. Training and policy development is not a problem for Bangladesh. The country already has many laws and policies favourable to the environment. Developing countries like Bangladesh need help with establishing modern hazardous substances removal and treatment plants. Without providing technology and funds, training alone will not bring any positive change. In Bangladesh, a similar project run by the United Nations Development Programme (UNDP)[152] has not been very successful. Moreover, some NGOs are doing similar work that has also accomplished little.[153] This emphasis on training, seminars and policy development suggests that most of the funds are used for so-called foreign consultants and local experts, and other trivial purposes. Despite all of these projects, in 2016, 22 workers died in the Bangladeshi shipbreaking industry.[154] This is the second-highest number of deaths in a single year in the last decade and the highest in the last six years. This clearly shows that, despite all the propaganda claiming success, the situation in the shipbreaking industry is deteriorating; it is certainly not improving.

Without changing current beaching methods and the overall operational systems of Bangladeshi shipbreaking yards, no amount of research, analysis or

148 IMO, *Safe and Environmentally Sound Ship Recycling in Bangladesh–Phase I* (2017) <www.imo.org/en/OurWork/Environment/SupportToMemberStates/MajorProjects/Pages/Ship-recycling.aspx>.

149 Ibid.

150 Ibid.

151 Ibid.

152 Matthew Russell Lee, *Ship-Breakers Missed by UN's Budget for Travel and Consultants in Bangladesh* (18 August 2006) <www.innercitypress.com/unhq081806.html> (a report on a UNDP project in Bangladesh).

153 YPSA, *YPSA's Works in Shipbreaking* (2012) <www.shipbreakingbd.info/YPSAworks.html>.

154 NGO Shipbreaking Platform, *Substandard Shipbreaking: A Global Challenge* (February 2017) <www.shipbreakingplatform.org/shipbrea_wp2011/wp-content/uploads/2017/01/Worldwide-overview_FINAL_2017.pdf>.

training will make any real difference. Despite current and completed development projects, deaths and casualties of shipbreaking workers remain as regular incidents in the shipbreaking yards of Bangladesh. As observed in Chapter 1 of this book, at least 10 workers were killed or severely injured in a single month during 2016.[155]

4.4 European shipbreaking regulation

Initially, the EU adopted the EC WSR to implement the Basel Ban in 1997.[156] This regulation was replaced in 2006.[157] Preamble Paragraph 35 of the regulation 'noted that a ship may become waste as defined in Article 2 of the Basel Convention and that at the same time it may be defined as a ship under other international rules'.[158] Therefore, it was clear that the EC WSR is applicable to obsolete ships. However, ship owners are able to avoid the implementation of this regulation by reflagging their ships using flags of convenience before sending the ship to a developing country shipbreaking yard.

In 2013, the European Parliament and Council adopted a separate regulation for ship recycling; the previously adopted Regulations on Waste Shipments will no longer be applicable for ships covered by this specialised regulation.[159] The EU SRR implements the Hong Kong Convention in EU member states. Therefore, most of the provisions mirror the Hong Kong Convention and do not deserve a detailed discussion. However, the EU SRR includes some additional safety and environmental requirements. According to the EU SRR, the application of the EC WSR, which implements the Basel Convention, is excluded for ships falling under the scope of the EU SRR. Exclusion of the application of the Basel Convention on the assumption that the Hong Kong Convention establishes an equivalent level of control is highly problematic.[160]

The EU SRR prohibits or restricts the installation or use of hazardous materials listed in Annex 1 relating to the regulation on ships.[161] It requires that all new ships flying a member state's flag must carry on board an inventory of hazardous

155 NGO Shipbreaking Platform, *Platform News–Surge of Fatal Accidents in Chittagong: 10 Shipbreaking Workers Killed or Severely Injured in One Month Only* (27 June 2016) <www.shipbreakingplatform.org/platform-news-surge-of-fatal-accidents-in-chittagong/>.

156 *Council Regulation 120/97 of 20 January 1997, Amending Regulation (EC) No. 259/93 on the Supervision and Control of Shipments of Waste within, into and Out of the European Community*, 1997 OJ (L 22) 14.

157 *Regulation (EC) No. 1013/2006 of the European Parliament and of the Council of 14 June 2006 on Shipments of Waste*, 2006 OJ (L 190) 1.

158 Ibid.

159 EU SRR, art 27.

160 See generally, Ludwig Krämer, *The Commission Proposal for a Regulation on Ship Recycling, the Basel Convention and the Protection of the Environment* (4 September 2012) <www.shipbreakingplatform.org/shipbrea_wp2011/wp-content/uploads/2012/12/Legal-Analysis-of-EC-proposal_Ludwig-Kramer_FINAL-1.pdf>.

161 EU SRR, art 4.

materials.[162] This rule is applicable for ships flying the flag of a third-party calling at a port or anchorage of a member state.[163] According to the EU SRR, ships flying the flag of an EU member state can only be recycled in a ship recycling facility that is included in the European List of Ship Recycling Facilities on a date not later than 31 December 2018.[164] The first such list was created in December 2016, and it includes 18 shipyards located in European countries.[165] However, ship recycling facilities in countries outside Europe can also be included in the European List if they fulfil conditions included in the regulation.[166] The EU SRR provides conditions that may be more stringent than the Hong Kong Convention. One such condition is that ship recycling facilities are operated from built structures.[167] Accordingly, South Asian, particularly Bangladeshi, shipbreaking yards using the beaching method may not be eligible to be listed. The European Commission adopted technical guidance on requirements and procedures for inclusion of facilities located in third countries on the European List of Ship Recycling Facilities.[168]

The EU SRR has some serious flaws. The regulation fails to introduce any meaningful provision to prevent avoidance of the European regulation by reflagging of European ships under flags of convenience before sending them to developing country shipbreaking yards. This creates serious doubt about the future success of the regulation considering the failure of the EC WSR with respect to obsolete ships. To make the situation worse, an end-of-life flag of convenience business has emerged to facilitate substandard shipbreaking. As observed in a report published by the NGO Shipbreaking Platform:

> Nearly 40% of all end-of-life ships beached in South Asia were imported under flags of convenience . . . These 'end-of-life flags' are hardly used during the operational life of a ship and offer special 'discount rates' for last voyages and quick and easy short-term registration without any nationality requirements . . . while during operational life 22% of the global fleet uses a European flag, less than 8% of the ships sold for breaking still fly a European flag – which means European flag state jurisdiction only covers a very small amount of end-of-life vessels.[169]

162 EU SRR, art 5.
163 EU SRR, art 12
164 EU SRR, art 6(2)(a) and art 32.
165 European Commission, *European List of Ship Recycling Facilities* (19 December 2016) <http://ec.europa.eu/environment/waste/ships/pdf/list_ship_recycling_facilities.pdf>; European Commission, *Commission Adopts First European List of Ship Recycling Facilities Safe for Workers and Environmentally Sound* (20 December 2016) <http://ec.europa.eu/environment/pdf/20_12_2016_news_en.pdf>.
166 EU SRR, art 15.
167 EU SRR, art 13(c).
168 European Commission, *Technical Guidance Note under Regulation (EU) No. 1257/2013 on Ship Recycling (2016/C 128/01)* (12 April 2016) <http://eur-lex.europa.eu/legal-content/EN/TXT/PDF/?uri=CELEX:52016XC0412(01)&from=EN>.
169 Patrizia Heidegger et al., *What a Difference a Flag Makes: Why Ship Owners' Responsibility to Ensure Sustainable Ship Recycling Needs to go beyond Flag State Jurisdiction* (NGO Shipbreaking Platform, 2015) 1.

The EU SRR may even unintentionally encourage more end-of-life flags of convenience. Like the Hong Kong Convention, the EU SRR fails to implement the polluter pays principle. It does not create a direct financial consequence for ship owners. There is a new proposal for creating a financial instrument to ensure compliance. A report commissioned by the European Commission proposes a new financial instrument – the Ship Recycling Licence.[170] According to this proposal, all ships that visit EU ports must buy a Ship Recycling Licence.[171] To obtain this licence, ship owners must pay a contribution consisting of two parts: the first part of the contribution is a small fee to cover the administration costs of issuing the licence;[172] the second is a levy that will be transferred to a new Ship Recycling Fund. If, at the end of its life, a ship is recycled in a ship recycling facility from the European List, the ship owner will be repaid the capital amount.[173] If the last owner of the ship fails to recycle the ship in a facility that is included in the European List, the accrued rights to the payment of the capital amount will be forfeited.[174] This proposal is yet to be adopted by the EU, but it has received strong support from environmental NGOs.[175] However, both the European Community Shipowners' Associations and the International Chamber of Shipping are strongly opposing this proposal.[176]

Similar to the Hong Kong Convention, the EU SRR treats shipbreaking as a technical issue and fails to address the issue of environmental injustice suffered by the workers and people of developing shipbreaking countries. The EU SRR and its proposed associated financial mechanisms may be useful in bringing the shipbreaking industry back to European soil in the future when most ships being recycled no longer contain hazardous materials, but they are having no effect whatsoever in addressing the ongoing environmental injustice and gross violation of labour rights in the South Asian shipbreaking industry.

4.5 Conclusion

Seven years after its adoption, only five states have become parties to the Hong Kong Convention, and the convention is yet to enter into force.[177] Although it

170 Ecorys, 'DNV GL and Erasmus University: The Erasmus School of Law' *Financial Instrument to Facilitate Safe and Sound Ship Recycling Final Report* (June 2016) <http://ec.europa.eu/environment/waste/ships/pdf/financial_instrument_ship_recycling.pdf>

171 Ibid.

172 Ibid.

173 Ibid.

174 Ibid.

175 NGO Shipbreaking Platform, *Make the Polluter Pay! Why We Need the European Ship Recycling Licence* (October 2016) <www.shipbreakingplatform.org/shipbrea_wp2011/wp-content/uploads/2016/10/Position-Paper-FINANCIAL-INCENTIVE.pdf>.

176 ECSA, *Shipowners Reject Proposals for Ships to Pay for EU Ship Recycling Licences* <www.ecsa.eu/9-latest-news/267-shipowners-reject-proposals-for-ships-to-pay-for-eu-ship-recycling-licences>.

177 IMO, *Status of Multilateral Conventions and Instruments in Respect of Which the International Maritime Organization or Its Secretary-General Performs Depositary or Other Functions* (14 March 2017) 511 <www.imo.org/en/About/Conventions/StatusOfConventions/Documents/Status%20-%202017.pdf>.

was expected that the Hong Kong Convention would establish a more effective and comprehensive regulatory framework, to some extent it even fails to establish an equivalent level of control to the Basel Convention.[178] As discussed in this chapter, the Hong Kong Convention has a number of fundamental flaws that may make it largely ineffective. The convention also fails to address the issue of environmental injustice and violation of labour rights.

As noted earlier, the Hong Kong Convention is imposing more regulations on developing shipbreaking countries rather than on developed countries that benefit from the shipping itself. To strike a balance, the convention includes an article on technical assistance and cooperation. However, as noted earlier, the convention makes transfer of technology subject to national laws, regulations and policies. This means that this provision will remain a paper tiger, like similar provisions of other IMO conventions. Regardless, funding and technology transfer is not sufficient to ensure environmental justice in the shipbreaking industry. As discussed in the next chapter, in the context of Bangladesh, lack of political will of the national government and institutional bias may create serious hindrances in ensuring environmentally sound management of the shipbreaking industry and the protection of labour rights.

178 Orellana et al., above n 122; UNHRC Special Rapporteur Comment, above n 123.

5 Environmental justice and regulatory developments for the shipbreaking industry in Bangladesh

5.1 Introduction

This chapter discusses the effectiveness of the national legal and institutional framework of Bangladesh in ensuring environmental justice in the shipbreaking industry. As discussed in Chapter 1, the shipbreaking industry in Bangladesh developed haphazardly. Initially there was no specialised regulation for this industry. Nevertheless, like any industry, the shipbreaking industry is required to follow the environmental and labour laws of the country, although the implementation and enforcement of environmental and labour laws in this industry is seriously lacking. Following repeated directions from the Bangladesh Supreme Court, the government developed specific regulations for this industry. However, practical implementation and enforcement of these regulations is yet to be achieved due to the reluctance of the relevant government departments, the lack of willingness of the shipbreaking industry and the industry's influence over regulatory institutions.

Section 5.2 examines whether the existing legal framework of Bangladesh is adequate to ensure environmentally sound management of the shipbreaking industry. Section 5.3 outlines Bangladeshi laws relating to the working environment and labour rights, and argues that the owners of shipbreaking yards are continuously violating the labour laws of the country. Section 5.4 describes early initiatives for regulatory development to control shipbreaking activities in Bangladesh. Section 5.5 assesses the role played by legal activism in the regulatory development and enforcement of existing laws. Section 5.6 critically examines recent regulatory developments and identifies serious lacunae in the regulatory system. Section 5.7 discusses the institutional framework for ensuring environmentally sound recycling of ships. In Bangladesh, different government agencies are working in the same area, with overlapping and conflicting duties and responsibilities. Interagency conflict is more apparent than interagency cooperation. Relevant government agencies are also handicapped by a lack of resources and the widespread practice of corruption. Moreover, the government's policy of rapid development at the cost of the environment and labour rights severely reduces the ability of relevant government agencies to ensure environmental justice. Further, the highly influential owners of shipbreaking companies have enormous power over government policy.

5.2 Environmentally sound management and existing laws

Bangladesh's *Environment Conservation Act 1995* is an umbrella environmental statute that provides for overall environmental conservation in the country. This act could be used as an effective instrument for protection of the environment around shipbreaking yards. It establishes the Department of Environment headed by a Director General whose powers and functions include taking all necessary steps to ensure conservation of the environment, improvement of environmental standards and control and mitigation of pollution of the environment.[1]

The act defines 'waste' as 'any solid, liquid, gaseous, radioactive substance, the discharge, disposal and dumping of which may cause harmful change to the environment'[2] and a 'hazardous substance' as 'a substance, the chemical or biochemical properties of which are such that its manufacture, storage, discharge or unregulated transportation can be harmful to the environment'.[3] In 2010, the act was amended to include a definition of 'hazardous waste', as 'any waste, due to its own physical or chemical characteristics or due to its contact with other waste or substance, may cause harm to the environment by toxicity, infection, flammability, explosion, radioactivity, decay or any other detrimental activities'.[4] A plain reading of these definitions reveals that an obsolete ship with hazardous substances can be treated as hazardous waste within the purview of the *Environment Conservation Act.*

The act broadly defines pollution in a way that certainly brings within its ambit the pollution produced by the shipbreaking industry in coastal and marine areas of Chittagong.[5] Section 7 of the act gives necessary power to the Director General to take action against polluters, including, inter alia, mitigation, realisation of compensation, realisation of payment for corrective action and initiation of judicial proceedings.[6] However, instances in which the Director General invokes these powers against shipbreaking industries are rare.

The act defines an environmental pollutant as a 'solid, liquid or gaseous substance which causes harmful effect to the environment and also includes heat, sound and radiation'.[7] Shipbreaking yards regularly discharge toxic substances that are treated as environmental pollutants under the act, such as asbestos,

1 *Environment Conservation Act 1995* (Act No. I of 1995), s. 3 and 4.
2 *Environment Conservation Act 1995.*
3 *Environment Conservation Act 1995.*
4 *Environment Conservation Act 1995*, s. 2 (AAA).
5 The *Environment Conservation Act* defines pollution as 'the contamination or alteration of the physical, chemical or biological properties of air, water or soil, including change in their temperature, taste, odor, density, or any other characteristics, or such other activity which, by way of discharging any liquid, gaseous, solid, radioactive or other substances into air, water or soil or any component of the environment, destroys or causes injury or harm to public health or to domestic, commercial, industrial, agricultural, recreational or other useful activity, or which by such discharge destroys or causes injury or harm to air, water, soil, livestock, wild animal, bird, fish, plant or other forms of life'. *Environment Conservation Act 1995*, s. 2.
6 *Environment Conservation Act 1995*, s. 7.
7 *Environment Conservation Act 1995*, s. 2.

PCBs, lead, arsenic, TBT, PAHs, chromates, mercury and slag oil. Section 9 of the act empowers the Director General to take action against the discharge of environmental pollutants.[8] However, practical exercise of this power is rare in the shipbreaking industry.

According to Section 12 of the act, no industrial enterprise can be established without clearance from the Director General.[9] The shipbreaking yards contribute significantly to marine environmental pollution and pose a great threat to all living creatures by releasing polluting agents in all three forms: solid, liquid and gaseous. However, unfortunately the *Environmental Conservation Rules 1997* incorporate 'Ship-breaking' in the list of Orange B category industries rather than incorporating it in the Red List with respect to the industry's environmental clearance.[10] The industries listed in the Orange B list are subject to less stringent measures for environmental clearance than are Red List industries. Although the rule gives the shipbreaking industry some flexibility, the industry is still not interested in complying with environmental clearance provisions. Although the Department of Environment submitted a notification to the Supreme Court showing that ship dismantling has been temporarily included in the Red List,[11] no formal gazette notification for amendment of the *Environmental Conservation Rules 1997* is available.

Apart from the *Environment Conservation Act*, some other laws of Bangladesh are also relevant for the shipbreaking industry. These laws include, inter alia, the *Merchant Shipping Ordinance 1983*, the *Territorial Waters and Maritime Zones Act 1974*, the *Bangladesh Coast Guard Act 2016* and the *Explosive Act 1884*.

As observed in Chapter 3, some international conventions relating to vessel-source pollution may be relevant to the shipbreaking industry; unfortunately, none of those conventions have been incorporated or implemented into Bangladesh's legal framework. Bangladesh does not have any comprehensive law directly dealing with vessel-source marine pollution. The umbrella law regulating maritime affairs in Bangladesh is the *Merchant Shipping Ordinance 1983*.[12] Questions about implementing the MARPOL Convention did not arise while enacting this ordinance because all the annexes of the MARPOL Convention came into effect for Bangladesh in 2002. Although the ordinance was subsequently amended several times, the issue of implementing the MARPOL and other IMO conventions was not addressed by these amendments. The *Merchant Shipping Ordinance* is not suitable to meet present-day need. This ordinance elaborates

8 *Environment Conservation Act 1995*, s. 9.

9 *Environment Conservation Act 1995*, s. 12.

10 Environment Conservation Rules (1997) <http://doe.portal.gov.bd/sites/default/files/files/doe.portal.gov.bd/page/5a9d6a31_d858_4001_b844_817a27d079f5/Environment%20Conservation%20Rule-1997.pdf>.

11 Department of Environment, Notification 2169 dated 14 November 2007, signed by the Director General.

12 *Merchant Shipping Ordinance*, 1983 (Ordinance No. XXVI of 1983), as amended by the *Merchant Shipping (Amendment) Act 1995* (Act No. II of 1995) and the *Merchant Shipping (Amendment) Act 2004* (Act No. VII of 2004).

on the powers and functions of the Department of Shipping, the Mercantile Marine Department, Shipping Offices, Surveyors and all other shipping-related government bodies. Some of these institutions are involved in the regulation of the shipbreaking industry. For example, there was a circular from the Bangladesh government that permission from the Mercantile Marine Department was required before beaching a vessel for breaking, and the Department of Shipping is entrusted with the duty of dealing with IMO-related matters.

The Bangladesh *Coast Guard Act 2016* empowers the Coast Guard to take action against environmental pollution in the maritime area.[13] The Coast Guard is also entrusted with enforcing any warrant or any other order of any court or other authority with respect to any ship or any person on the ship.[14]

The *Territorial Waters and Maritime Zones Act 1974* demarcates the territorial waters, contiguous zone, economic zone and continental shelf of Bangladesh.[15] This act also contains some provisions to prevent marine environmental pollution. According to Section 6 of this act, the government may, by gazette notification, establish conservation zones in the sea for the maintenance of living resources. Section 8 of the act empowers the government to take such measures as it deems appropriate for preventing and controlling marine pollution and preserving the quality and ecological balance in the marine environment in high seas adjacent to the territorial waters.

Although Bangladesh has ratified important international marine environmental conventions including UNCLOS and the MARPOL Convention, national laws have not been updated to implement these international conventions. In 2004, the Department of Shipping drafted a *Marine Environment Conservation Act* to implement a number of IMO marine environmental conventions including the MARPOL Convention. The draft act had some serious flaws.[16] In November 2008, the government prepared an improved draft titled the *Marine Environment Protection Act*. Unfortunately, this draft was never presented before the Bangladesh Parliament for enactment. Therefore, major IMO marine environmental conventions remain unimplemented in Bangladesh.

5.3 Labour rights and existing laws

As discussed in Chapter 1, death and injury of workers in Bangladeshi shipbreaking yards is very common. It is pertinent to examine the liability of shipbreaking company owners and operators in this regard. Existing civil, criminal and labour laws can be used to establish civil and criminal liability of shipbreaking company owners and operators if the relevant government departments are willing to enforce the law properly.

13 *Bangladesh Coast Guard Act 2016* (Act No. XI of 2016), s. 10.
14 *Bangladesh Coast Guard Act 2016*, s. 7 10.
15 *Territorial Waters and Maritime Zones Act*, 1974 (Act No. XXVI of 1974), ss. 3, 4, 5, 6 and 7.
16 Md Saiful Karim, 'Implementation of the MARPOL Convention in Bangladesh' (2009) 5 *Macquarie Journal of International and Comparative Environmental Law* 51.

Death or serious injury due to lack of safety measures is not an accident; it is an inevitable result of the negligence of shipbreaking company owners and operators. The beaching method is an inherently dangerous activity. Shipbreaking company owners should be absolutely responsible for death and injuries in this industry. As observed by the Supreme Court of India in *M.C. Mehta v. Union of India*:

> We are of the view that an enterprise which is engaged in a hazardous or inherently dangerous industry which poses a potential threat to the health and safety of the persons working in the factory and residing in the surrounding areas *owes an absolute and no delegable duty to the community to ensure that no harm results to anyone on account of hazardous or inherently dangerous nature of the activity which it has undertaken*. The enterprise must be held to be under an obligation to provide that the hazardous or inherently dangerous activity in which it is engaged must be conducted with the highest standards of safety and if any harm results on account of such activity, the enterprise must be absolutely liable to compensate for such harm and it should be no answer to the enterprise to say that it had taken all reasonable care and that the harm occurred without any negligence on its part.[17]

In this case, the Supreme Court of India established absolute liability for certain hazardous and inherently dangerous activities even if the operator takes 'all reasonable care and that the harm occurred without any negligence'. However, the situation in the Bangladeshi shipbreaking industry is even worse than this: in this hazardous and inherently dangerous industry, worker casualties have become a regular occurrence due to the gross negligence of shipbreaking company owners and operators. Therefore, they should not only bear the civil liability; they should be held criminally responsible for killing workers.

According to Section 299 of Bangladesh Penal Code: '[w]hoever causes death by *doing an act . . . with the knowledge that he is likely by such act to cause death*, commits the offence of culpable homicide'.[18] Intentionally and knowingly sending workers to cut gigantic tankers or ships without pre-cleaning and without gas-freeing for hot work undoubtedly should be treated as *an act which is likely to cause death* of such workers. If eventually a death occurs, the owner and operator of the industry should be liable for this death. One of the main elements here is with the knowledge that likely to cause death. It should be noted that in this situation gross negligence may amount to knowledge.[19] Moreover, in many cases, superior courts in the Indian subcontinent have decided that *knowledge* about the *probable consequence* of an act will be sufficient for establishing an offence

17 *M C Mehta v. Union of India* (1987) AIR 1086 (emphasis added).

18 Penal Code, 1860 (Act No. XLV of 1860) (emphasis added).

19 D.A. Desai, M.L. Jain and N.R. Madhava Menon (eds), *Ratanlal and Dhirajlal's Law of Crimes* (Bharat Law House, 1993, 23rd ed.) 1047.

of culpable homicide.[20] It is difficult to believe that, after so many deaths in the Bangladeshi shipbreaking industry, shipbreaking company owners and operators do not have *the knowledge of the likely consequence* of sending workers with a gas-powered blowtorch to cut gigantic ships without maintaining proper Safe-for-hot-work and Safe-for-entry procedures.[21] If the law enforcing authorities are serious, it should not be difficult to prove an offence of culpable homicide. Moreover, according to Section 304A of the Penal Code of Bangladesh, causing the death of any person by doing any rash or negligent act not amounting to culpable homicide shall also be a punishable crime. The acts of shipbreakers causing death of workers also fulfils the elements of a Section 304A crime.

It is unsurprising that Bangladeshi law enforcement authorities do not initiate criminal proceedings against shipbreakers. As discussed earlier, the government clearly favours the shipbreakers and does not hesitate to change laws to favour shipbreakers. Moreover, the widespread corruption of the law enforcing agencies is also responsible for this culture of impunity. As observed by a worker in a Bangladeshi shipbreaking yard:

> Workers still die in the shipbreaking yards. Many workers suffer injuries and some have died. Workers die due to lack of safety gear. Families do not receive proper compensation for deceased family members. Owners and management are exempt from punishment. They bribe police to settle everything. The owners have never been arrested for killing workers.[22]

The main law related to labour rights in Bangladesh is the *Bangladesh Labour Act 2006* (hereinafter Labour Act). Before 2006, around 44 labour-related laws were in operation. The 2006 act replaces and revises most of these laws, and regulates issues of employment, collective bargaining and trade unions, wages, compensation, dispute settlement, health, safety, welfare and working conditions and environment for workers.[23] However, shipbreaking company owners are very reluctant to implement this act, with some even claiming that this law is not applicable for shipbreaking because shipbreaking is not an industry. However, in accordance with present and previously applicable labour laws, shipbreaking is always an industry.[24] Therefore, providing rights under the Labour Act is an

20 Ibid., 1048.

21 As observed by Hari Singh Gour, 'Now Knowledge implies consciousness. That consciousness is necessarily of future contingency the happening of which may depend upon a variety of circumstances all of which cannot possibly be present in the mind of offender'. Hari Singh Gour, *The Penal Law of India* (revised by M.C. Desai, Gyanendra Kumar and R.B. Sethi) (Vol. III, Law Publishers (India) Pvt. Limited, 1990) 2227.

22 Charles Kernaghan, 'Murder in the Shipbreaking Yards, Chittagong, Bangladesh', *Report, Institute for Global Human and Labour Rights* (November 2015) <www.globallabourrights.org/reports/document/Murder-in-the-Shipbreaking-Yards-1.pdf>.

23 *Bangladesh Labour Act, 2006* (Act No. XLII of 2006).

24 Md Saiful Karim, 'Violation of Labour Rights in the Ship-Breaking Yards of Bangladesh: Legal Norms and Reality' (2009) 25 *The International Journal of Comparative Labour Law*

obligation of shipbreaking company owners. Moreover, to please shipbreaking company owners, the Ministry of Industries made a specific gazette notification declaring shipbreaking and ship recycling to be an industry that will receive all facilities, like any other industry.[25] Although shipbreaking company owners were enthusiastic about this declaration because of the financial benefits they gain as an industry, they remain reluctant to comply with the Labour Act. Using an obscure appointment system and middlemen, shipbreaking company owners most of the time deprive their workers of legally entitled amenities, the right to form trade unions, and other protection and benefits as required under the Labour Act.[26]

Moreover, the very weak and grossly inadequate compensation system in the Labour Act is responsible for rampant killings in the guise of accidents. The highest value of a life is 100,000 taka [US$1,284] to shipbreaking yard owners in Bangladesh. Shipbreaking company owners, when not able to cover up a killing due to local media and NGO activists, pay this small compensation and then ask the relatives of a deceased worker to sign a no-claim agreement. The author has had the misfortune of viewing one such agreement signed between a shipbreaking yard owner and the parents of a young shipbreaking worker (20 years old) who died by suffocating on toxic gas in the shipbreaking yard. The words in that agreement reveal the arrogant and cruel attitude of shipbreaking company owners in Bangladesh. Any person who has a minimum respect for human rights, justice and human dignity would find the document distressing. The agreement says that the shipbreaking yard owner has no responsibility but to show sympathy when a worker dies through suffocation by toxic gas while working in his shipbreaking yard. The agreement also says that the shipbreaking company owner is paying this money to the family members of the dead worker simply as a grant, despite admitting that the worker died due to suffocation by toxic gas. This clearly shows that the shipbreaking yard owner sent him to cut the ship without a proper 'gas-free-for-man-entry' system or procedure. The incident occurred due to the reckless behaviour of the shipbreaking yard owner and was clearly not an accident but an inevitable incident caused by the shipbreaking yard owner. The owner should bear civil and criminal responsibility for this culpable homicide.

Worker compensation under the Labour Act is for compensation for injury by accident, but killings of shipbreaking workers in Bangladeshi shipbreaking yards are not just accidents. Therefore, the minimal compensation under the Labour Act is not enough. These so-called 'accidental' deaths are not accidental in the true sense because they are the result of gross negligence and reckless acts of shipbreaking company owners who direct illiterate labourers to cut gigantic ships using oxy-acetylene torches without proper 'gas-free-for-man-entry' and

---

and Industrial Relations 379; see also, *Bangladesh Environmental Lawyers Association v. Ministry of Shipping*, Writ Petition No. 7260 of 2008 (Unreported judgment dated 17 March 2009) (hereinafter *MT Enterprise* case [Judgment]).

25 Ministry of Industries Notification Number 36.061.016.07.00.012.2010 (part 1)/08 dated 21 March 2011, Published in *Bangladesh Gazette* on 21 April 2011.

26 Kernaghan, above n 22; Karim, above n 24.

'gas-free-for-hot-work' processes, or ask barefooted workers with no protective gear to carry large, heavy iron plates. Therefore, compensation for a death in the shipbreaking industry should be far higher than the normal compensation under the Labour Act. Exemplary compensation is justified considering the liability of the owners of this ultra-hazardous industry.

5.4 Initial attempts to regulate the shipbreaking industry

Although in the last 40 years shipbreaking in Bangladesh has developed into a major industry, until recently no comprehensive legislation had been developed to regulate shipbreaking. This gigantic industry was initially regulated by a circular issued by the Department of Customs in 1987.[27] The circular listed a number of clearances and certificates to be obtained from different government departments before a ship could be admitted for breaking in the Chittagong Port area.[28] The list includes, inter alia, permission for beaching from the Mercantile Marine Department, permission for beaching from the Chittagong Port, and a gas-free certificate from the Department of Explosives.[29] As this circular was issued long before the enactment of the *Environment Conservation Act*, obtaining environmental clearance under the act was not included as a condition of beaching an obsolete ship for scrapping purposes.

The Mercantile Marine Department had previously issued a circular that required shipbreaking enterprises to comply with some safety protection procedures prior to obtaining a beaching permit.[30] The circular introduced a compulsory surveying system for beaching permission.[31] However, in 1997 the BSBA filed a writ petition[32] against the Customs Department and the Mercantile Marine Department challenging the legality of a clause in the Customs Department's circular that provides for beaching permission from the Mercantile Marine Department. The court issued a *rule nisi* calling upon the respondents to demonstrate why said clause should not be declared illegal, and suspended the operation of the clause pending a hearing on the rule.[33] However, the parties involved in the writ petition never took the initiative for a final hearing of this petition. The court's decision effectively prevented the Mercantile Marine Department from taking any measures relating to pre-beaching survey of ships, which has undoubtedly increased the likelihood of environmental pollution and accidents. This writ was

27 Government of the People's Republic of Bangladesh, Custom House, Chittagong, General Notification 15 (20 April 1987).

28 Ibid.

29 Ibid.

30 Government of the People's Republic of Bangladesh, Mercantile Marine Department, Chittagong, Circular (29 May 1983).

31 Ibid.

32 *Bangladesh Ship Breakers Association v. Commissioner of Customs* (Writ Petition No. 2048 of 1997) (10 April 1997).

33 Ibid.

most likely orchestrated by shipbreaking company owners to delay or defy the implementation of the existing laws.

A vast sector such as shipbreaking cannot be guided by just a circular. There was a need for comprehensive legislation covering all aspects of shipbreaking operations so that the sector could operate in a sustainable manner. Such legislation was also needed for implementation of relevant international laws, regulations, guidelines and codes of practice. However, absence of a specialised law for the shipbreaking industry does not necessarily mean that there was no law regulating this industry. Proper enforcement of existing environmental, criminal and labour laws could have improved the situation. However, the relevant government departments showed very little interest in properly enforcing the existing laws.

5.5 Legal activism

Environmental activist organisations have undertaken a lengthy legal battle against the uncontrolled operation of shipbreaking industries in breach of the fundamental right to a decent environment, and right to life of the workers as guaranteed by the Constitution of Bangladesh, as well as other applicable laws and regulations of the country. On 19 April 2003, the BELA filed a writ petition before the HCD of the Supreme Court of Bangladesh to stop pollution of the marine environment caused by the disposal of hazardous wastes and labour rights violations in the shipbreaking industry.[34] The BELA contended that the available records suggest that no shipbreaking industries have environmental clearance as required by the *Environment Conservation Act*.[35] The BELA named all relevant government departments and the BSBA as respondents in the petition. In this case, the BELA mainly sought to compel the respondents to comply with the relevant provisions of the environmental and labour laws of the country and of the Basel Convention. Final hearing for this writ petition was never completed, mainly because the subject matter of this case was covered in subsequent writ petitions by the same organisation.

A great controversy arose in Bangladesh when some shipbreakers imported or tried to import a number of ultra-hazardous ships that had been blacklisted by Greenpeace. Greenpeace-blacklisted ships that despite repeated requests had failed to submit an inventory of hazardous wastes or provide a statement from any credible organisation regarding decontamination of toxic substances.[36]

The first attempted import of a Greenpeace-listed hazardous ship involved the *SS Norway*. Following a red alert issued by Greenpeace against the purchase of the *SS Norway* by a Bangladeshi shipbreaker, the BELA served a justice demand notice requesting that government agencies stop the entry of the *SS Norway* into

34 *Bangladesh Environmental Lawyers Association v. Bangladesh*, para 40 (Writ Petition No. 2911 of 2003).

35 Ibid.

36 Greenpeace, *50 Ships in the Spotlight* (25 June 2003) <http://archive.li/qdhK7>.

the territorial waters of Bangladesh.[37] In the notice, the BELA also informed the respective governmental and nongovernmental agencies about future legal action if they failed to prohibit the entry of this ship containing hazardous substances to Bangladesh.[38]

Subsequently, the government of Bangladesh in an inter-ministerial meeting declared that, according to the Basel Convention and other international regulations, the country had a right to decline to import any ship that can damage its environment, and hence decided to refuse the entry of the *SS Norway* into the territorial waters of Bangladesh.[39] The Environment Minister told journalists that '[w]e have information that the ship is carrying toxic materials like asbestos and mono-carbon and asked the authorities concerned to keep vigil so that it cannot enter our territory'.[40] The Ministry of Shipping wrote to the Department of Shipping, the Chittagong Port Authority and the Mercantile Marine Department in Chittagong directing them to take effective steps to ensure that this hazardous ship could not be imported to Bangladesh for scrapping.[41] Upon receipt these instructions, the Department of Shipping issued a letter to the Governor of Bangladesh Bank requesting him to instruct all banks to ensure that a No Objection Certificate (NOC) be obtained from the Department of Shipping before opening a Letter of Credit for importing any ship to Bangladesh.[42] Following these interventions from different governmental and nongovernmental institutions, the attempted import of the *SS Norway* to Bangladesh was finally abandoned.[43]

After the failure to import the toxic ship *SS Norway* to Bangladesh for scrapping, a shipbreaker tried to import another toxic ship for scrapping, a single-hull oil tanker called the *MT Alfaship*, despite successive refusals by the Department of Shipping to give a NOC.[44] The Department of Shipping informed the importer that because the scrapping of this ship would be extremely hazardous to the environment of the country, it was not possible to give a NOC to open a Letter of Credit for importation of the ship into Bangladesh for scrapping.[45] However, a controversy arose when the Bangladesh Navy informed the Department

37 BELA, *Justice Demand Notice No. LN/2006–16* (14 February 2006).

38 Ibid.

39 Government of the People's Republic of Bangladesh, Ministry of Environment and Forest, Letter No. POBOMO/Sha-6/Paper Clipping/2–2005/51 (16 February 2006).

40 New Age, 'Government Bans Toxic Material-Laden Ship from Entering Bangladesh' *New Age* (online) 17 February 2006 <www.newagebd.com/2006/feb/17/front.html#3>.

41 Government of the People's Republic of Bangladesh, Ministry of Shipping, Letter No. NOUPAM/JAHAJ/8(3)/2005/54 (2 February 2006).

42 Government of the People's Republic of Bangladesh, Department of Shipping, Letter No. 064/CNS/SCRP/9734(1) (22 February 2006).

43 New Age, above n 40.

44 Government of the People's Republic of Bangladesh, Department of Shipping, Letter No. Shipping-181-JA: AA:/2006/0029 (4 April 2006); see also, Government of the People's Republic of Bangladesh, Department of Shipping, Letter No. Shipping-181-JA: AA:/2006/3869(8) (23 April 2006) (hereinafter DoS Letter No. Shipping-181-JA: AA:/2006/3869(8)).

45 DoS Letter No. Shipping-181-JA: AA:/2006/3869(8), ibid.

of Shipping that it needed a court order to prevent any commercial ship from entering the territory of Bangladesh.[46]

Despite refusal by the Department of Shipping to allow the *MT Alfaship* to be brought into Bangladesh for scrapping purposes, the ship reached the outer anchorage of Chittagong Port.[47] Against this backdrop, the BELA filed a writ petition before a division bench of the HCD of the Bangladesh Supreme Court.[48] Upon hearing the petition, the court called upon the respondents to defend their failure to stop the entry of the vessel into the territorial waters of the country.[49] It also directed the respondents to explain why the arrival of the vessel without permission from the concerned authority should not be declared illegal.[50] At the same time, the court required the government to show why it should not be directed to take proper steps for banning the import of the 50 hazardous vessels listed by Greenpeace into the country.[51]

Pending hearing on the rule, the Supreme Court directed different government authorities to not allow the *MT Alfaship* to proceed further towards Chittagong Port or the internal waters of Bangladesh for two months.[52] After a hearing, the importer ultimately decided not to break the ship in Bangladesh, and the ship left the country's territorial waters.[53] In this case, a division bench of the HCD of the Supreme Court of Bangladesh directed the government to make a regulation to prohibit the import of hazardous ships for scrapping, thereby complying with the country's obligation under the Basel Convention.[54]

In this case, the petitioner contended that according to the Basel Convention it is required that the vessel (as waste) can only be imported after PIC from exporting, importing and transit states. Moreover, there must be a declaration stating that the importing country has an environmentally sound facility that meets the environmentally sound management rules of the exporting country.[55] The petitioner further contended that the concerned Bangladeshi departments never consented to the import of the ship into Bangladesh and, hence, that both the notification and the environmentally sound management requirements of the Basel Convention were violated by the shipbreaker in importing the *MT Alfaship* to Bangladesh for recycling.[56] The petitioner also argued that, although refusing

46 Commodore Commanding BNS Flotilla, Letter No. COMBAN/OPS-138/1033 (25 April 2006).

47 BELA, *Justice Demand Notice* (28 April 2006).

48 *Bangladesh Environmental Lawyers Association v. Bangladesh*, Writ Petition No. 3916 of 2006 (Unreported, Bangladesh Supreme Court High Court Division) (hereinafter *MT Alfaship* case).

49 Ibid.

50 Ibid.

51 Ibid.

52 Ibid.

53 Ibid.

54 Ibid.

55 Ibid., at para 23.

56 Ibid., at para 24.

to allow entry of the *SS Norway*, the Bangladesh government took the position that, according to the Basel Convention, Bangladesh reserves the right to refuse to import hazardous materials carriers.[57] Consequently, in this case, the Supreme Court directed the government to take immediate steps so that ships containing hazardous materials cannot enter Bangladesh for shipbreaking purposes.[58] Thus, this decision appears to create the legal obligation for government authorities to refuse entry of any hazardous ships to Bangladesh.

In another incident, despite the Supreme Court's embargo on the importation of hazardous ships to Bangladesh, an importer tried to import another ocean liner, the *MT Apsheron*, which is one of the hazardous ships blacklisted by Greenpeace. Following a vigorous protest by the media and environmental activists, the government on 14 January 2007 denied the ocean liner *MT Apsheron* entry to Bangladesh until it was first decontaminated somewhere outside the country.[59]

Environmental activists and researchers have long demanded that the Supreme Court of Bangladesh come forward and take a more proactive role in guiding the government in taking necessary steps to ensure the fundamental right to a healthy environment[60] by stressing environmental compliance within the shipbreaking industry. A proactive role is needed in the shipbreaking industry, where some of the most sacred human rights (e.g. the right to life, health and a safe working environment) are blatantly dishonoured. The Bangladesh Supreme Court has indeed played an instrumental role in the development of a regulatory framework for this industry.

In another case brought by the BELA, also related to the importation of a Greenpeace-listed hazardous ship named the *MT Enterprise*, a division bench of the HCD of the Bangladesh Supreme Court, comprised of Justice Md. Imman Ali and Justice Sheikh Abdul Awal, gave a number of directions to the government. The vessel in question changed its name several times. The *MT Enterprise* case reveals serious inadequacies in the Bangladeshi regulatory and institutional framework. Although this writ petition was prompted by importation of a particular vessel, the HCD of the Supreme Court critically and comprehensively examined the regulatory framework for shipbreaking industry generally. The broader context of this decision is discussed here rather than specific issues related to the vessel *MT Enterprise*. In his judgment, Justice Md. Imman Ali provided valuable guidance and direction for safe and environmentally sound management of the shipbreaking industry. In an initial order issued in the same case, the court

57 Ibid., at paras 11, 12, 25.

58 Ibid.

59 Staff Correspondent, 'Toxic Ship Barred from Chittagong Port' *The Daily Star* (online) 15 January 2007 <www.thedailystar.net/2007/01/15/d7011501044.htm>.

60 In Bangladesh, like 'other common law countries with written constitution, neither the Constitution nor the judiciary is supreme, and the Supreme Court is the final interpreter of law . . . The function of the judiciary includes the enhancement of rule of law, to promote the fundamental rights, and to administer the law impartially between citizen and state and between citizen and citizen. The judiciary can mould principles of law and give them a sense of coherence and direction'. Jona Razzaque, 'Access to Environmental Justice: Role of the Judiciary in Bangladesh' (2000) 4 *Bangladesh Journal of Law* 1, 1.

ordered the Department of Environment to submit a report including the number of shipbreaking yards/projects operating without obtaining an environmental clearance certificate.[61] Subsequently, the Department of Environment submitted a report showing that none of the shipbreaking companies have environmental clearance.[62] This case also reveals that the concerned government department gave NOC for the vessel *MT Enterprise* without proper scrutiny.[63]

The HCD gave a number of directions to the government after hearing the *MT Enterprise* case. The court directed the Ministry of Environment and Department of Environment 'to immediately take steps to ensure closure of all shipbreaking yards which are operating without necessary Environmental Clearance as required by law'.[64] However, this direction was initially stayed by the Appellate Division of the Bangladesh Supreme Court. Following the judgment, some shipbreaking yards obtained environmental clearance certificates. However, the BELA filed a contempt of court petition in 2015 claiming that shipbreaking yards are not following the conditions listed in their environmental clearance.[65] After hearing the applicant, a division bench of the HCD of the Bangladesh Supreme Court issued a contempt rule against 14 senior government officials, including secretaries of different ministries and the president of the BSBA asking them to 'explain why proceedings should not be initiated against them and why they should not be punished for deliberately and persistently ignoring safety of workers and protection of environment in gross violation of its March 2009 judgment'.[66] The case is currently pending before the HCD.

In the *MT Enterprise* case, the court also directed the Ministry of Environment to frame rules and regulations for the proper handling and management of hazardous materials and wastes, in light of the *Environment Conservation Act*, the Basel Convention and the Labour Act.[67] To comply with this direction, the Ministry of Environment framed the Hazardous Wastes and Shipbreaking Wastes Management Rules, 2011 and the Ministry of Industries formulated the Ship Breaking and Recycling Rules, 2011. These rules are briefly discussed in the next section.

61 *Bangladesh Environmental Lawyers Association v. Ministry of Shipping (MT Enterprise)*, Writ Petition No. 7260 of 2008 (Unreported order dated 30 November 2008).
62 *MT Enterprise* case (Judgment), above n 24.
63 Ibid.
64 Ibid.
65 NGO Shipbreaking Platform, *Press Release–Bangladesh High Court Issues Contempt Rule against 14 Government Officials: Ministries and Shipbreakers Asked to Account for Non-Compliance with 2009 Judgement* (12 April 2016) <www.shipbreakingplatform.org/press-release-bangladesh-high-court-issues-contempt-rule-against-14-government-officials-ministries-and-shipbreakers-asked-to-account-for-non-compliance-with-2009-judgement/> (hereinafter NGO Shipbreaking Platform Press Release); *Bangladesh Environment Lawyers Association (BELA) v. Shafique Alam Mehedi and Others*, Contempt Petition(H) 304 of 2015.
66 Staff Correspondent, 'Safety in Ship-Breaking: 14 Govt High Officials Face Contempt Rule' *The Daily Star* (online) 12 April 2016 <www.thedailystar.net/backpage/14-govt-high-officials-face-contempt-rule-1208011>.
67 *MT Enterprise* case (Judgment), above n 24.

5.6 Regulatory developments for shipbreaking

Due to the direction from the Supreme Court, as well as national and international media attention, some initiatives have been taken by the Bangladesh government with respect to regulatory reform to ensure environmentally sustainable shipbreaking operations. However, the serious influence of the industry on the government's decision making process has handicapped initiatives for regulatory reform. As discussed in this section, the government has frequently changed its position in response to the demands of shipbreaking company owners. The following section briefly discusses the Import Policy Order, the Hazardous Wastes and Shipbreaking Wastes Management Rules, the Ship Breaking and Recycling Rules and the *Draft Ship Recycling Act.*

5.6.1 Changes in the Import Policy Order

The *Imports and Exports (Control) Act 1950* provides power to the Bangladesh government to publish orders relating to prohibition, restriction and control of the import to Bangladesh of goods of any specified description.[68] The Bangladesh government usually adopts a new Import Policy Order under this law every three years. According to the Bangladesh Import Policy Order 2006–2009, unless otherwise specified in the order, importing any kind of waste was restricted.[69] This order did not recognise obsolete ships as an importable item in Bangladesh. If this order were to be applied strictly, it would have been impossible to import end-of-life ships containing hazardous wastes. However, in violation of this law while it was operational, shipbreaking company owners regularly imported obsolete ships with inbuilt hazardous wastes for scrapping. The government always showed leniency in enforcing this law against shipbreaking company owners. However, there was a short-lived attempt from the Ministry of Commerce to apply and strengthen this provision. In the Import Policy Order 2009–2012, the following provision was added along with the above provision of restriction for import of waste:

> In case of import of scrap vessels (HS Heading No. 89.08), a certificate containing the goods is *free from all poisonous and hazardous garbage materials* issued from the government of exporting country or an authority approved by the government, must be submitted with shipping documents.[70]

For a short period, this provision prevented the import of obsolete ships with hazardous materials without pre-cleaning. This provision received serious opposition from the shipbreaking industry.[71] A newspaper report shows that the Ministry

68 *Imports and Exports (Control) Act, 1950* (Act No. XXXIX of 1950), s. 3(1).
69 Import Policy Order 2006–2009 (No. S.R.O. 73-LAW/2007) Annexure-1, para 1.6.
70 Import Policy Order 2009–2012 (No. S.R.O. 22-LAW/2010).
71 Kawsar Khan, 'Ship-Breaking Conundrum' *The Daily Star* (online) 10 March 2010 <www.thedailystar.net/news-detail-129383>; Staff Correspondent Ctg, 'Ctg Ship-Breakers Protest

of Environment, rather than advocating for effective environmental regulation, requested that the Ministry of Commerce to change this newly introduced provision.[72] The then Minister for Commerce initially said to a journalist that the government would not change this rule.[73] However, less than three months later, the government changed its position and replaced the above provision with the following:

> In case of import of scrap vessels (HS Heading No. 89.08), a certificate to the effect that 'no *poisonous or hazardous waste except inbuilt materials of the ship* is not being carried' issued by the last exporter or owner and a declaration of the importer must be submitted with shipping documents.
>
> Provided that, provisions of *Bangladesh Environment Protection Act 1995* (Act No. 1 of 1995) and rules and regulations thereon shall be observed in case of ship breaking.[74]

A similar provision has been added to subsequent import policy orders.[75] The new provision in import policy orders permits the import of hazardous waste if it is part of the inbuilt materials of a ship. This change of law indicates the serious influence that the shipbreaking industry has over the government decision-making process. Shipbreaking company owners in Bangladesh defy almost all provisions of the *Environment Conservation Act*; therefore, permitting them to import poisonous or hazardous wastes in the inbuilt materials of a ship is undoubtedly a serious concern.

Despite changes in favour of the shipbreaking industry, one provision in the current Import Policy Order of Bangladesh may nevertheless make import of some obsolete vessels illegal. The current Import Policy Order prohibits import of POPs listed in the Stockholm Convention.[76] The policy specifically prohibits import of POPs including, inter alia, PCBs and hexachlorobenzene (HCB), which are listed as POPs in the Stockholm Convention.[77] PCBs may be present in older ships.[78] A 2015 study by a group of researchers from Norway and Bangladesh found high concentrations of PAHs, PCBs and HCB at sites near the

---

New Policy' *The Daily Star* (online) 23 February 2010 <www.thedailystar.net/news-detail-127519>.

72 Pinaki Roy, 'Environment Ministry Favours Polluters: Writes to Commerce Ministry to Allow Scrap Ship without Pre-Export Cleaning' *The Daily Star* (online) 20 February 2010 <www.thedailystar.net/news-detail-127111>.

73 See, Staff Correspondent, 'Already Imported Old Ships Will Get Exemption' (translated from Bengali) *Daily Prothom Alo* (online) 23 February 2010 <http://archive.prothom-alo.com/detail/news/44413>.

74 S. R. O. No. 107-Law/2010 of 11 April 2010.

75 Import Policy Order 2012–2015 (No. S.R.O. 411-Ain/2012); Import Policy Order 2015–2019 (No. S.R.O. 28-Law/2016 of 15 February 2016).

76 Import Policy Order 2015–2019 (No. S.R.O. 28-Law/2016 of 15 February 2016), annex 1.

77 Ibid.

78 EPA, *Polychlorinated Biphenyls (PCBs) in Ships* <www.epa.gov/pcbs/polychlorinated-biphenyls-pcbs-ships>.

shipbreaking yards in Chittagong.[79] Therefore, under the Import Policy Order 2015–2019 it is illegal to import ships containing PCBs or HCB to Bangladesh. However, it is highly unlikely that the government will enforce this provision against the shipbreaking industry.

5.6.2 *Hazardous wastes and shipbreaking wastes management rules, 2011*

To comply with the direction of the Supreme Court in the *MT Enterprise* case, the Ministry of Environment framed the Hazardous Wastes and Shipbreaking Wastes Management Rules on 22 December 2011 in exercise of the powers conferred by Section 20 of the Bangladesh *Environment Conservation Act.*[80] These rules implement the Basel Convention and provide that the importer and exporter of hazardous substances must comply with the provisions of the Basel Convention.[81] The rules provide for constituting a National Technical Committee for Hazardous Waste and Shipbreaking comprised of government officials, scientific and academic institutions, and representatives of environmentalist organisations and the shipbreaking industry.[82] This is in line with the following direction given by the Supreme Court in the *MT Enterprise* case:

> The Government is directed to set up a High Level Technical Committee comprising representatives from the Ministry/Department of Shipping, the Ministry/Department of Environment, Ministry of Labour and Manpower, Retired Naval officers, Academicians/Experts in the field of Marine Engineering, Marine Biology Specialists in the field of Environment, Soil Science and Ecology, Hazardous Waste Management and relevant NGOs, such as BELA.[83]

However, six years after the formulation of this rule and eight years after the Supreme Court's judgment in the *MT Enterprise* case, this committee is yet to be established. Last year the Supreme Court issued a contempt of court ruling against the government because of its failure to implement the above direction.[84] An environmental NGO claimed that this High Level Technical Committee 'has never been made functional – thus, there is no impartial supervision of the industry'.[85]

The rules outline provisions for export, import and management of hazardous wastes, and make it mandatory to obtain clearance prior to import hazardous

79 Therese H. Nøst et al., 'High Concentrations of Organic Contaminants in Air from Ship Breaking Activities in Chittagong, Bangladesh' (2015) 49 *Environmental Science and Technology* 11372.

80 *Hazardous Wastes and Shipbreaking Wastes Management Rules*, 2011 (SRO No. 369-Law/2011).

81 Ibid., Rule 17.

82 Ibid., Rule 3.

83 *MT Enterprise* case (Judgment), above n 24.

84 Staff Correspondent, above n 73.

85 NGO Shipbreaking Platform Press Release, above n 65.

materials in Bangladesh. They clearly prohibit issuance of any clearance certificate for import of hazardous wastes or Greenpeace-blacklisted vessels to Bangladesh. The original rules framed on 22 December 2011 contained a provision that clearance cannot be issued for importation of a sea-going vessel, oil tanker or fishing trawler for breaking purposes unless there is a certificate from the government or a government-appointed expert from the exporting country that the ship has been decontaminated and has no hazardous wastes.[86] This is effectively a provision for pre-cleaning. However, like the amendment to the Import Policy Order discussed above, this provision was also short-lived. Less than one year after the enactment, on 15 November 2012, the government changed the rule and lifted this requirement. The requirement for a certificate from the exporting country was replaced by the requirement for a certificate issued by the relevant Bangladeshi authority under the Import Policy Order discussed above.[87] This means that a certificate issued by the last exporter or owner, and a declaration from the importer that no poisonous or hazardous waste *except inbuilt materials* of the ship is being carried will be sufficient to import.[88] Unfortunately, most of the hazardous wastes in a ship may be in the form of *inbuilt materials*. This is an example of how an apparently simple change can make an entire law ineffective for practical purposes. It can be assumed that this change was made with the aim of making the law ineffective and creating room for the import of obsolete ships with inbuilt hazardous materials or wastes. It is clear that the amended Hazardous Wastes and Shipbreaking Wastes Management Rules, 2011 will not be able to prevent import of obsolete ships with hazardous wastes. Rather, the rules will encourage such import.

Nevertheless, the rules contain some provisions that may be helpful in minimising environmental harm from the shipbreaking industry. Rule 15 elaborates on a provision for operation of the shipbreaking industry. This rule makes separate environmental clearance for each ship mandatory before breaking. It also provides that before submitting an application for environmental clearance, the ship must be inspected by a government inspection team to determine the quantity of hazardous materials and hazardous wastes. It also outlines measures for safe and environmentally sound shipbreaking. However, as with many other laws, shipbreaking company owners in Bangladesh are flouting this rule with impunity. One newspaper report suggests that from January to November 2016, 190 ships were imported for dismantling in Chittagong. Only 12 of these imports received environmental clearance from the Department of Environment.[89]

86 *Hazardous Wastes and Shipbreaking Wastes Management Rules*, 2011 (SRO No. 369-Law/2011) (21 December 2011) Rule 15(D).

87 SRO No. 386-Law/2012 amending the *Hazardous Wastes and Shipbreaking Wastes Management Rules* (15 November 2012).

88 Ibid.

89 Mintu Chowdhury, 'Bangladesh Ship-Breakers Contend No Need for Environmental Clearance' *Bdnews24.com* (online) 7 November 2016 <http://bdnews24.com/bangladesh/2016/11/07/no-need-to-environmental-clearance-say-ship-breakers-in-bangladesh>.

5.6.3 Ship Breaking and Recycling Rules, 2011

The Ministry of Industries formulated the Ship Breaking and Recycling Rules, 2011 in pursuance to the direction of the Supreme Court in the *MT Enterprise* case.[90] These rules mainly implement the Hong Kong Convention.

The rules provide for the constitution of a Ship Building and Ship Recycling Board (SBSRB) providing a one-stop service for the ship recycling industry. This board will operate under the Ministry of Industries in association with other relevant government agencies including the National Board of Revenue (NBR), Department of Environment, Department of Shipping, Department of Explosives, Department for Factories and Establishment, Mercantile Marine Department, Port Authority and Department of Labour. The SBSRB has power to give NOC to facilitate a Letter of Credit to import a scrap vessel after evaluation and examination of the ship and relevant documents and in cooperation with all relevant government departments. However, there is no information available about the constitution of this board. As discussed in the next section, the concept of the SBSRB will probably be replaced by another board under the proposed *Ship Recycling Act.*

These rules elaborate on the procedures for arrival of ships to ship recycling yards, the procedure for beaching permission, the ship recycling process including the SRFP and SRP, worker safety and hazardous waste management, environmental compliance and management of OHS. Although the rules make some provisions for safe and environmentally sound ship recycling, there are some serious loopholes. Considering the approach of some government departments discussed above it would not be surprising if those loopholes were created deliberately. For example, clause 3(3) of the rules provides that the Department of Environment should provide environmental clearance to a ship without examining the inbuilt hazardous and toxic materials of the ship.[91] Nevertheless, the rules contain some good provisions, including the requirement for certificates for 'gas-free-for-man-entry' and 'gas-free-for-hot-work', which could bring positive change to the shipbreaking industry. However, none of these provisions has been properly implemented in practice. Deaths, disabilities and environmental pollution remain common occurrences in the Bangladeshi shipbreaking industry more than half a decade after formulation of the Ship Breaking and Recycling Rules, 2011. As observed by a group of environmentalist organisations:

> The political clout of the shipbreaking industry, amongst them members of Parliament and other powerful politicians as well as some of the most

90 *Ship Breaking and Recycling Rules, 2011* (Ministry of Industries Gazette Notification dated 12 December 2011, an amended gazette notification published on 11 January 2012).

91 'In cooperation with the SBSRB the Department of Environment simultaneously examines the ship for Hazardous Waste and material excluding in built hazardous and toxic materials and they may issue an environment clearance certificate for that particular ship'. *Ship Breaking and Recycling Rules, 2011*, Rule 3(3).

influential industrialists in the country, managed hastily issued environmental clearances for their yards. For the import of end-of-life vessels to Bangladesh, the authorities blindly accept fake certificates stating that all the old ships are free of hazardous waste.[92]

Against this backdrop, rather than implementing existing laws and rules, the Ministry of Industries decided to enact a new law. The next section briefly discusses that draft law.

5.6.4 Draft Bangladesh Ship Recycling Act

On 30 January 2017, the Cabinet of Bangladesh approved the *Draft Bangladesh Ship Recycling Act 2017*.[93] The draft has been placed before the parliament for enactment on 10 July 2017.[94] The draft law includes provisions for establishing ship recycling zones and yards. According to the draft act, the government can declare a ship recycling zone through gazette notification.[95] The Cabinet Secretary of Bangladesh informed journalists after a cabinet meeting that the government will establish a ship recycling zone in Chittagong for ship recycling companies.[96]

According to the draft act, seeking government permission will be mandatory for establishing a ship recycling yard within the zone. No ship recycling yard can be established outside a ship recycling zone. Ship recycling yards operating within the declared zone prior to declaration of the zone must seek permission to continue from the government within a timeframe to be determined by the government. If an existing ship recycling yard fails to apply for permission, operation of the yard cannot continue and its assets will be forfeited.[97] Establishing a ship recycling yard without government permission or operating a ship recycling yard outside the declared zone will be an offence punishable by imprisonment for a time not exceeding two years, a fine of 1–3 million taka, or both.[98]

The draft law provides for establishing a new board called the Bangladesh Ship Recycling Board. The act will require a NOC from the board for the import of obsolete vessels to Bangladesh for recycling. Import or collection of a ship for recycling, and beaching and recycling of a ship without a NOC from the board, will be an offence punishable by imprisonment for a maximum of two years, a fine of 1–3 million taka, or both. The draft act provides the board with a duty to ensure implementation of international law and conventions with respect to

92 NGO Shipbreaking Platform Press Release, above n 65.

93 Tribune Online Report, 'Cabinet Clears Draft Ship Recycling Law' *Dhaka Tribune* (online) 30 January 2017 <http://archive.dhakatribune.com/environment/2017/jan/30/cabinet-clears-draft-ship-recycling-law>.

94 *Draft Bangladesh Ship Recycling Act*, (Bangladesh National Parliament, Bill No 16/2017).

95 *Draft Bangladesh Ship Recycling Act*, s. 4.

96 Tribune Online Report, above n 93.

97 *Draft Bangladesh Ship Recycling Act*, s. 5.

98 *Draft Bangladesh Ship Recycling Act*, s. 25.

ship recycling activities.[99] The functions and powers of the board will be the following:

- Overall supervision of ship recycling activities;
- Periodic monitoring and evaluation of ship recycling yards;
- Approval of ship recycling plan;
- Approval of ship recycling facility plan;
- Evaluation of hazardous waste management related activities of ships;
- Coordination with concerned ministry, institution and department for assurance of workers' health and safety and elimination of occupational risks;
- Coordination with concerned ministry, institution and department for undertaking activities in light of environment related laws for ensuring environmentally sound ship recycling;
- Providing recommendation and proposal to the government for development of ship recycling industry;
- Providing recommendation to government for establishment of new ship recycling zone or extension of existing ship recycling zone for development of ship recycling industry;
- Receiving national and international assistance for ship recycling activities and signing contract with national and international institutions or organisations for this purpose with the prior approval of the government;
- Establishing mutual relationship with national and international organisations, research institutions and universities; and
- Other duties entrusted by the government.[100]

The proposed Bangladesh Ship Recycling Board will be constituted under the chairpersonship of an Additional Secretary of the Ministry of Industries, including a joint secretary from the Ministry of Industries, a joint secretary from the Ministry of Forests and Environment, a joint secretary from the Ministry of Labour and Employment, a joint secretary from the Energy and Mineral Resources Division of the Ministry of Power, Energy and Mineral Resources, a commissioner from the NBR, a representative of the Chittagong Port Authority, the President of the Ship Recycling Industry Association, and two more members representing ship recycling industry owners nominated by the government. The board will also have a Director General who will act as its member-secretary.

The most important difference between the proposed Bangladesh Ship Recycling Board and the SBSRB discussed in the previous section is that it includes three shipbreaking company owners (or so-called ship *recycling* industry owners) as members. This is highly problematic because the proposed board does not include representatives from the scientific community or civil society organisations. To clarify, the only nongovernmental members of the board will be three

99 *Draft Bangladesh Ship Recycling Act*, s. 7.
100 *Draft Bangladesh Ship Recycling Act*, s. 11.

shipbreaking company owners, meaning that the so-called ship recycling industry will have more representation than the lead ministry, the Ministry of Industries.

This situation seems even more problematic after careful consideration of the decision-making processes of the proposed board. At meetings of the board every member will have one vote and decisions will be made by a simple majority of members present and voting. One-third of the members will constitute a voting quorum for any meeting. The board will have only 11 members, including three shipbreaking company owners. Therefore, it will be possible to have a meeting at which the three shipbreaking industry owners and just one government official member is present (4 out of 11, more than one-third) and at such a meeting the shipbreaking company owners could make any decision. Even if only five members of the board, including the three shipbreaking company owners, were present at a meeting, the shipbreaking owners could still make any decision because they would have the majority. In any case, with 3 of the 11 members being shipbreaking company owners, they will have a serious influence on the board. This is unacceptable because the board will have the power to make decisions regarding approvals of SRPs and SRFPs. Shipbreaking company owners may have a pecuniary interest and bias in this respect. The inclusion of shipbreaking company owners – or so-called ship recycling industry owners – on the board will create a serious conflict of interest and represent a gross violation of the principles of natural justice; in short, the board will not be able to make unbiased decisions.

It is not unusual to have industry members on government advisory committees. However, the powers and functions listed for this board are not advisory in nature. As mentioned earlier, the board will have the power to approve applications in which ship recycling owners have a pecuniary interest; board members should not be applicant and decision maker at the same. It is hoped that the parliament will consider this important legal issue and change the formation of the board before enacting this law.

It is also frustrating that rather than operationalising the High Level Technical Committee as directed by the Supreme Court in the *MT Enterprise* case, the government is going to create a board dominated by shipbreaking company owners without any representation of other stakeholders and national labour rights organisations. This attitude indicates that positive change will not come to the Bangladeshi shipbreaking industry in the near future. The future of environmental justice in the shipbreaking industry is gloomy.

5.7 Institutional aspects

The institutional framework in Bangladesh for regulation of shipbreaking is fragmented. The Department of Environment is responsible for implementing the Basel Convention and enforcing the *Environmental Conservation Act* in the shipbreaking industry of Bangladesh. Bangladesh has been a party to the Basel Convention from 1993 through accession but yet to ratify the Basel Ban amendment and the Basel Protocol on Liability and Compensation. Bangladesh appointed its Secretary of the Ministry of Environment and Forest as National Focal Point and Competent Authority as required by the Basel Convention.[101] The Ministry of Environment and Forests is also responsible for implementation of the Stockholm Convention.[102] The Ministry of Labour and Employment is responsible for labour rights-related matters.

The Department of Shipping under the Ministry of Shipping is responsible for implementation of IMO conventions. However, following recent changes in the allocation of business, the Ministry of Industries has become the key regulatory agency for shipbreaking and ship recycling activities in Bangladesh. Other government ministries and agencies, such as the Mercantile Marine Department, NBR, Chief Inspector of Factories and Establishment, Coast Guard, Chief Inspector of Explosives, Chittagong Port Authority, Fire Service and Civil Defence, Bangladesh Police and Bangladesh Navy also bear varying degrees of responsibility with respect to the shipbreaking industry.

In Bangladesh, different government agencies are working in the same areas with overlapping and conflicting duties and responsibilities. Until the Supreme Court specifically ordered it, the relevant government agencies did not propose that the government enact implementing legislation for the Basel Convention or other international legal instruments. After repeated directions from the apex court, various government agencies took the initiative for regulatory development. However, the interests of the concerned departments were directed more towards a bureaucratic power grab rather than establishing an effective legal and institutional structure for prevention of pollution and ensuring the safety of workers. Despite achieving the powers they desired, they have shown very little interest in the enforcement of those powers in an effective manner. For example, as discussed earlier, the Department of Shipping played a proactive role in refusing to give NOCs for two ships carrying hazardous materials. However, as soon as its newly found power with respect to shipbreaking was confirmed, the department began showing its true colours. In the *MT Enterprise* case, the court expressed serious dissatisfaction about an officer who provided a NOC to the ship when admittedly she was not able to collect the necessary information about the Greenpeace blacklisting of said ship. The court also expressed serious concerns that the department had not taken any action against the officer.[103]

As shown in Table 5.1, although the Department of Environment under the Ministry of Environment and Forest is responsible for implementation of the Basel Convention, it has no role in the process of import clearance. Although the *Environment Conservation Act 1995*, a forward-looking legal instrument, gives the Department of Environment ample power to regulate the shipbreaking industry, it has never honestly attempted to apply the provisions of the act to that industry. Department of Environment officials sometimes speak as if they were a

101 Secretariat of the Basel Convention, *Country Contacts* <www.basel.int/Countries/CountryContacts/tabid/1342/Default.aspx>.

102 Secretariat of the Stockholm Convention Clearing House, *Country Contacts* <http://chm.pops.int/Countries/CountryContacts/tabid/304/Default.aspx>.

103 *MT Enterprise* case (Judgment), above n 24.

Table 5.1 Key Government and Business Agencies Involved in Shipbreaking

Name	*Role*
Ministry of Industries ↓ Ship Recycling Board (Proposed)	• Regulation of industrial operations • Leading role in the proposed Ship Recycling Board • Leading role in the so-called one-stop service for shipbreaking company owners • Enforcement of the Ship Breaking and Recycling Rules, 2011 • Enforcement of the *Bangladesh Ship Recycling Act* (approved by the Cabinet, yet to be enacted by the Parliament) • Providing No Objection Certificates (NOCs) for import of ships for breaking/recycling
Ministry of Environment and Forest ↓ Department of Environment	• Overall management and protection of the environment • Implementation of international environmental conventions including the Basel Convention on the Control of Transboundary Movement of Hazardous Wastes and their Disposal • Enforcement of the *Environment Conservation Act 1995*, Environment Conservation Rules, 1997 and Hazardous Wastes and Shipbreaking Wastes Management Rules, 2011
Ministry of Shipping ↓ Department of Shipping ↓ Mercantile Marine Department	• Implementation of International Maritime Organization conventions including the Hong Kong Convention • Control of the beaching of ships for scrapping • NOCs to ships entering Chittagong Port
Ministry of Commerce	• Implementation and enforcement of the Import Policy Order
National Board of Revenue (NBR) ↓ Bangladesh Customs	• Control import of obsolete ships for scrapping
Ministry of Labour and Employment ↓ Chief Inspector of Factories and Establishment	• Promotion of labour welfare • Registration of shipbreaking yards as factories/industries • Monitoring working conditions of shipbreaking enterprises • Enforcement of the *Bangladesh Labour Act 2006* and other labour laws
Chief Inspector of Explosives Chittagong Port Authority Fire Service and Civil Defence	• Responsible for regulating ship scrapping activities as shipbreaking company owners are required to obtain permission from these agencies before scrapping a ship in Bangladesh
Bangladesh Navy and Coast Guard	• Responsible for stopping entry of ships to the territorial waters of Bangladesh if needed
Bangladesh Police and other law enforcing agencies	• Investigation and prosecution of criminal offences under the Penal Code, particularly culpable homicide and causing death by negligence of workers in shipbreaking yards
Bangladesh Ship Breakers Association (BSBA)	• Shipbreaking operations require membership in and permission from this association

mouthpiece of the shipbreaking industry. A director of the Department of Environment said in a newspaper interview: 'we [Department of Environment] are unable to take tough legal action as there is huge demand for recycled steel in the country'.[104] It is certainly not the duty of a Department of Environment official to consider how the demand for recycled steel should be fulfilled. They have a mandate to conserve the environment of the country by applying existing environmental laws. It is their duty, not merely a discretionary power, to apply the existing laws. An administrative department or a civil bureaucracy cannot seize the role of lawmaker. The *Environment Conservation Act 1995* is a law enacted by parliament that all stakeholders must follow. The Department of Environment has no jurisdiction to decide whether or not they will apply it to shipbreaking. As a government institution, the Department of Environment is legally obliged to apply existing laws relating to environmental conservation wherever applicable. Moreover, after the decisions in the *MT Alfaship* and *MT Enterprise* cases, such an approach may be in contempt of the country's highest court. The court, in its judgment, also highlighted the government authorities' negligence in enforcing the applicable laws of the country.[105]

Recent statistics shows that Bangladesh is scrapping the largest number of ships.[106] Proper enforcement of environmental law will not be a bottleneck in the growth of this industry. It should be a driving force for sustainable development of this industry and the country. The attitude of considering environmental protection as a burden to the industry in the long run will do real harm to the industry, the environment and the economy of the country. If the country fails to properly implement present and upcoming international regulations, the shipbreaking industry in Bangladesh will not be able to operate in the future. The Bangladeshi regulatory system should be strengthened as soon as possible to overcome the challenges of upcoming developments in international law. In the future, this industry may have to compete with an environmentally compliant industry in Europe.[107] Strengthening the national regulatory system is needed

104 'Chittagong Set to Become Graveyard of Toxic Ships' *New Age* (online), 5 June 2005 <www.newagebd.com/2005/jun/05/front.html#1>.

105 *MT Enterprise* case (Judgment), above n 24; *MT Alfaship* case, above n 48.

106 NGO Shipbreaking Platform, *Substandard Shipbreaking: A Global Challenge* (February 2016) <www.shipbreakingplatform.org/shipbrea_wp2011/wp-content/uploads/2016/04/Worldwide-overview_FINAL.pdf>.

107 This can be predicted from a comment of the former EU Environment Commissioner Stavros Dimas: 'We will look at the viability of re-establishing ship recycling facilities in the EU. European waste shipment law is very strict in preventing movements of hazardous waste to developing countries. That is why we need facilities where ships that reach the end of their life can be safely disposed of. In some – or even many – cases, this could be in the EU'. He also observed that 'Community funds, like the structural funds, might also serve as a source of support. If we are clever and forward-looking, we might be able to provide new economic possibilities for the less developed regions of the EU that have suffered from the closure of shipyards'. Stavros Dimas, *Solutions for the Responsible Recycling of Ships* (Open Hearing, European Parliament, Brussels, 25 April 2006) <www.shipbreakingplatform.org/shipbrea_wp2011/wp-content/uploads/2011/11/DIMAS-SPEECH-06-259_EN.pdf>.

not only for the protection of the marine and coastal environment but also for the very existence of the industry itself.[108]

The Ministry of Industries submitted an affidavit of compliance on 8 July 2014 in the *MT Enterprise* case, claiming that no person under the age of 16 years was employed in the shipbreaking industry.[109] The ministry also submitted that the court direction for sufficient firefighting appliances was being followed in the yards.[110] In the same affidavit, the ministry made claims about compliance with other directives of the court.[111] However, the ministry did not present any credible proof for these assertions. On the contrary, newspaper reports showed that child labours are still working in this hazardous industry.[112] As observed earlier, the number of deaths in the shipbreaking industry increased in 2015 and 2016. Therefore, it appears that the Ministry of Industries most likely made an incorrect statement in the affidavit in compliance. This is an indication that regulatory institutions of the government support shipbreaking company owners and try to mislead the court.

Although the fact remains that various government departments have not taken necessary initiatives in this regard, they suffer from a chronic lack of resources, infrastructure, equipment and, most importantly, adequate and qualified manpower. Unless these lacunae in the enforcement machinery are properly and promptly addressed, the relevant conventions, legislation and regulations will all stand in abeyance. Institutional capacity building must not be limited to providing training and coordination. Implementation of international conventions involves a huge amount of investment for facilities and equipment. The government of Bangladesh must invest reasonable funds into providing pollution-detection equipment to concerned departments.

5.8 Conclusion

The overall conditions in shipbreaking yards on the Chittagong Coast are not yet in line with international standards concerning the safe and environmentally sound management of hazardous wastes. Apart from the failure to establish a well-defined legal framework in line with international standards, the government has failed to apply existing international and national legal requirements in the shipbreaking industry. It is time to bring the Bangladeshi regulatory framework

108 John F. Sawyer, 'Shipbreaking and the North–South Debate: Economic Development or Environmental and Labor Catastrophe?' (2002) 20 *Penn State International Law Review* 535, 562.

109 *Bangladesh Environmental Lawyers Association v. Ministry of Shipping (MT Enterprise)*, Writ Petition No. 7260 of 2008 (affidavit in compliance dated 8 June 2014, submitted by the Ministry of Industries, Respondent Number 2).

110 Ibid.

111 Ibid.

112 Shashank Bengali, 'Adult and Underage Workers Risk Their Lives in Bangladesh's Rising Ship-Breaking Industry' *Los Angeles Times* (online) 9 March 2016 <www.latimes.com/world/asia/la-fg-bangladesh-ships-20160309-story.html>.

into conformity with relevant international laws, rules, guidelines and codes of practice for ensuring safe and environmentally sound shipbreaking operations in Bangladesh. At the same time, government authorities must take serious and honest steps to implement existing national laws.

The situation in the industry may improve if the industry takes the initiative to establish pre-cleaning facilities using state-of-the-art technology and implement proper health and safety measures. In any case, the government and the industry should not justify serious environmental pollution and violation of labour rights for economic reasons. However, taking only a 'command and control approach' without creating financial incentives for environmental compliance may not be successful in the long run. The government should introduce market-based mechanisms to ensure financial incentives for an environmentally compliant shipbreaking industry. The government may offer a lower rate of import tax for pre-cleaned ships for scrapping. Moreover, the government may offer a 'tax holiday' or fix a subsidised price to attract local and foreign entrepreneurs to the establishment of environmentally compliant shipbreaking facilities after closing non-complaint shipbreaking yards.

This chapter has shown that NGO-inspired judicial activism has failed to ensure environmental justice in the shipbreaking industry. NGOs have undertaken legal battles by initiating a number of lawsuits in the Supreme Court of Bangladesh against the uncontrolled operations of shipbreaking companies in breach of the fundamental right to a decent environment and right to life of the workers, as well as other applicable laws and regulations. In these proceedings, the Supreme Court has taken a proactive role by directing the government to frame necessary rules for ensuring safe and environmentally sound management of the shipbreaking industry. However, none of these initiatives has altered the real scenario in the shipbreaking yards. Serious environmental pollution and violation of labour rights are still going on unabated. This chapter has argued that without an honest initiative from the government and the industry, activism from NGOs will not be successful in making any meaningful change. Workers are caught in a vicious cycle of poverty and are mostly ignorant of the dangers posed by this industry. The lack of capability to choose makes them helpless.

6 The shipbreaking industry and the forgotten people

The shipbreaking industry in Bangladesh is a perfect example of *matsyanyaya*, where big fish can freely eat small fish. Shipping companies from developed countries and rich shipbreaking company owners from Bangladesh are profiting from this industry. The victims are the poor shipbreaking workers and the natural environment of the surrounding area, neither of which has any voice or influence. The poor and mostly illiterate workers do not have the capacity to make choices or decisions. The natural environment also cannot speak. This is an example of how local and foreign commercial entities work together to oppress and exploit the most marginalised segments of society. This industry is a stain on humanity and an example of disparity in the so-called 'liberal capitalised world'. It also shows us the hollow foundation of international and national regulatory systems that can only uphold the interests of the powerful, influential and wealthy parts of society.

International and national regulatory systems have failed to ensure environmental justice in the shipbreaking industry. The Constitution of Bangladesh makes emancipation of workers from all forms of exploitation a fundamental responsibility of the state. Ironically, despite this constitutional aspiration and responsibility, Bangladesh hosts one of the most exploitative and deadly industries in the world, where the violation of labour rights and the killing of labourers are regular occurrences, with full impunity.

Bangladesh's regulatory system is an isomorphic mimicry that resembles all of the characteristics of a modern governance system on paper; but it is an ineffective system where bad drives out the good.[1] As observed by Akbar Ali Khan (a former Cabinet Secretary of Bangladesh), the Bangladesh bureaucracy is an example of Murphy's Law: 'anything that can go wrong will go wrong'.[2]

The repeated initiatives from the highest court of the country fell on deaf ears due to the notorious tendency of some government officials for ill-motivated interpretation of the court's decisions as well as their infamous skills in making

1 Akbar Ali Khan, *Gresham's Law Syndrome and Beyond: An Analysis of the Bangladesh Bureaucracy* (University Press Limited, 2015).
2 Ibid.

frequent changes to regulations in favour of the shipbreaking industry. As observed by the Supreme Court in an order in the *MT Enterprise* case:

> We wish to reiterate that the matters raised in the judgment [of the *MT Enterprise* case] are of critical importance for the future generations of this country and there is no scope for giving a go by to the intendment of the judgment by producing a narrow and technical and perhaps motivated interpretation.[3]

The regulatory mockery occurring in the shipbreaking industry is an example of how bad drives out the good. Every attempt at good governance in the regulatory apparatus for shipbreaking has faced a blow that is evident in the frequent changes to laws and responsible institutions to uphold the vested interests and greed of some highly influential individuals. The final episode of this hideous saga is witnessing a virtual transfer of government regulatory power to the shipbreaking industry through the proposed establishment of a so-called Bangladesh Ship Recycling Board – dominated by shipbreaking company owners – as the main decision making body for this sector.

Regulatory developments at the international level portray an even more depressing scenario. International legal developments in shipbreaking can be characterised by the shifting of responsibility to the shoulders of developing shipbreaking countries rather than finding a way to internalise the cost of disposal of hazardous wastes by the shipping industry that is the generator of these wastes. This is a violation of international environmental law principles and norms, particularly the polluter pays principle.

As discussed in Chapter 4, environmental justice and the human rights of the workers received no attention in the negotiation of the Hong Kong Convention. The global community considered environmentally sound and safe shipbreaking as a mere technical issue, turning a blind eye to the human face of the problem. The workers only received attention in the submissions of NGOs with a very limited scope of participation and certainly no voting rights. Even the governments of developing shipbreaking countries mainly represented the interests of the shipbreaking industry in their respective countries and totally failed to consider the poor workers. More frustratingly, they showed a tendency to deny environmental pollution and labour rights violations in their shipbreaking industries. This is unsurprising. As discussed in Chapter 4, in some IMO meetings an advisor of the BSBA participated as a representative of Bangladesh. The workers of the shipbreaking yards – dead, disabled or alive – are truly forgotten people. No one really represents them in the true sense in the international negotiation process, let alone in more local decision making forums.

The ability of shipbreaking workers to influence decision and policy making within Bangladesh is very limited due to their lack of capacity and vulnerable condition. Environmental justice for Bangladeshi shipbreaking workers remains elusive.

3 *Bangladesh Environmental Lawyers Association v. Ministry of Shipping*, Writ Petition No. 7260 of 2008 (*MT Enterprise*) (Unreported order dated 11 May 2010).

Bibliography

Books

Adamson, Joni, Evans, Mei and Stein, Rachel, *The Environmental Justice Reader: Politics, Poetics, & Pedagogy* (University of Arizona Press, 2002).
Ahmed, Naim, *Public Interest Litigation: Constitutional Issues and Remedies* (Bangladesh Legal Aid and Services Trust, 1999).
Ako, Rhuks, *Environmental Justice in Developing Countries: Perspectives from Africa and Asia-Pacific* (Routledge, 2013).
Alam, M. Shah, *Selected Writings on International Law, Constitutional Law and Human Rights* (New Warsi Book Corporation, 2016).
Anand, Ruchi, *International Environmental Justice: A North – South Dimension* (Ashgate, 2004).
Anton, Donald K. and Shelton, Dinah L., *Environmental Protection and Human Rights* (Cambridge University Press, 2011).
Basu, Kaushik et al., *International Labour Standards: History, Theory, and Policy Options* (John Wiley & Sons, 2008).
Bell, Karen, *Achieving Environmental Justice: A Cross-National Analysis* (Policy Press, 2014).
Bilchitz, David, *Poverty and Fundamental Rights: The Justification and Enforcement of Socio-Economic Rights* (Oxford University Press, 2008).
Boer, Ben, *Environmental Law Dimensions of Human Rights* (Oxford University Press, 2015).
Bryant, Bunyan I., *Environmental Justice: Issues, Policies, and Solutions* (Island Press, 1995).
Bullard, Robert Doyle, *Dumping in Dixie: Race, Class, and Environmental Quality* (Westview Press, 2000).
Bullard, Robert Doyle, *The Quest for Environmental Justice: Human Rights and the Politics of Pollution* (Sierra Club Books, 2005).
Chowdhury, Badrul Haider, *Evolution of the Supreme Court of Bangladesh* (University of Dhaka, 1990).
Cole, Luke W. and Foster, Sheila R., *From the Ground Up: Environmental Racism and the Rise of the Environmental Justice Movement* (New York University Press, 2001).
de Sadeleer, Nicolas, *Environmental Principles: From Political Slogans to Legal Rules* (Oxford University Press, 2002).
Desai, D.A., Jain, M.L. and Madhava Menon, N.R. (eds.), *Ratanlal and Dhirajlal's Law of Crimes* (Bharat Law House, 1993, 23rd ed.).

Dobson, Andrew, *Justice and the Environment: Conceptions of Environmental Sustainability and Theories of Distributive Justice* (Oxford University Press, 1998).
Dobson, Andrew (ed.), *Fairness and Futurity: Essays on Environmental Sustainability and Social Justice* (Oxford University Press, 1999).
Eni-Ibukun, Tomilola Akanle, *International Environmental Law and Distributive Justice* (Routledge, 2014).
Fraser, Nancy, *Justice Interruptus: Critical Reflections on the 'Postsocialist' Condition* (Routledge, 1997).
Gour, Hari Singh, *The Penal Law of India* (revised by M.C. Desai, Gyanendra Kumar and R.B. Sethi) (Vol. III, Law Publishers (India) Pvt. Limited, 1990).
Grear, Anna and Kotzé, Louis J., *Research Handbook on Human Rights and the Environment* (Edward Elgar Publishing, 2015).
Haque, Muhammad Ekramul, *Protection of Economic, Social and Cultural Rights: A Critical Analysis of the Fundamental Principles of State Policy in the Constitution of Bangladesh* (PhD thesis, Monash University, 2012).
Honkonen, Tuula, *The Common but Differentiated Responsibility Principle in Multilateral Environmental Agreements: Regulatory and Policy Aspects* (Kluwer Law International, 2009).
Hoque, Kazi Ebadul, *Administration of Justice in Bangladesh* (Asiatic Society of Bangladesh, 2003).
Hoque, Ridwanul, *Judicial Activism in Bangladesh: A Golden Mean Approach* (Cambridge Scholars Publishing, 2011).
Hossain, Kamal, *Economic and Social Justice under the Constitution of Bangladesh* (University of Chittagong, 2016).
Islam, Mahmudaul, *Constitutional Law of Bangladesh* (Mullick Brothers, 2012).
Kamal, Mustafa, *Bangladesh Constitution: Trends and Issues* (University of Dhaka, 1994).
Karim, Md Saiful, *Prevention of Pollution of the Marine Environment from Vessels: The Potential and Limits of the International Maritime Organisation* (Springer, 2015).
Khan, Akbar Ali, *Gresham's Law Syndrome and beyond: An Analysis of the Bangladesh Bureaucracy* (University Press Limited, Dhaka, 2015).
Kummer, Katharina, *International Management of Hazardous Wastes: The Basel Convention and Related Legal Rules* (Oxford University Press, 1995).
Laszlo, Ervin et al., *Obstacles to the New International Economic Order* (Pergamon Press, 1980).
Lessmann, Ortrud and Rauschmayer, Felix (eds.), *The Capability Approach and Sustainability* (Routledge, 2016).
Margai, Florence, *Environmental Health Hazards and Social Justice: Geographical Perspectives on Race and Class Disparities* (Routledge, 2010).
Molenaar, Erik Jaap, *Coastal State Jurisdiction over Vessel-Source Pollution* (Kluwer Law International, 1998).
Mukherjee, Janam, *Hungry Bengal: War, Famine and the End of Empire* (Oxford University Press, 2015).
Munim, Fazle Kaderi Mohammad Abdul, *Rights of the Citizen under the Constitution and Law* (Bangladesh Institute of Law and International Affairs, 1975).
Nussbaum, Martha and Sen, Amartya (eds.), *The Quality of Life* (Oxford University Press, 1992).
Okereke, Chukwumerije, *Global Justice and Neoliberal Environmental Governance: Ethics, Sustainable Development and International Co-Operation* (Routledge, 2008).
Pellow, David Naguib and Brulle, Robert J. (eds.), *Power, Justice, and the Environment: A Critical Appraisal of the Environmental Justice Movement* (MIT Press, 2005).

Picolotti, Romina and Taillant, Jorge Daniel, *Linking Human Rights and the Environment* (University of Arizona Press, 2010).

Rajamani, Lavanya, *Differential Treatment in International Environmental Law* (Oxford University Press, 2006).

Rawls, John, *A Theory of Justice* (Oxford University Press, 1971).

Razzaque, Jona, *Public Interest Environmental Litigation in India, Pakistan and Bangladesh* (Kluwer, 2004).

Rodgers, Gerry et al., *The International Labour Organization and the Quest for Social Justice, 1919–2009* (International Labour Office, 2009).

Schlosberg, David, *Defining Environmental Justice: Theories, Movements, and Nature* (Oxford University Press, 2007).

Segger, Marie-Claire Cordonier and Weeramantry, Christopher Gregory (eds.), *Sustainable Justice: Reconciling Economic, Social and Environmental Law* (Martinus Nijhoff Publishers, 2005).

Sen, Amartya, *Development as Freedom* (Oxford University Press, 1999).

Sen, Amartya, *The Idea of Justice* (Allen Lane, 2009).

Shrader-Frechette, Kristin, *Environmental Justice: Creating Equity, Reclaiming Democracy* (Oxford University Press, 2002).

Steady, Filomina Chioma, *Environmental Justice in the New Millennium: Global Perspectives on Race, Ethnicity, and Human Rights* (Springer, 2009).

Tan, Alan Khee-Jin, *Vessel-Source Marine Pollution: The Law and Politics of International Regulation* (Cambridge University Press, 2006).

Tharoor, Shashi, *An Era of Darkness: The British Empire in India* (Aleph Book Company, 2016).

Walker, Gordon, *Environmental Justice: Concepts, Evidence and Politics* (Routledge, 2012).

Westra, Laura, *Environmental Justice and the Rights of Indigenous Peoples: International and Domestic Legal Perspectives* (Earthscan, 2012).

Young, Iris Marion, *Justice and the Politics of Difference* (Princeton University Press, 1990).

Zarsky, Lyuba, *Human Rights and the Environment: Conflicts and Norms in a Globalizing World* (Earthscan, 2012).

Book chapters

Al Faruque, Abdullah and Karim, Md Saiful, 'Environmental Law of Bangladesh' in Nicholas A. Robinson, Elizabeth Burleson and Lin-Heng Lye (eds.), *Comparative Environmental Law and Regulation* (Thomson Reuters, 2016) 7A:1.

Barry, Brian, 'Sustainable and Intergenerational Justice' in Andrew Dobson (ed.), *Fairness and Futurity: Essays on Environmental Sustainability and Social Justice* (Oxford University Press, 1999) 94.

Birnie, Patricia, 'The Status of Environmental "Soft Law": Trends and Examples with Special Focus on IMO Norms' in Henrik Ringbom (ed.), *Competing Norms in the Law of Marine Environmental Protection* (Kluwer Law International, 1997) 31.

de Sadeleer, Nicolas Michel, 'The Polluter-Pays Principle in EU Law – Bold Case Law and Poor Harmonisation' in Hans Christian Bugge (ed.), *Pro Natura* (Universitetsforlaget, 2012) 405.

Farooque, Mohiuddin, 'Institutional and Legal Aspects in Resolving Conflicts of Development and Environment in Bangladesh' in Ock-Kyung Kim and James Ypsilantis (eds.), *People, Development and Environment: Complex Interlinkages in Bangladesh* (IUCN, 1993) 141.

Farooque, Mohiuddin, 'Regulatory Framework and Some Examples of Environmental Contamination in Bangladesh' in Bangladesh Environmental Lawyers Association (BELA) (ed.), *Selected Writings of Mohiuddin Farooque: Environmental Order the Security of Survival* (BELA, 2004) 20.

Gonzalez, Carmen G., 'Environmental Justice and International Environmental Law' in Shawkat Alam et al. (eds.), *Routledge Handbook of International Environmental Law* (Routledge, 2013) 77.

Preston, Brian J., 'The Effectiveness of the Law in Providing Access to Environmental Justice: An Introduction' in Paul Martin et al. (eds.), *The Search for Environmental Justice* (Edward Elgar Publishing, 2015) 23.

Rummel-Bulska, Iwona, 'The Basel Convention and the UN Convention on the Law of the Sea' in Henrik Ringbom (ed.), *Competing Norms in the Law of Marine Environmental Protection* (Kluwer Law International, 1997) 83.

Journal articles

Abdullah, Hasan Muhammad et al., 'Monitoring the Drastic Growth of Ship Breaking Yards in Sitakunda: A Threat to the Coastal Environment of Bangladesh' (2013) 185 *Environmental Monitoring and Assessment* 3839.

Adeola, Francis O., 'Cross-National Environmental Injustice and Human Rights Issues: A Review of Evidence in the Developing World' (2000) 43 *American Behavioral Scientist* 686.

Ahmed, M. Jamaluddin et al., 'Physicochemical Assessment of Soil Pollutants Due to the Ship Breaking Activities and Its Impact on the Coastal Zone of Chittagong, Bangladesh' (2013) 2 *European Chemical Bulletin* 1053.

Amechi, Emeka Polycarp, 'Enhancing Environmental Protection and Socio-Economic Development in Africa: A Fresh Look at the Right to a General Satisfactory Environment under the African Charter on Human and Peoples' Rights' (2009) 5 *Law, Environment and Development Journal* 60.

Bafundo, Nina E., 'Compliance with the Ozone Treaty: Weak States and the Principle of Common but Differentiated Responsibility' (2006) 21 *American University International Law Review* 46.

Baileya, Sarah A., 'An Overview of Thirty Years of Research on Ballast Water as a Vector for Aquatic Invasive Species to Freshwater and Marine Environments' (2015) 18 *Aquatic Ecosystem Health and Management* 261.

Ballet, Jérôme, Koffi, Jean-Marcel and Pelenc, Jérôme, 'Environment, Justice and the Capability Approach' (2013) 85 *Ecological Economics* 28.

Barrios, Paula, 'The Rotterdam Convention on Hazardous Chemicals: A Meaningful Step toward Environmental Protection?' (2004) 16 *Georgetown International Environmental Law Review* 679.

Bax, Nicholas et al., 'Marine Invasive Alien Species: A Threat to Global Biodiversity' (2003) 27 *Marine Policy* 313.

Bedi, Heather Plumridge, 'Right to Food, Right to Mine? Competing Human Rights Claims in Bangladesh' (2015) 59 *Geoforum* 248.

Begg, David, 'Poverty and Human Rights in Bangladesh' (2000) 1 *Melbourne Journal of International Law* 149.

Betten, Lammy, 'International Implementation of Economic and Social Rights by ILO' (1988) 6 *Netherlands Quarterly of Human Rights* 29.

Bodansky, Daniel, 'Protecting the Marine Environment from Vessel-Source Pollution: UNCLOS III and beyond' (1991) 18 *Ecology Law Quarterly* 719.

Boyle, Alan E., 'Marine Pollution under the Law of the Sea Convention' (1985) 79 *American Journal of International Law* 347.

Carlton, James T., 'Transoceanic and Interoceanic Dispersal of Coastal Organisms: The Biology of Ballast Water' (1985) 23 *Oceanography and Marine Biology Annual Review* 313.

Carlton, James T., 'Patterns of Transoceanic Marine Biological Invasions in the Pacific Ocean' (1987) 41 *Bulletin of Marine Science* 452.

Charney, Jonathan I., 'The Marine Environment and the 1982 United Nations Convention on the Law of the Sea' (1994) 28 *International Lawyer* 879.

Ciesla, David, 'Developments in Vessel-Based Pollution: The International Maritime Organizations Ballast Water Convention and the European Union's Regulation to Phase Out Single-Hull Oil Tankers' (2004) 15 *Colorado Journal of International Environmental Law and Policy* 107.

Clarke, Gerard, 'The Evolving ASEAN Human Rights System: The ASEAN Human Rights Declaration of 2012' (2012) 11 *Northwestern University Journal of International Human Rights* 1.

Cohen, Matt, 'U.S. Shipbreaking Exports: Balancing Safe Disposal with Economic Realities' (2005) 28 *Environs: Environmental Law and Policy Journal* 237.

Cusack, Marguerite M., 'International Law and the Transboundary Shipment of Hazardous Waste to the Third World: Will the Basel Convention Make a Difference?' (1990) 5 *American University International Law Review* 393.

David, Matej and Perkovič, Marko, 'Ballast Water Sampling as a Critical Component of Biological Invasions Risk Management' (2004) 49 *Marine Pollution Bulletin* 313.

Davidson, Ian C. and Simkanin, Christina, 'The Biology of Ballast Water 25 Years Later' (2012) 14 *Biological Invasions* 9.

Desgagne, Richard, 'Integrating Environmental Values into the European Convention on Human Rights' (1995) 89 *American Journal of International Law* 26.

Dodds, David, 'Breaking Up Is Hard to Do: Environmental Effects of Shipwrecking and Possible Solutions under India's Environmental Regime' (2007) 20 *Pacific McGeorge Global Business and Development Law Journal* 207.

Donner, Patrick, 'Ballast Water Treatment Ashore – Better for the Environment and for Seafarers' (2010) 9 *WMU Journal of Maritime Affairs* 191.

Firestone, Jeremy and Corbett, James J., 'Coastal and Port Environments: International Legal and Policy Responses to Reduce Ballast Water Introductions of Potentially Invasive Species' (2006) 7 *Sustainable Development Law and Policy* 45.

French, Duncan, 'Developing States and International Environmental Law: The Importance of Differentiated Responsibilities' (2000) 49 *International and Comparative Law Quarterly* 35.

Frey, R. Scott, 'Breaking Ships in the World-System: An Analysis of Two Ship Breaking Capitals, Alang-Sosiya, India and Chittagong, Bangladesh' (2015) 21 *Journal of World-Systems Research* 25.

Gaines, Sanford E., 'The Polluter-Pays Principle: From Economic Equity to Environmental Ethos' (1991) 26 *Texas International Law Journal* 463.

Gilman, Nils, 'The New International Economic Order: A Reintroduction' (2015) 6 *Humanity* 1.

Gollasch, Stephan et al., 'Critical Review of the IMO International Convention on the Management of Ships' Ballast Water and Sediments' (2007) 6 *Harmful Algae* 585.

Gregson, Nicky et al., 'Following Things of Rubbish Value: End-of-Life Ships, "Chock-Chocky" Furniture and the Bangladeshi Middle Class Consumer' (2010) 41 *Geoforum* 846.

Griffin, Andrew, 'MARPOL 73/78 and Vessel Pollution: A Glass Half Full or Half Empty' (1994) 1 *Indiana Journal of Global Legal Studies* 489.

Hackett, David P., 'An Assessment of the Basel Convention on the Control of Transboundary Movements of Hazardous Wastes and Their Disposal' (1990) 5 *American University International Law Review* 291.

Hagen, Paul E. and Walls, Michael P., 'The Stockholm Convention on Persistent Organic Pollutants' (2005) 19 *Natural Resources and Environment* 49.

Hallegraeff, Gustaaf M. and Bolch, Christopher J., 'Transport of Toxic Dinoflagellate Cysts via Ships' Ballast Water' (1991) 22 *Marine Pollution Bulletin* 27.

Hasana, Asma Binta et al., 'Enrichment Factor and Geo-Accumulation Index of Trace Metals in Sediments of the Ship Breaking Area of Sitakund Upazilla (Bhatiary – Kumira), Chittagong, Bangladesh' (2013) 125 *Journal of Geochemical Exploration* 130.

Hasana, Asma Binta et al., 'Trace Metals Pollution in Seawater and Groundwater in the Ship Breaking Area of Sitakund Upazilla, Chittagong, Bangladesh' (2013) 71 *Marine Pollution Bulletin* 317.

Hayes, Keith R. and Sliwa, Cathryn, 'Identifying Potential Marine Pests – a Deductive Approach Applied to Australia' (2003) 46 *Marine Pollution Bulletin* 91.

Hossain, M. Zahid, 'A Few Data on the Accident of Shipbreaking, Chittagong' (2006) 6 *Social Action* 13.

Hossain, Md M. Maruf and Islam, Mohammad Mahmudul, 'Shipbreaking Activities and Its Impact on the Coastal Zone of Chittagong, Bangladesh: Towards Policy Implications' (2006) 6 *Social Action* 3.

Huggins, Anna and Karim, Md Saiful 'Shifting Traction: Differential Treatment and Substantive and Procedural Regard in the International Climate Change Regime' (2016) 5 *Transnational Environmental Law* 427.

Hung, Hayley, Katsoyiannis, Athanasios A. and Guardans, Ramon, 'Ten Years of Global Monitoring under the Stockholm Convention on Persistent Organic Pollutants (POPs): Trends, Sources and Transport Modelling' (2016) 217 *Environmental Pollution* 1.

Karim, Md Saiful, 'UNCLOS and Regional Action for Protection of the Marine Environment: Perspectives of the South Asian Seas Region' (2008) 29 *Bangladesh Institute of International and Strategic Studies Journal* 415.

Karim, Md Saiful, 'Implementation of the MARPOL Convention in Bangladesh' (2009) 5 *Macquarie Journal of International and Comparative Environmental Law* 51.

Karim, Md Saiful, 'Violation of Labour Rights in the Ship-Breaking Yards of Bangladesh: Legal Norms and Reality' (2009) 25 *The International Journal of Comparative Labour Law and Industrial Relations* 379.

Karim, Md Saiful, 'Environmental Pollution from Shipbreaking Industry: International Law and National Legal Response' (2010) 22 *Georgetown International Environmental Law Review* 185.

Karim, Md Saiful, 'Implementation of the MARPOL Convention in Developing Countries' (2010) 79 *Nordic Journal of International Law* 303.

Karim, Md Saiful, Vincents, Okechukwu Benjamin and Rahim, Mia Mahmudur, 'Legal Activism for Ensuring Environmental Justice' (2012) 7 *Asian Journal of Comparative Law* 346.

Karim, Md Saiful, 'Proposed REDD+ Project for the Sundarbans: Legal and Institutional Issues' (2013) 3 *International Journal of Rural Law and Policy* 1.

Keselj, Tatjana, 'Port State Jurisdiction in Respect of Pollution from Ships: The 1982 United Nations Convention on the Law of the Sea and the Memoranda of Understanding' (1999) 30 *Ocean Development and International Law* 127.

Kettlewell, Ursula, 'The Answer to Global Pollution? A Critical Examination of the Problems and Potential of the Polluter-Pays Principle' (1992) 3 *Colorado Journal of International Environmental Law and Policy* 429.

Kindt, John Warren, 'Vessel-Source Pollution and the Law of the Sea' (1984) 17 *Vanderbilt Journal of Transnational Law* 287.

Kummer, Katharina, 'The International Regulation of Transboundary Traffic in Hazardous Wastes: The 1989 Basel Convention' (1992) 41 *International and Comparative Law Quarterly* 530.

Kummer, Katharina, 'Prior Informed Consent for Chemicals in International Trade: The 1998 Rotterdam Convention' (1999) 8 *Review of European Community and International Environmental Law* 323.

Kusumaningdyah, Widha, Eunike, Agustina and Yuniarti, Rahmi, 'Modelling Tradeoff in Ship Breaking Industry Considering Sustainability Aspects: A System Dynamics Approach' (2013) 17 *Procedia Environmental Sciences* 785.

Lallas, Peter L., 'The Stockholm Convention on Persistent Organic Pollutants' (2001) 95 *American Journal of International Law* 692.

Lee, Eddy, 'Declaration of Philadelphia: Retrospect and Prospect' (1994) 133 *International Labour Review* 467.

Legatski, Richard A., 'Port State Jurisdiction over Vessel-Source Marine Pollution' (1977) 2 *Harvard Environmental Law Review* 448.

Lipman, Zada Marie, 'International Regulation of Hazardous Chemicals and Its Efficacy in Promoting Sustainability for Developing Countries' (2006) 2 *International Journal of Environmental, Cultural, Economic and Social Sustainability* 85.

Lipman, Zada Marie, 'Transboundary Movement of Hazardous Waste: Environmental Justice Issues for Developing Countries' (1999) *Acta Juridica* 266.

Lucier, Cristina A. and Gareau, Brian J., 'Obstacles to Preserving Precaution and Equity in Global Hazardous Waste Regulation: An Analysis of Contested Knowledge in the Basel Convention' (2016) 16 *International Environmental Agreements: Politics, Law and Economics* 493.

McCarthy, Susan A. and Khabaty, Farukh M., 'International Dissemination of Epidemic *Vibrio cholerae* by Cargo Ship Ballast and Other Nonpotable Waters' (1994) 60 *Applied and Environmental Microbiology* 2597.

McConnell, Moira L. and Gold, Edgar, 'The Modern Law of the Sea: Framework for the Protection and Preservation of Marine Environment?' (1991) 23 *Case Western Reserve Journal of International Law* 23.

McDorman, Ted L., 'The Rotterdam Convention on the Prior Informed Consent Procedure for Certain Hazardous Chemicals and Pesticides in International Trade: Some Legal Notes' (2004) 13 *Review of European Community and International Environmental Law* 187.

Melanson, Richard A., 'Human Rights and the American Withdrawal from the ILO' (1979) 1 *Universal Human Rights* 43.

Mintz, Joel A., 'Two Cheers for Global POPs: A Summary and Assessment of the Stockholm Convention on Persistent Organic Pollutants' (2002) 14 *Georgetown International Environmental Law Review* 319.

Mollah, Awal Hossain, 'Judicial Activism and Human Rights in Bangladesh: A Critique' (2014) 56 *International Journal of Law and Management* 494.

Munim, Fazle Kaderi Mohammad Abdul, 'The Challenges of Social Justice' (1984) 7 *Law and International Affairs* 1.

Nøst, Therese H. et al., 'High Concentrations of Organic Contaminants in Air from Ship Breaking Activities in Chittagong, Bangladesh' (2015) 49 *Environmental Science and Technology* 11372.

Okere, B. Obinna, 'Fundamental Objectives and Directive Principles of State Policy under the Nigerian Constitution' (1983) 32 *International and Comparative Law Quarterly* 214.

Olivier, Marius, 'International Labour and Social Security Standards: A Developing Country Critique' (2013) 29 *International Journal of Comparative Labour Law and Industrial Relations* 21.

O'Shea, Sharonne and Cangelosi, Allegra, 'Trojan Horses in Our Harbors: Biological Contamination from Ballast Water Discharge' (1996) 27 *University of Toledo Law Review* 381.

Oxman, Bernard H., 'The Duty to Respect Generally Accepted International Standards' (1991) 24 *New York University Journal of International Law and Politics* 110.

Patel, Vilas et al., 'Response of Bacterial Community Structure to Seasonal Fluctuation and Anthropogenic Pollution on Coastal Water of Alang – Sosiya Ship Breaking Yard, Bhavnagar, India' (2014) 161 *Bioresource Technology* 362.

Patel, Vilas et al., 'Taxonomic Profiling of Bacterial Community Structure from Coastal Sediment of Alang – Sosiya Shipbreaking Yard Near Bhavnagar, India' (2015) 101 *Marine Pollution Bulletin* 736.

Pillay, Anashri, 'Revisiting the Indian Experience of Economic and Social Rights Adjudication: The Need for a Principled Approach to Judicial Activism and Restraint' (2014) 63 *International and Comparative Law Quarterly* 385.

Rajamani, Lavanya, 'Public Interest Environmental Litigation in India: Exploring Issues of Access, Participation, Equity, Effectiveness and Sustainability' (2007) 19 *Journal of Environmental Law* 293.

Rajamani, Lavanya, 'The Right to Environmental Protection in India: Many a Slip between the Cup and the Lip?' (2007) 16 *Review of European Community and International Environmental Law* 274.

Razzaque, Jona, 'Access to Environmental Justice: Role of the Judiciary in Bangladesh' (2000) 4 *Bangladesh Journal of Law* 1.

Razzaque, Jona, 'Linking Human Rights, Development and Environment: Experiences from Litigation in South Asia' (2007) 18 *Fordham Environmental Law Review* 587.

Reddy, M. Srinivasa et al., 'Distribution, Enrichment and Accumulation of Heavy Metals in Coastal Sediments of Alang – Sosiya Ship Scrapping Yard, India' (2004) 48 *Marine Pollution Bulletin* 1055.

Reed, Kenneth R., 'Economic Incentives for Pollution Abatement: Applying Theory to Practice' (1970) 12 *Arizona Law Review* 51.

Renshaw, Catherine Shanahan, 'The ASEAN Human Rights Declaration 2012' (2013) 13 *Human Rights Law Review* 557.

Rousmaniere, Peter and Raj, Nikhil, 'Shipbreaking in the Developing World: Problems and Prospects' (2007) 13 *International Journal of Occupational and Environmental Health* 359.

Roy, Anjan Kumer Dev, Alam, Khorshed and Gow, Jeff, 'A Review of the Role of Property Rights and Forest Policies in the Management of the Sundarbans Mangrove Forest in Bangladesh' (2012) 15 *Forest Policy and Economics* 46.

Sahu, Geetanjoy, 'Workers of Alang-Sosiya: A Survey of Working Conditions in a Ship-Breaking Yard, 1983–2013' (2014) 49 *Economic and Political Weekly* 52.

Sawyer, John F., 'Shipbreaking and the North – South Debate: Economic Development or Environmental and Labor Catastrophe?' (2002) 20 *Penn State International Law Review* 535, 562.

Schachte, William L. Jr., 'The Value of the 1982 UN Convention on the Law of the Sea: Preserving our Freedoms and Protecting the Environment' (1992) 23 *Ocean Development and International Law* 55.

Schlosberg, David, 'Theorising Environmental Justice: The Expanding Sphere of a Discourse' (2013) 22 *Environmental Politics* 37.

Shelton, Dinah, 'What Happened in Rio to Human Rights?' (1992) 3 *Yearbook of International Environmental Law* 75.

Sohn, Louis B., 'Generally Accepted International Rules' (1986) 61 *Washington Law Review* 1073.

Stevens, Candice, 'Interpreting the Polluter Pays Principle in the Trade and Environment Context' (1994) 27 *Cornell International Law Journal* 577.

Stone, Christopher D., 'Common but Differentiated Responsibilities in International Law' (2004) 98 *American Journal of International Law* 276.

Takahashi, C.K. et al., 'Ballast Water: A Review of the Impact on the World Public Health' (2008) 14 *Journal of Venomous Animals and Toxins Including Tropical Diseases* 395.

Tsimplis, Michael, 'Alien Species Stay Home: The International Convention for the Control and Management of Ships' Ballast Water and Sediments 2004' (2005) 19 *International Journal of Marine and Coastal Law* 411.

Ward, Halina, 'Common but Differentiated Debates: Environment, Labour and the World Trade Organization' (1996) 45 *International and Comparative Law Quarterly* 592.

Wiles, Ellen, 'Aspirational Principles or Enforceable Rights? Future for Socio-Economic Rights in National Law' (2006) 22 *American University International Law Review* 35.

Williams, R.J. et al., 'Cargo Vessel Ballast Water as a Vector for the Transport of Non-Indigenous Marine Species' (1988) 26 *Estuarine, Coastal and Shelf Science* 409.

Wirth, David A., 'Trade Implication of the Basel Convention Amendment Banning North-South Trade in Hazardous Wastes' (1998) 7 *Review of European Community and International Environmental Law* 237.

Wolf, Francis, 'ILO Experience in the Implementation of Human Rights' (1975) 10 *Journal of International Law and Economics* 599.

Zahedi, Nancy S., 'Implementing the Rotterdam Convention: The Challenges of Transforming Aspirational Goals into Effective Controls on Hazardous Pesticide Exports to Developing Countries' (1999) 11 *Georgetown International Environmental Law Review* 707.

Reports

Andersen, Aage Bjørn, Bjørnbom, Erik and Sverud, Terje, *Technical Report: Decommissioning of Ships – Environmental Standards: Ship-Breaking Practices/On Site Assessment: Bangladesh – Chittagong*, Det Norske Veritas Report No. 2000–3158 (12 May 2000) <www.shipbreakingplatform.org/shipbrea_wp2011/wp-content/uploads/2011/11/dnvbangladesh.pdf>

Dao, Ruben, 'Childbreaking yards – child labour in the ship recycling industry in Bangladesh' Report, FIDH and YPSA (2008) <www.fidh.org/IMG/pdf/bgukreport.pdf>

FIDH, 'Where do the "floating dustbins" end up? Labour rights in shipbreaking yards in South Asia: The cases of Chittagong (Bangladesh) and Alang (India)' Report, FIDH (December 2002) <www.fidh.org/IMG/pdf/bd1112a.pdf>

Heidegger, Patrizia et al., *What a Difference a Flag Makes: Why Ship Owners' Responsibility to Ensure Sustainable Ship Recycling Needs to go beyond Flag State Jurisdiction* (NGO Shipbreaking Platform, 2015).

The Hong Kong Convention and IMO's position in relation to the preliminary assessment by the UNHRC Special Rapporteur (2011) <archive.basel.int/ships/oewg-vii12-comments/comments/imo.doc>

Hossain, Md M. Maruf and Islam, Mohammad Mahmudul, *Ship Breaking Activities and Its Impact on the Coastal Zone of Chittagong, Bangladesh: Towards Sustainable Management* (Young Power in Social Action, 2006).

International Law and Policy Institute, *Shipbreaking Practices in Bangladesh, India and Pakistan: An Investor Perspective on the Human Rights and Environmental Impacts of Beaching* (International Law and Policy Institute, 2016).

Kernaghan, Charles, 'Murder in the shipbreaking yards, Chittagong, Bangladesh' Report, Institute for Global Human and Labour Rights (November 2015) <www.globallabourrights.org/reports/document/Murder-in-the-Shipbreaking-Yards-1.pdf>

Krämer, Ludwig, *The Commission Proposal for a Regulation on Ship Recycling, the Basel Convention and the Protection of the Environment* (4 September 2012) <www.shipbreakingplatform.org/shipbrea_wp2011/wp-content/uploads/2012/12/Legal-Analysis-of-EC-proposal_Ludwig-Kramer_FINAL-1.pdf>

NGO Shipbreaking Platform, *Substandard Shipbreaking: A Global Challenge* (February 2016) <www.shipbreakingplatform.org/shipbrea_wp2011/wp-content/uploads/2016/04/Worldwide-overview_FINAL.pdf>

Orellana, Marcos A. et al., *Shipbreaking and the Basel Convention: Analysis of the Level of Control Established under the Hong Kong Convention* (Centre for International Environmental Law, 2011).

Organisation for Economic Co-operation and Development (OECD), *The Polluter-Pays Principle: OECD Analyses and Recommendations* (OECD, 1992).

Rahman, Ataur and Ullah, A.Z.M. Tabarak, *Ship Breaking: A Background Paper*, International Labour Organization Report (1999).

Sarraf, Maria et al., *The Ship Breaking and Recycling Industry in Bangladesh and Pakistan*, World Bank Report No. 58275-SAS (2010) <http://documents.worldbank.org/curated/en/2010/12/13695952/ship-breaking-recycling-industry-bangladesh-pakistan>

Special Rapporteur on the adverse effects of the movement and dumping of toxic and dangerous products and wastes on the enjoyment of human rights, *Preliminary Assessment of Whether the Hong Kong Convention Establishes an Equivalent Level of Control and Enforcement as That Established under the Basel Convention* (2011) <www.shipbreakingplatform.org/shipbrea_wp2011/wp-content/uploads/2011/12/UN-special-rapporateur-on-Basel-IMO-conventions-comparison.doc>

Ulfstein, Geir, *Legal Aspects of Scrapping of Vessels*, A Study for the Norwegian Ministry of Environment (9 March 1999) <www.shipbreakingplatform.org/shipbrea_wp2011/wp-content/uploads/2011/11/MD1999dismantling-ships-academic-survey.pdf>

YPSA, *Workers in Shipbreaking Industries: A Base Line Survey of Chittagong (Bangladesh)* (Young Power in Social Action, 2005).

UN, IMO and other international organisations' documents

Analysis of Inconsistencies between the IMO Guidelines on Ship Recycling and the Basel Convention (Submitted by Greenpeace International), IMO Doc. MEPC 51/INF.11 (6 February 2004).

ASEAN Human Rights Declaration, (2012) <http://aichr.org/?dl_name=ASEAN-Human-Rights-Declaration.pdf>

Comments on the Report of the Correspondence Group (Submitted by Greenpeace International), IMO Doc. MEPC 47/3/5 (11 January 2002).

Consideration of the Draft International Convention for the Safe and Environmentally Sound Recycling of Ships: Statement of Concern (Submitted by Greenpeace International and FOEI), IMO Doc. SR/CONF/CW/INF.1 (14 May 2009).

Consideration of the Draft Text of the International Convention for the Safe and Environmentally Sound Recycling of Ships: Texts Approved on Thursday, 14 May 2009, for Consideration by the Drafting Committee, IMO Doc. SR/CONF/CW/5 (14 May 2009).

Council Recommendation of 3 March 1975 Regarding Cost Allocation and Action by Public Authorities on Environmental Matters, 75/436/Euratom, ECSC, EEC, OJ L 194 (25 July 1975).

Council Regulation 120/97 of 20 January 1997, Amending Regulation (EC) No 259/93 on the Supervision and Control of Shipments of Waste Within, into and out of the European Community, O.J. (L 22) 14 (1997).

Decisions Adopted by the Third Meeting of the Conference of the Parties to the Basel Convention, at Dec. III/1, U.N. Doc. UNEP/CHW.3/35 (28 November 1995).

Declaration on the Establishment of a New International Economic Order, UN Doc. A/RES/S-6/3201 (1974).

Declaration of the United Nations Conference on the Human Environment, UN Doc. A/Conf.48/14/Rev.1 (1972).

Declaration on the Right to Development, UN Doc. A/41/53 (1986).

Development of the Capacity of Ship Scrapping for the Smooth Implementation of the Amendments to Annex I of MARPOL 73/78, Resolution MEPC. (53) 32, IMO Doc. MEPC 32/20, Annex 7 (6 March 1992).

Development of the Draft International Convention for the Safe and Environmentally Sound Recycling of Ships (Submitted by India), IMO Doc. MEPC 55/3/12 (17 August 2006).

Ensuring Sustainable Green and Safe Ship Dismantling – Concerning Beaching and the Establishment of a Mandatory Fund (Submitted by Greenpeace International and FOEI), IMO Doc. SR/CONF/14 (9 February 2009).

Environmental Comparison of the Beaching Method with Other Methods of Recycling of Ships (Submitted by India), IMO Doc. SR/CONF/36 (1 May 2009).

Establishment of an International Ship Recycling Trust Fund, IMO Doc. Circular Letter No.2703 (20 April 2006).

Guidelines for the Authorization of Ship Recycling Facilities, 2012 (Resolution MEPC.211(63)), IMO Doc. MEPC 63/23, Annex 5 (14 March 2012).

Guidelines for the Development of the Inventory of Hazardous Materials, 2011 (Resolution MEPC.197(62)), IMO Doc. MEPC 62/24, Annex 3 (26 July 2011).

Guidelines for the Development of the Inventory of Hazardous Materials, 2015 (Resolution MEPC.269(68)), IMO Doc. MEPC 68/21/Add.1, Annex 17 (29 May 2015).

Guidelines for the Development of the Ship Recycling Plan (SRP), 2011, IMO Doc. MEPC 62/24, Annex 2 (26 July 2011).

Guidelines for Safe and Environmentally Sound Ship Recycling, 2012 (Resolution MEPC.210(63)), IMO Doc. MEPC 63/23, Annex 4 (14 March 2012).

Human Rights and Environment, Final Report Prepared by Mrs Fatma Zohra Ksentini, Special Rapporteur, UN. E/CN.4/Sub.2/1994/9 (6 July 1994).

IMO Guidelines on Ship Recycling, IMO Doc. A23/Res.962 (4 March 2004).

Implications of the United Nations Convention on the Law of the Sea for the International Maritime Organization, IMO Doc. LEG/MISC.7 (19 January 2012).

International Labour Organization (ILO), *Safety and Health in Shipbreaking: Guidelines for Asian Countries and Turkey* (ILO, 2004).

Johannesburg Declaration on Sustainable Development, UN Doc. A/CONF.199/20 (4 September 2002); *The Future We Want, General Assembly Resolution 66/288*, UN Doc A/RES/66/288 (11 September 2012).

Legal Aspects of the Full and Partial Dismantling of Ships (Submitted by Basel Action Network & Greenpeace International) 1, UN Doc. UNEP/CHW/LWG/5/4/Add.1 (21 May 2002).

Legal Aspects of the Full and Partial Dismantling of Ships: Comments Provided by Parties and Others, UNEP Doc. UNEP/CHW/OEWG/3/INF/5 (24 February 2004).

Marine Environment Protection Committee, 55th Session, 9–13 October 2006, List of Participants, IMO Doc. MEPC 55/INF.1 (15 November 2006).

Marine Environment Protection Committee 60th Session, 22–26 March 2010, List of Participants, IMO Doc. MEPC 60/INF.1 (26 March 2010).

National Workshop on the Development of the International Convention for the Safe and Environmentally Sound Recycling of Ships (Submitted by India), IMO Doc. MEPC 57/3/5 (25 January 2008).

New Legally Binding Instrument on Ship Recycling, IMO Doc. A24/Res.981 (6 February 2006).

Opening Address by Mr EE Mitropoulos Secretary-General International Maritime Organization, IMO Doc. SR/CONF/INF.3 (11 May 2009).

Permanent Sovereignty over Natural Resources, UN Doc. A/5217 (1962).

Potential Environmental Effects of Ships Ballast Water Discharges in Considering the Involvement of IMO in Regulating the Scrapping of Ships (Submitted by Friends of the Earth International), IMO Doc. MEPC 44/16 (3 December 1999).

Preparation of Oil Tankers for Ship Recycling (Submitted by India), IMO Doc. SR/CONF/26 (2 April 2009).

Proposal for a New Legally Binding Instrument on Recycling of Ships: Industry Comments (Submitted by ICS, BIMCO, INTERTANKO, INTERCARGO, IPTA, WNTI), IMO Doc. MEPC 54/3/11 (27 January 2006).

Proposal for a New Legally Binding Instrument on Recycling of Ships (Submitted by Norway), IMO Doc. MEPC 54/3 (5 December 2005).

Proposal for Consideration of the Committee for Developing a New Annex under MARPOL 73/78 for Ship Recycling (Submitted by India), IMO Doc. MEPC 47/3/4 (7 January 2002).

Proposal for Providing Clarity in the Convention and Reaffirming the Importance of Safe-for-Hot Work and Safe-for-Entry Conditions During Recycling (Submitted by the United States), IMO Doc. SR/CONF/33 (29 April 2009).

Proposals for Ship Recycling Plan, Ready for Recycling and Final Surveys, IMO Doc. MEPC 57/3/18 (8 February 2008).

Recommendation of the Council on Guiding Principles concerning International Economic Aspects of Environmental Policies, OECD Council Recommendation C (72)128 (26 May 1972), 14 ILM 236 (1975).

Recommendation of the Council on the Implementation of the Polluter-Pays Principle, OECD Council Recommendation C (74)223 (14 November 1974), 14 ILM 234 (1975).

Recycling of Ships: Additional Information Related to Ship Scrapping (Submitted by the Netherlands), IMO Doc. MEPC 44/16/1 (23 December 1999).

Recycling of Ships: Comments on Document MEPC 48/3 (Submitted by India), IMO Doc. MEPC 48/3/2 (9 August 2002).

Recycling of Ships: Proposal for an Enforceable Legally Binding System for the Recycling of Ships (Submitted by Denmark), para 3, IMO Doc. MEPC 53/3/7 (13 May 2005).

Recycling of Ships: Proposal for an IMO Work Plan (Submitted by Norway), IMO Doc. MEPC 44/16/2 (24 December 1999).

Recycling of Ships: Report of the Correspondence Group (Submitted by the Coordinator of the Correspondence Group), IMO Doc. MEPC 46/7, 6 (18 January 2001).

Recycling of Ships: Report of the Correspondence Group (Submitted by the Coordinator of the Correspondence Group), IMO Doc. MEPC 48/3 (3 July 2002).

Recycling of Ships: Report of the Correspondence Group (Submitted by the Coordinator of the Correspondence Group), IMO Doc. MEPC 49/3/1 (28 March 2003).

Recycling of Ships (Submitted by Brazil), IMO Doc. MEPC 44/16/3 (24 December 1999).

Recycling of Ships (Submitted by India), IMO Doc. MEPC 46/7/1 (14 February 2001).

Recycling of Ships (Submitted by the International Chamber of Shipping (ICS) on Behalf of the Industry Working Party on Ship Recycling), IMO Doc. MEPC 47/3/2 (30 November 2001).

Regulation (EC) No 1013/2006 of the European Parliament and of the Council of 14 June 2006 on Shipments of Waste, Council Regulation 1013/2006, 2006 OJ (L 190) 1 (2006).

Regulation (EU) No 1257/2013 of the European Parliament and of the Council of 20 November 2013 on Ship Recycling and Amending Regulation (EC) No 1013/2006 and Directive 2009/16/EC, 2013, OJ (L 330) 1 (2013).

Report of the Conference of the Parties to the Basel Convention on the Control of Transboundary Movements of Hazardous Wastes and Their Disposal, UNEP Doc. UNEP/CHW.6/40 (10 February 2003).

Report of the Conference of the Parties to the Basel Convention on the Control of Transboundary Movements of Hazardous Wastes and Their Disposal, 63, UN Doc. UNEP/CHW.7/33 (25 January 2005).

Report of the Correspondence Group (Submitted by the Coordinator of the Correspondence Group), IMO Doc. MEPC 46/7 (18 January 2001).

Report of the Correspondence Group (Submitted by the Coordinator of the Correspondence Group), IMO Doc. MEPC 47/3/3 (30 November 2001).

Report of the Fifth Meeting of the Conference of the Parties to the Basel Convention, UNEP Doc. UNEP/CHW.5/29 (10 December 1999).

Report of the Independent Expert on the Issue of Human Rights Obligations Relating to the Enjoyment of a Safe, Clean, Healthy and Sustainable Environment, John H. Knox, UN Doc. A/HRC/22/43 (24 December 2012).

Report of the Independent Expert on the Question of Human Rights and Extreme Poverty, UN Doc. A/65/259 (9 August 2010).

Report of the Marine Environment Protection Committee on Its Forty-Second Session, IMO Doc. MEPC 42/22 (16 November 1998).

Report of the Marine Environment Protection Committee on Its Forty-Third Session, IMO Doc. MEPC 43/21 (6 July 1999).

Report of the Marine Environment Protection Committee on Its Forty-Fourth Session, IMO Doc. MEPC 44/20 (12 April 2000).

Report of the Marine Environment Protection Committee on Its Forty-Sixth Session, IMO Doc. MEPC 46/23 (16 May 2001).

Report of the Marine Environment Protection Committee on Its Forty-Seventh Session, IMO Doc. MEPC 47/20 (18 March 2002).

Report of the Marine Environment Protection Committee on Its Forty-Eighth Session, IMO Doc. MEPC 48/21 (24 October 2002).

Report of the Marine Environment Protection Committee on Its Forty-Ninth Session, IMO Doc. MEPC 49/22 (8 August 2003).

Report of the Marine Environment Protection Committee on Its Fifty-Third Session, IMO Doc. MEPC 53/24 (25 July 2005).

Report of the Open-Ended Working Group of the Basel Convention on the Work of Its Second Session, UN Doc. UNEP/CHW/OEWG/2/12 (16 December 2003).

Report of the Second Intersessional Meeting of the Working Group on Ship Recycling, IMO Doc. MEPC 56/3 (11 May 2007).

Report of the Second Meeting of the Conference of the Parties to the Basel Convention, 19–20, UN Doc. UNEP/CHW.2/30 (25 March 1994).

Report of the Special Rapporteur on the Adverse Effects of the Movement and Dumping of Toxic and Dangerous Products and Wastes on the Enjoyment of Human Rights, UN Doc. A/HRC/12/26 (15 July 2009).

Report of the Third Intersessional Meeting of the Working Group on Ship Recycling, IMO Doc. MEPC 57/3 (25 January 2008).

Report of the World Commission on Environment and Development: Our Common Future, UN Doc. A/42/427, Annex (4 August 1987).

Resolution of Human Rights Council 16/11 Human Rights and the Environment, UN Doc. A/HRC/RES/16/11 (12 April 2011).

Revised Specific Guidelines for the Assessment of Vessels, IMO Doc. LC 38/16, Annex 7 (18 October 2016).

Rio Declaration on Environment and Development, UN Doc. A/CONF.151/26 (Vol. I) (1992).

Statements by Delegations and Observers at the Closing Session of the Conference Friday, 15 May 2009, IMO Doc. SR/CONF/INF.8 (21 May 2009).

Technical Guidelines for the Environmentally Sound Management of the Full and Partial Dismantling of Ships, UN Doc. UNEP/CHW/6/23 (8 August 2002).

Transforming Our World: The 2030 Agenda for Sustainable Development, GA Res 70/1, UN Doc. A/RES/70/1 (21 October 2015).

UN, *The Millennium Development Goals Report 2015* (UN, 2015).

UNDP, *Millennium Development Goals* (2006) <www.undp.org/content/undp/en/home/sdgoverview/mdg_goals.html>

United Nations Millennium Declaration, GA Res 55/2, UN Doc A/RES/55/2 (18 September 2000).

Universal Declaration of Human Rights, GA Res 217(III), UN Doc. A/RES/3/217A (10 December 1948).

Urgent Considerations for Correcting Deficiencies in the Draft Convention on the Safe and Environmentally Sound Recycling of Ships (Submitted by Greenpeace), IMO Doc. MEPC 55/3/7 (10 August 2006).

Work Programme of the Committee and Subsidiary Bodies: Scrapping of Ships (Note by the International Chamber of Shipping (ICS)), IMO Doc. MEPC 43/18/10 (14 May 1999).

Work Programme of the Committee and Subsidiary Bodies: Scrapping of Ships (Submitted by Denmark), IMO Doc. MEPC 43/18/9 (14 May 1999).

Work Programme of the Committee and Subsidiary Bodies: Scrapping of Ships (Submitted by Greenpeace International and the ICFTU), IMO Doc. MEPC 43/18/6 (2 April 1999).

Work Programme of the Committee and Subsidiary Bodies: Scrapping of Ships (Submitted by Norway), IMO Doc. MEPC 43/18/1 (12 February 1999).

Newspaper reports

Bengali, Shashank, 'Adult and Underage Workers Risk Their Lives in Bangladesh's Rising Ship-Breaking Industry' *Los Angeles Times* (online) 9 March 2016 <www.latimes.com/world/asia/la-fg-bangladesh-ships-20160309-story.html>

Chowdhury, Mintu, 'Bangladesh Ship-Breakers Contend No Need for Environmental Clearance' *Bdnews24.com* (online) 7 November 2016 <http://bdnews24.com/bangladesh/2016/11/07/no-need-to-environmental-clearance-say-ship-breakers-in-bangladesh>

Dey, Arun Bikash, 'Two Ship Breaking Yard Burn Victims Groaning at CMCH' *The Daily Star* (online) 22 January 2014 <www.thedailystar.net/two-ship-breaking-yard-burn-victims-groaning-at-cmch-7908>

The Economist, 'Bangladesh and Development: The Path through the Fields' *The Economist* (online) 3 November 2012 <www.economist.com/news/briefing/21565617-bangladesh-has-dysfunctional-politics-and-stunted-private-sector-yet-it-has-been-surprisingly>

Khan, Kawsar, 'Ship-Breaking Conundrum' *The Daily Star* (online) 10 March 2010 <www.thedailystar.net/news-detail-129383>

Lal, M.B., 'How Our British Rulers "Legalised" Bribery' *The Hindu* (online) 10 September 2011 <www.thehindu.com/opinion/open-page/how-our-british-rulers-legalised-bribery/article2442485.ece#comments>

Mahmud, Iftekhar, '150 Industrial Projects Around Sundarbans' *Daily Prothom Alo* (online) 9 August 2016 <http://en.prothom-alo.com/bangladesh/news/115689/150-industrial-projects-around-Sundarbans>

New Age, 'Government Bans Toxic Material-Laden Ship from Entering Bangladesh' *New Age* (online) 17 February 2006 <www.newagebd.com/2006/feb/17/front.html#3>

Roy, Pinaki, 'Critical Area at a Stake: Nearly 150 Industrial Units Springing Up within 10 kms of Sundarbans' *The Daily Star* (online) 4 October 2016 <www.thedailystar.net/frontpage/critical-area-stake-1293748>

Roy, Pinaki, 'Environment Ministry Favours Polluters: Writes to Commerce Ministry to Allow Scrap Ship without Pre-Export Cleaning' *The Daily Star* (online) 20 February 2010 <www.thedailystar.net/news-detail-127111>

Staff Correspondent, 'Already Imported Old Ships Will Get Exemption' (Translated from Bengali) *Daily Prothom Alo* (online) 23 February 2010 <http://archive.prothom-alo.com/detail/news/44413>

Staff Correspondent, 'Burnt Worker of Ctg Ship-Breaking Yard Dies in CMCH' *The Daily Star* (online) 10 September 2015 <www.thedailystar.net/city/burnt-worker-ctg-ship-breaking-yard-dies-cmch-140662>.

Staff Correspondent, 'Ctg Ship Breaking Yard Worker Dies' *The Daily Star* (online) 7 July 2015 <www.thedailystar.net/city/ctg-ship-breaking-yard-worker-dies-108625>

Staff Correspondent, 'Four Workers Die Due to Toxic Gas in Sitakunda Ship-breaking Yards' (title translated from Bengali), *The Daily Prothom Alo* (online) 4 April 2014 <www.prothom-alo.com/bangladesh/article/184267/সীতাকুণ্ডে-জাহাজভাঙা-ইয়ার্ডে-বিষক্রিয়ায়-চার>

Staff Correspondent, 'One-Third of Bangladesh Ship-Breaking Workers at High Risk of Lung Diseases: Study' *Bdnews24.com* (online) 2 February 2017 <http://bdnews24.com/bangladesh/2017/02/02/one-third-of-bangladesh-ship-breaking-workers-at-high-risk-of-lung-diseases-study>

Staff Correspondent, 'Safety in Ship-Breaking: 14 Govt High Officials Face Contempt Rule' *The Daily Star* (online) 12 April 2016 <www.thedailystar.net/backpage/14-govt-high-officials-face-contempt-rule-1208011>

Staff Correspondent, 'Ship-Breaking Worker Killed' *The Daily Star* (online) 3 June 2014 <www.thedailystar.net/ship-breaking-worker-killed-26819>

Staff Correspondent, 'Toxic Ship Barred from Chittagong Port' *The Daily Star* (online) 15 January 2007 <www.thedailystar.net/2007/01/15/d7011501044.htm>

Staff Correspondent, 'Worker Dies in Ctg Ship Breaking Yard Accident' *The Daily Star* (online) 7 June 2015 <www.thedailystar.net/city/worker-dies-ctg-ship-breaking-yard-accident-93400>

Staff Correspondent Ctg, 'Ctg Ship-Breakers Protest New Policy' *The Daily Star* (online) 23 February 2010 <www.thedailystar.net/news-detail-127519>

Staff Correspondent Ctg, 'Worker Dies at Chittagong Shipbreaking Yard' *The Daily Star* (online) 18 April 2016 <www.thedailystar.net/backpage/worker-dies-ship breaking-yard-ctg-1210384>.

Star Business Report, 'Barua Praises Role of Ship-Breakers' *The Daily Star* (online) 11 February 2011 <www.thedailystar.net/news-detail-173747>

Star Online Report, '3 Burnt in Ctg Ship-Breaking Yard Fire' *The Daily Star* (online) 19 January 2014 <http://archive.thedailystar.net/news2014/3-burnt-in-ctg-ship-breaking-yard-fire-7455>

Star Online Report, 'Cylinder Blast Hurts 8 at Ctg Ship Breaking Yard' *The Daily Star* (online) 5 September 2015 <www.thedailystar.net/country/cylinder-blast-hurts-4-ctg-ship-breaking-yard-138238>

Star Online Report, 'Worker Killed in Ctg Ship Breaking Yard' *The Daily Star* (online) 3 June 2013 <www.thedailystar.net/news/worker-killed-in-ctg-ship-breaking-yard>

TNN, 'India Ahead of IMO on Ship Recycling Norms', *The Economic Times* (online) 28 January 2008 <http://economictimes.indiatimes.com/rssarticleshow/msid-2736359,prtpage-1.cms>

Tribune Online Report, 'Cabinet Clears Draft Ship Recycling Law' *Dhaka Tribune* (online) 30 January 2017 <http://archive.dhakatribune.com/environment/2017/jan/30/cabinet-clears-draft-ship-recycling-law>

Online materials

Basel Action Network (BAN), *The French Deception: PCBs and the Clemenceau* (1 February 2006) 4, <http://archive.ban.org/library/the_french_deception.pdf>

Basel Action Network, *Legal Analysis of Letter from Mr Raja to Ms Hedegaard Regarding the Legal Application of the Basel Convention to the Kong Frederik IX (aka Riky)* (3 May 2005) <http://archive.ban.org/library/BAN_analysis_Ricky.pdf>

Department for Environment, Food and Rural Affairs, *UK Ship Recycling Strategy* (February 2007) 6 <http://webarchive.nationalarchives.gov.uk/20081105144808/www.defra.gov.uk/environment/waste/strategy/pdf/shiprecycle-strategy.pdf>

Ecorys, DNV GL and Erasmus University – the Erasmus School of Law, *Financial Instrument to Facilitate Safe and Sound Ship Recycling Final Report* (June 2016) <http://ec.europa.eu/environment/waste/ships/pdf/financial_instrument_ship_recycling.pdf>

ECSA, *Shipowners Reject Proposals for Ships to Pay for EU Ship Recycling Licences* <www.ecsa.eu/9-latest-news/267-shipowners-reject-proposals-for-ships-to-pay-for-eu-ship-recycling-licences>

EPA, *Polychlorinated Biphenyls (PCBs) in Ships* <www.epa.gov/pcbs/polychlorinated-biphenyls-pcbs-ships>

European Commission, *Commission Adopts First European List of Ship Recycling Facilities Safe for Workers and Environmentally Sound* (20 December 2016) <http://ec.europa.eu/environment/pdf/20_12_2016_news_en.pdf>

European Commission, *European List of Ship Recycling Facilities* (19 December 2016) <http://ec.europa.eu/environment/waste/ships/pdf/list_ship_recycling_facilities.pdf>

European Commission, *Technical Guidance Note under Regulation (EU) No 1257/2013 on Ship Recycling (2016/C 128/01)* (12 April 2016) <http://eur-lex.europa.eu/legal-content/EN/TXT/PDF/?uri=CELEX:52016XC0412(01)&from=EN>

Greenpeace, *50 Ships in the Spotlight* (25 June 2003) <http://archive.li/qdhK7>

Greenpeace, *No More Ships for Scrap to India or Bangladesh: Green Groups Expose* (11 July 2005) <www.greenpeace.org/india/en/news/no-more-ships-for-scrap-to-ind/>

Greenpeace, *Oil Tanker Phase Out Threatens Asian Workers and Environment* (4 April 2005) <www.greenpeace.org/international/en/press/releases/shipbreak/>

ILO, *Declaration on Fundamental Principles and Rights at Work*, adopted by the International Labour Conference, 86th Session, Geneva (June 1998) <www.ilo.org/dyn/normlex/en/f?p=1000:62:0::NO:62:P62_LIST_ENTRIE_ID:2453911:NO>

ILO, *Safety and Health in Shipbreaking: Guidelines for Asian Countries and Turkey* (2004) <www.ilo.org/public/english/region/asro/beijing/download/ship_breaking.pdf>

IMO, *Safe and Environmentally Sound Ship Recycling in Bangladesh – Phase I* (2017) <www.imo.org/en/OurWork/Environment/SupportToMemberStates/Major-Projects/Pages/Ship-recycling.aspx>

IndustriALL, *Four Workers Die in a Series of Accidents in Bangladeshi Shipbreaking Yards* (7 June 2016) <www.industriall-union.org/four-workers-die-in-a-series-of-accidents-in-bangladeshi-shipbreaking-yards>.

International Federation for Human Rights (FIDH), *Bangladesh Shipbreaking Still Dirty and Dangerous with at Least 20 Deaths in 2013* (13 December 2013) <www.fidh.org/en/region/asia/bangladesh/14395-bangladesh-shipbreaking-still-dirty-and-dangerous-with-at-least-20-deaths>

International Maritime Organization (IMO), *GISIS: Port Reception Facilities* (2016) <https://gisis.imo.org/Public/PRF/SearchPort.aspx>

Lee, Matthew Russell, *Ship-Breakers Missed by UN's Budget for Travel and Consultants in Bangladesh* (18 August 2006) <www.innercitypress.com/unhq081806.html>

Mikelis, Nikos, *Developments and Issues on Recycling of Ships* (2006) <www.imo.org/includes/blastDataOnly.asp/data_id%3D17980/Developments.pdf>

NGO Shipbreaking Platform, *Make the Polluter Pay! Why We Need the European Ship Recycling Licence* (October 2016) <www.shipbreakingplatform.org/shipbrea_wp2011/wp-content/uploads/2016/10/Position-Paper-FINANCIAL-INCENTIVE.pdf>

NGO Shipbreaking Platform, *Platform News – Surge of Fatal Accidents in Chittagong: 10 Shipbreaking Workers Killed or Severely Injured in One Month Only* (27 June

2016) <www.shipbreakingplatform.org/platform-news-surge-of-fatal-accidents-in-chittagong/>
NGO Shipbreaking Platform, *Press Release – Bangladesh High Court Issues Contempt Rule against 14 Government Officials: Ministries and Shipbreakers Asked to Account for Non-Compliance with 2009 Judgement* (12 April 2016) <www.shipbreakingplatform.org/press-release-bangladesh-high-court-issues-contempt-rule-against-14-government-officials-ministries-and-shipbreakers-asked-to-account-for-non-compliance-with-2009-judgement/>
NGO Shipbreaking Platform, *Substandard Shipbreaking: A Global Challenge* (February 2016) <www.shipbreakingplatform.org/shipbrea_wp2011/wp-content/uploads/2016/04/Worldwide-overview_FINAL.pdf>
NGO Shipbreaking Platform, *Why Ships Are Toxic* (2017) <www.shipbreakingplatform.org/main-aspects/why-ships-are-toxic/>
Ramsar Sites Information Service, *Sundarbans Reserved Forest* (1 January 2003) <https://rsis.ramsar.org/ris/560>
Schuler, Mike, *NGO Shipbreaking Platform: Use of 'Polluting' South Asia Scrap Yards Accelerating* (1 February 2017) <http://gcaptain.com/ngo-shipbreaking-platform-use-of-polluting-south-asia-scrap-yards-accelerating/>
Secretariat of the Basel Convention, *Amendment to the Basel Convention on the Control of Transboundary Movements of Hazardous Wastes and Their Disposal* (2017) <www.basel.int/Countries/StatusofRatifications/BanAmendment/tabid/1344/Default.aspx>
Secretariat of the Basel Convention, *Country Contacts* <www.basel.int/Countries/CountryContacts/tabid/1342/Default.aspx>
Secretariat of the Stockholm Convention, *What Are POPs?* (2008) <http://chm.pops.int/TheConvention/ThePOPs/tabid/673/Default.aspx>
Secretariat of the Stockholm Convention Clearing House, *Country Contacts* <http://chm.pops.int/Countries/CountryContacts/tabid/304/Default.aspx>
Stavros Dimas, *Solutions for the Responsible Recycling of Ships* (Open Hearing, European Parliament, Brussels, (25 April 2006) <www.shipbreakingplatform.org/shipbrea_wp2011/wp-content/uploads/2011/11/DIMAS-SPEECH-06-259_EN.pdf>
UNESCO World Heritage Centre, *The Sundarbans* <http://whc.unesco.org/en/list/798>
YPSA, *Death Trap! Accident Information for 2012* (2012) <www.shipbreakingbd.info/death_trap_2012.html>
YPSA, *Death Trap! A List of Dead Workers from the Year of 2005 to 2012* (September 2012) <www.shipbreakingbd.info/death_trap.html>
YPSA, *Overview of Ship Breaking in Bangladesh* (2012) <www.shipbreakingbd.info/overview.html>

Index

For Product Safety Concerns and Information please contact our EU representative GPSR@taylorandfrancis.com
Taylor & Francis Verlag GmbH, Kaufingerstraße 24, 80331 München, Germany

www.ingramcontent.com/pod-product-compliance
Ingram Content Group UK Ltd.
Pitfield, Milton Keynes, MK11 3LW, UK
UKHW022123190926
475702UK00013B/1615
9780367871208